THE GHOST TALKS

SERENADE

(Pat Enright for the Democratic National Committee)

The Ghost Talks

by Charles Michelson

G. P. PUTNAM'S SONS   NEW YORK

Designed by Robert Josephy

To three fine friends

who, under the guise of secretaries, saved me from errors, guided and guarded me, straightened out my complications, and generally smoothed my professional path I extend my thanks. So this book is dedicated to

WILLIAM JANSON, VIRGINIA FRALEY,

and

EDNA GOLDSBOUROUGH

The author and publishers wish to thank the *American Magazine* for permission to use two articles which appeared in the April and May issues of that magazine and which were based on material in this book.

CONTENTS

ILLUSTRATIONS

INTRODUCTION

I CAN IMAGINE no literary task easier than the compilation of a book from the writings of fellows like myself to picture the manifold superexcellences of Franklin Roosevelt, spiced with just enough quotation of his enemies to bring out the fullness of the sweet flavor of the whole—unless it be the production of a volume compounded of generally unfavorable writings, with merely a pinch of praise—like dusting salt on watermelon to make it more savory to a critical palate.

The foregoing is, in a measure, forestalling complaint that in this production of my experiences and reflections I have dealt overlightly with the faults and errors of the administration and unduly emphasized its accomplishments. If the anticipated criticism is valid, I can only say that any favoritism I show is unconscious, but I cannot disclaim partisanship. I was an Al Smith partisan in 1928; I was a Roosevelt partisan in '32; I was a Hull man in the controversy between the Secretary of State and Ray Moley at the London Economic Conference, and could only write about those things as I saw them; and it would be idle to insist that I was not affected by my environment.

As to the New Deal, somebody has to give me a clearer definition of that term before I know whether or not I am a New Dealer. As an imprecation the term has its uses; as a rallying slogan it is not without its appeal; but actually all of those enlisted under that banner are not mystical theorists, any more than all anti-New-Dealers are reactionaries opposed to every liberal thought.

Contemporary history is the most alluring form of fiction. Truth takes its color from the tint of the glasses through which the painstaking observer surveys and analyzes it.

The impartial commentator is an abstraction: no man capable of intelligent thought reaches a status that entitles him to parade his conclusions, without having at the same time found a theory or philosophy satisfactory to himself; and, once having so ranged himself, he becomes perforce a partisan.

Take my friends the newspaper columnists, for example. They have a particular brand of merchandise to dispose of. Their market is the world of journalism, and ninety per cent of the newspapers big enough to pay well for the higher type of commentators are Republican and, more especially, anti-Roosevelt. If you are a produce wholesaler, you are not going to ship apples to a merchant who wants potatoes. It may not be as gross as that simile indicates; for these same columnists are graduates of these same newspapers, for the most part, and after writing miles of editorials along a special line for years are natural converts to principles they advocated. There is still another angle to this situation. There are headlines in criticism; denunciation makes good reading, eulogy does not.

I imagine that the historians of the future are going to have a terrible time appraising the status and influence of Franklin D. Roosevelt in the procession of human affairs. The data on which they will have to base their estimates are as various as they are contradictory. The man who is pictured as a marvel of altruism, a spotless example of all that is good and noble, whose farsightedness approaches that of a biblical seer and prophet; and at the same time as an individual who surreptitiously essays the destruction of our economic system, who has been so devious that nobody could trust him, so selfish that his own political future outweighed his patriotism, so weak that he was swayed by dreamers, and so despotic that he wanted all power to reside in himself—such a man never did exist; never could exist.

The difficulty appears to be rooted in the deification of our chief executive; whether it be a satanic or a celestial deification, it is the attribution to a president of qualities extreme in every direction.

Actually the election of an American citizen to be sheriff—or president—makes little change in his general quality or character. If he was a strong citizen, he will be a strong official. If he was a trimmer, he will continue to trim. Those who dislike him call Roosevelt an enemy to business; yet when the war came upon us, he drafted the biggest figures in industry to head the different production and supply divisions. But, say his critics, he would not give them the authority requisite for the performance of their tasks, and the outcome was confusion and controversy.

Accepting that statement as a fact: it still is not the whole story. These big business men are stout, opinionated fellows. They did not win to the top by being either modest or unassertive, or prone to give up their own judgments when opposed by similar men. Theoretically the President might have knocked their heads together and ordered them to agree, or fired one or both parties to an administration row. Actually his job was to get production, and that enterprise would hardly have been promoted by indiscriminate firing of these titans of industry.

The Jesse Jones—Henry Wallace collision illustrates the point. Here was Jones, invaluable in his handling of billions of money to the end that such war projects as merited loans got them, and that the government's interests were protected where the security was hazardous. Here was the Vice-President, charged with getting things done, and finding himself delayed at the money source. If you don't like Jones, you may say that his banker supercaution was misplaced when it came to war emergencies. If you don't like Wallace, you may say that he is harebrained and that Jesse Jones was right in going slow.

It certainly would have been perilous for either of the two to hold absolute authority. The President could not dispense with Jones's eminent and proven capacity in conducting the R.F.C., and he could not fire the Vice-President even if he were so minded. Had he undertaken to decide for one as against the other, it would have involved a long and deep study of the relative values of the two positions to arrive at a just verdict; and if the president of the United States in the midst of a mighty war undertook an investigation of every point on which his high deputies disagreed, he could not do anything else. Moreover, the discord in this case was so pronounced and so publicized, it was evident that the two men could not be brought into accord. Wherefore the President took the only practicable course, which was to relieve both of the duties that had brought about the collision and entrust the responsibilities to somebody else.

There never was an errorless war or a flawless administration in this or any other country. There never was a president who satisfied all the people. When we reach into the bull pen of American citizenry and pull out one for the big job, we must realize that he is not a supernatural human! He is usually a politician, which means that he gained the eminence that brought him his opportunity through politics, plus a record in the successive steps of his rise that commends itself to the voting public.

Roosevelt, like most of his predecessors, was a politician. I have never known or read of a president who did not continue to be a politician when he got the office. Roosevelt's habits of economic thought were made known through his various campaigns, state and national. He was resourceful. If you like him, you say he was wise; if you don't, you say he was wily. He specialized in making people who came in contact with him believe he agreed with them. His friends call that amiability; his foes call it deceit. He was stubborn, vengeful, opportunist. There are pleasanter synonyms for these qualities; it all depends on the point of view.

Recently the President made a speech in which he promised certain awards, rewards, and considerations to the men in the armed forces as part recompense for their sacrifices. His political opponents saw in this a bid for the soldiers' vote for the fourth term. Could it not have been an effort to encourage and comfort those who were daring—and often finding—death for their country's sake?

Indeed, who can plot the dim line between self service and public service? I have never yet encountered an important personage who admitted that what he did was exclusively for his own sake. An example: I was with the Hearst organization, with some intervals, for thirty years. During that time we put over some queer exploits, but never in all that period did Mr.

Hearst admit an unworthy purpose. All was done in the public interest, even though the net result appeared to be increased circulation, advertising, or prestige.

Perhaps the mystery of Roosevelt's character would evaporate if his fellow citizens ceased regarding him as either a superman or a supermarplot and instead would take him as a highly intelligent person with much governmental experience and, presumably, the normal excellencies and defects of most of us.

He is accused of an excessive concern with his place in history. That may be a true bill; but does anybody suppose he is ambitious to have posterity's verdict sustain the picture drawn by his opponents?

The struggle between liberalism and conservatism is eternal; an advance by either school is hailed by the other as inevitably destructive, when probably it is nothing of the sort.

He is avid for power. Maybe; but with such a war on his hands, what official with confidence in his own judgment could do other than try to put his policies into effect?

He so manipulated the political situation as to break the tradition limiting presidential incumbency to two terms. I have frequently put the question to eminent citizens: suppose that you had been the Democratic president of the United States in 1940, whom would you have chosen to take your place with a world conflict tornadoing down upon the nation? Eliminating considerations of partisan politics, I have yet to get a satisfactory answer.

Other two-term presidents have wished for a third term and been turned down by their party convention. This one was renominated on the first ballot, and the people re-elected him. Again the matter is interpreted according to the viewpoint of the commentator. Re-election was wise if his motive, and if the people's motive, was based on the thought that with the impending war Roosevelt's experience made him the best-qualified man to steer the nation through a stormy period. The alternative is that, being convinced that no other available Democrat could be elected, and determined not to turn the

government over to the party opposed to him and to his policies, he therefore defied the tradition. Politics? certainly; electing a politician to the big office does not, and never did and
never will, mean that he ceases to be a politician.

If Roosevelt were the haloed Galahad he has been pictured
—without guile; frank, trusting, self-effacing, totally altruistic—
he never would have been president, or governor, or anything
else except perhaps an evangelical parson. It is because he had
certain sturdy, perhaps rude, qualities apart from the beatific
virtues; because he was capable of taking care of himself in
any sort of battle—polite or roughhouse—that he got where he is.

Doubtless I am prejudiced, but in writing about the President I can only state how he appeared to me.

Probably some of the matter of this book will be assailed as
inaccurate or erroneous. Once more I can only say I can but
paint the picture as I saw it. Obviously, I could not see it all,
any more than a war correspondent can see every detail of a
campaign or even a battle.

I was not of the policy-forming group; my part was neither
to reform the economic system nor to petrify it. My concern in
such matters was purely that of a political technician. If a
course seemed to me to advance the prestige of the party and
the administration, I was enthusiastic at its incubation. If it
seemed to me a hindrance to political success, I was against it;
but if such a policy was adopted, my business was to make
it palatable to the country, with no reservations on the score
of my personal views. Mine may not seem a noble conception of
my mission, but I was not the father confessor of the party or
the President; I was merely the press agent. Statesmanship was
not on the curriculum of the school of hard knocks that gave
such qualifications as I possessed for the fascinating job that
was mine for a dozen years. In this volume I have included a
loose account of the semesters of that school, from a puzzled
boyhood in a moribund mining camp through a glorious frontier vagrancy and a long and varied newspaper term, which
brought me ultimately to a listening post at the White House
press conferences.

THE GHOST TALKS

PART ONE

PRESS AGENT TO A SURPRISE PARTY

1. THE SAGA OF FRANKLIN THE ROOSE

How fate, well helped by the fated one, put a defeated candidate for vice-president, and one whom his party turned down for senator, in a way of becoming the most potent political figure of the world.

GOOD LUCK and good management must be accorded equal responsibility for the rise of Franklin Roosevelt.

During every phase of his advent to eminence his fairy godmother was on the job. Every time she waved her wand, she had the right people to translate the magic of opportunity into success. Innumerable times the cast of destiny's dice might have destroyed him, but the pixies of politics invariably outflanked the sinister gremlins of grief.

He was no towering Democratic figure, before 1928; his party had turned him down for a senatorial candidacy; he was only a minor sacrifice as the second man on its ticket in the hopeless 1920 election.

Had not the Democrats muffed the ball in the 1924 convention, John Raskob might have remained a Republican; there would have been no spectacular rejuvenescence of the Democratic party following the defeat of Al Smith by Herbert Hoover and the nomination of Roosevelt for governor in a strategic move to hold New York for Smith in 1928. If he had not carried New York, though Smith lost it, Roosevelt could probably not have won the presidential nomination in 1932; and but for the great depression, Hoover might well have been re-elected.

Had it not been for the imminence of war, Roosevelt would never have received the third-term nomination; would never, in fact, have gone after it.

His Aladdin's lamp has not failed him up to date.

If the Roosevelt forces had not double-crossed Jouett Shouse in 1932, Jouett would have double-crossed Franklin Roosevelt, and Al Smith, Bert Ritchie, or Newton Baker—or a Republican, possibly Herbert Hoover again—would have become president, and the New Deal would not have been.

I am not sure just what individual affixed the swastika on that occasion. Indeed only two men, Roosevelt and Bob Jackson, know exactly what was said over the telephone from Hyde Park to the Arrangements Committee in session in Chicago. By way of clarifying parenthesis, it is well to state that this was not Robert H. Jackson, now a Supreme Court justice, who once upon a time was backed for nomination to New York's governorship by the administration, but Secretary Jackson of the Democratic National Committee. In intimate political circles confusion of the names is averted by referring to one as the Good Bob Jackson and to the other simply as Bob Jackson.

Here was the situation at Chicago: Chairman John Raskob and Executive Chairman Shouse had labored for three years to refloat the Democratic party after it had gone down under the Hoover tidal wave of 1928. That epic reconstruction merits a chapter by itself. Suffice it to say here that Raskob, chagrined by the first failure of his career, had decided it was impossible to effect a political revolution in the brief months between a nomination and election day, and had undertaken the burden of getting together a machine that would give Al Smith another shot at the big target. Jim Farley had a different idea—but that, too, belongs in another compartment of this story.

The first job was to organize the 1932 convention. Of supreme importance was the selection of a temporary chairman; for though Farley had garnered a hypothetical majority of delegates, the two-thirds rule was still in effect. Moreover, Farley's flock was hypothetical indeed, for there were numerous contesting delegates, and on which delegates were seated depended the validity of that majority.

The program of the "Executive Committee"—that term is in quotation marks, for no executive committee had been appointed; I never saw even a pretended list of its members—was to put Shouse in as temporary chairman of the convention, which would have meant a torpedo under the prow of the Roosevelt craft. Both sides had perfectly good lists of members of the committee committed to their side. The difficulty was that certain members, bandwagon jumpers by habit and custom, were pledged to both factions, determined to land on the winning side in any event.

So the meeting eventuated with neither side certain. Then came the proposal, offered by Senator Byrd, that if Shouse would forego the temporary chairmanship, which carried with it the enunciation of the keynote speech, he might have the permanent chairmanship of the convention. Shouse agreed, but with the proviso that the proposal be personally validated by Governor Roosevelt. So Bob Jackson went to the phone and talked at some length with the Governor. He reported that Roosevelt had no objection. Here is where the controversy comes in. The Raskob faction believed, or affected to believe, that Roosevelt "recommended" the choice of Shouse for permanent chairman. Jackson reported to the convention, when that solemn body really came into session, that Governor Roosevelt had "commended" Shouse—a choice of wording whose obscure import was actualized when The National Committee, on permanent organization, subsequently presented the name of Senator Tom Walsh for the job. John W. Davis and Mrs. Bernice Pyke made eloquent arguments for Shouse, representing that the party's faith had been pledged to his selection. The counterargument was that while the committee had the authority to name temporary officers, it had no authority to direct the convention after that body was organized. In other words, to nominate a permanent chairman was not within its power.

Legalisms aside, Jouett Shouse had something to sell. His price for yielding the temporary chairmanship to Senator Barkley was that he should have the permanent chairmanship. Thus would be spared any embarrassment to the two-timers and double pledgers. Shouse believed, and was intended to believe, that his price was agreed on when Bob Jackson returned from telephoning to Albany and made his announcement to the Arrangements Committee: "We are happy to report that very satisfactory progress has been made in ironing out what might have been a cause for controversy. When I sit down, Governor Byrd of Virginia will move that Mr. Barkley be recommended temporary chairman of the convention by acclamation; and when that resolution is adopted, I shall offer the following resolution, which has been read to Governor Roosevelt over the telephone and which meets with his approval:

'This Committee commends to the Permanent Committee on Organization for consideration as Permanent Chairman of the National Convention, the name of the Honorable Jouett Shouse of Kansas.' "

That resolution was unanimously carried. After the session Shouse announced to the waiting newspaper correspondents— and that group comprised pretty much all the leading political writers—this report of the action of the committee:

"By unanimous action of the committee, it was decided to recommend to the National Committee the selection of Senator A. W. Barkley for temporary chairman, and the selection of Jouett Shouse as permanent chairman of the convention."

The newspapers all over the country carried the direct statement of the decision. For example the *New York Times* had this from its Washington correspondent:

"Agreement by the Arrangements Committee on Senator Barkley and Jouett Shouse, as temporary chairman and keynoter, and permanent chairman, respectively, was regarded here as a satisfactory arrangement."

Governor Roosevelt's comment carried on the same date was in these words:

"The Committee on Arrangements also recognized the long and tireless service of Jouett Shouse in charge of the National Committee by commending him to the consideration of the convention for the post of permanent chairman."

The editorials of the Democratic-minded press all were congratulatory over the harmony of the party and the skill in avoiding what had seemed to threaten a heavy clash.

There was never a word of contradiction or correction of the statement—or error—until it was suddenly sprung on the country that the National Committee had another candidate for the coveted post.

When the newspapers made the disclosure, Jouett Shouse volunteered this comment:

"I do not for a moment accept as in any way true or authorized the statements in the press that Governor Roosevelt purposes to oppose my election as permanent chairman of the coming Democratic convention.

"My reason for this belief is that the Governor himself not only endorsed the compromise effected at the meeting of the Committee of Arrangements at Chicago, wherein I agreed to waive being chosen temporary chairman as the majority of the committee was prepared to vote in favor of Senator Barkley (the Roosevelt choice), but the Governor himself dictated the resolution over the telephone, in which the terms of the agreement were set forth. Governor Roosevelt's character is all the assurance I require that no such violation of an obligation is or ever has been in his mind. That he, a candidate for the nomination as president, should purpose to interfere in my own state of Kansas to prevent my election as a delegate at large, and in the effort to make me ineligible for the chairmanship, cannot be other than distortion on the part of the newspapers which have taken somebody else's word as to the Governor's intention."

When the convention was called to order two months later, the Committee on Permanent Organization presented the name of Senator Tom Walsh for the permanent chairmanship—with only a minority report asking that Shouse get the job

—and the convention voted 626 to 528 for the great Montana senator.

It was all quite lawful—if oblique. Shouse and Raskob cannot have doubted that Roosevelt had committed himself, else they would have gone through with the fight in the Arrangements Committee. The episode was the precursor of a habit that has been useful throughout the period of presidential incumbency—F. D. R.'s genial trait of sending people away satisfied that he is quite in accord with them. Samples: Farley's faith in the idea that he had the President's word that he would not run for the third term, and faith of the various candidates for the vice-presidential nomination in 1940, each one thinking that he had been given the green light, despite the actuality that Roosevelt had determined on Henry Wallace for the second place on the ticket and would take nobody else.

I was there—at the 1932 convention—with Walsh's speech in one pocket and Shouse's in the other. I have been wrongfully charged with having written both. I had my mimeographs under the stairs leading to the platform and dared not issue either speech until after Missouri had voted, when it was evident that Walsh would be chosen.

With perfect legalism, impeccable courtesy, and calm logic, the Permanent Chairman squelched the Smith protestants as fast as they arose, and Roosevelt's majority persevered despite the roarings of the Smith boosters planted in the galleries.

That phase of the battle having been passed victoriously, the Rooseveltians did not trample the defeated. Bob Jackson came to me and said the convention wanted a resolution thanking Chairman Raskob for his service in rehabilitating the party. I hammered it out on the typewriter, but Raskob was in no frame of mind to be comforted with resolutions and declined the honor.

Jackson also wanted one praising me for my part in the campaign of preparation. Naturally I told him that if my boss refused, I could not do otherwise than go along with him. I went back to the convention and got there just in time to hear my Raskob resolution presented and unanimously adopted. It had been taken from my typewriter as soon as I was out of the way. Raskob blinked a little but swallowed his resentment and made a short speech of acknowledgment. Later he checked off twenty-five thousand dollars of the National Committee's debt to him as his contribution to the Roosevelt campaign.

Through three ballots Roosevelt's majority held, but he was still far shy of the requisite two-thirds majority, and his people were worried. Only by the most strenuous strong-arming by Senator Pat Harrison was Mississippi kept in line. Several other states were ready to quit Roosevelt. Another ballot and the prospects were that the line would break. Something had to be done and done quickly. So Farley went to work on Jack Garner, whose Texas and California votes were of the utmost importance. Likewise they wooed William Randolph Hearst— who was backing the Garner candidacy—over the long-distance phone to San Simeon. Hearst had two great newspapers in Chicago. Mayor Cermak, with Hearst's attorney in the windy city, represented him. Farley had, or thought he had, the publisher's nod. My postconvention information was that Mr. Hearst contended he had not agreed to go the whole way and was much put out about the deal, feeling that his representative had unduly committed him. Cermak was killed by the assassin's bullet meant for Roosevelt at Miami, so there was no opportunity to visit any displeasure the publisher may have felt against him. General Roy Keehn, the lawyer, ceased to be Mr. Hearst's attorney in Chicago.

Whatever the truth, the deal went through. My understanding at the time was that California, which state by alphabetical right came first in the balloting, was to yield to Texas, so that Garner's own state would announce the decision; but William Gibbs McAdoo could not forego the opportunity to get back at Al Smith. And did he enjoy telling how he had been the victim of the two-thirds rule! McAdoo had had 530 votes in the Madison Square Garden massacre in 1924, and maintained a majority for many ballots. Small wonder that he now had the time of his life driving the spikes into Smith's political coffin.

After Roosevelt's nomination I bade farewell to Raskob and Shouse, moved across the auditorium to Roosevelt headquarters, and reported to Farley, whom I had never met. He greeted me with a grin. Louis Howe came in, took me in tow, and escorted me to the nominee's room. Franklin Roosevelt was lying down resting from his rough trip in a plane from Albany. We were old friends, our acquaintance dating back to his incumbency as assistant secretary of the navy, when I was political reporter and chief of the New York *World's* Washington bureau.

Howe had asked me long before to press-agent the campaign if Roosevelt won in the convention; so had Ritchie and various others who hoped that the Smith-Roosevelt collision would bring about a deadlock and give a chance for dark-horsing. Having adopted politician propaganda as my field of activity, I agreed in every case. The "Executive Committee," of course, knew all about it.

"Glad to see you aboard the ship," was the candidate's greeting.

He did not seem particularly elated at his victory. Indeed, his frame of mind, not only after getting the first nomination but after each election, appeared to be that no other outcome was possible. We did not discuss policies or methods for the battle ahead. In fact, I cannot now recall any time when he sought to guide campaign publicity. Apparently he took it for granted that I knew my business, and so long as my functions seemed to be conducted with reasonable efficiency, it was all right with him.

When any question came up about which there might be a difference of opinion, I fought it out with Louis Howe. If the Governor was present, he declined to be referee or to take any greater part than nodding approval—not necessarily of the merits of a statement but rather of the manner of its presentation. Many pen pictures have been drawn of Louis Howe, that frail, gnomelike figure who played so great a part in the upcoming of Franklin Roosevelt. Though he was a devout worshiper at the shrine, he never was a yes man. Indeed, he was one of the few who spoke his mind, whether it was to State Senator Roosevelt or to President Roosevelt. Of all the advisers who have aided or plagued the great man during his long career, he—Howe—was the most loyal and most disinterested. He fulfilled the image drawn by Machiavelli—or maybe it was Jack Garner—of the duty and task of the confidential man for princes. I believe that Louis Howe's advice influenced Franklin Roosevelt more than that of any other individual. Not that he always accepted it. My experience is that he takes nobody's advice undiluted. His habit is to listen to all, letting each advocate believe that his is the only tenable course, and then do what he pleases.

I recall when he was on his big swing around the circle. It seemed important, because of the circumstance that President Hoover had scheduled a budget speech, that Roosevelt should shift his program, return as far as Pittsburgh, and there talk on federal finance, etc. Howe assembled half a dozen of us— Farley and a brace of senators among us—and we took the candidate on in relays by phone. He was then at Denver, or perhaps at Butte, Montana. In turn each of us impressed on him the vital necessity of heading off the Hoover broadside with an enunciation of his own fiscal program. We got nowhere, and it was decided that I would have to fly out there and endeavor to move him from his stubborn position. Fortunately, or unfortunately, there came a big storm that disrupted the then rather undependable air service, so I was not started. He pursued his own plans, and jeered us mildly for our insistence.

That western trip had been a matter of grave debate and many conferences. Farley and I had come to Washington and summoned a council of senators and representatives to consider the matter. It was unanimously decided that such a swing around the circle involved too many dangers. Our candidate's physical condition was being emphasized by the enemy propagandists, and there was the danger that he might collapse in mid-career, which would corroborate the foe's warning; or, in the course of a hundred impromptu train-end speeches, he might well make a slip that would be disastrous, etc.

So Farley and I repaired to the governor's mansion at Albany and reported that the high board of strategy agreed with us, and with Howe, that the project was too dangerous.

The Governor listened to our report and announced:

"Well, I'm going anyhow."

"Why take a chance?" was the query shot at him.

"Because I want to," was his reply. "And," he added, "I'm not going to take a doctor along either."

So he went on the pilgrimage, had an uninterrupted progress of enthusiasm, and returned to the East with his confidence of the election's outcome undiminished. He knew his capacity for endurance better than we did; he knew that the best answer to his opponents' insinuations of feeble health was to show himself to the people and demonstrate that he had the fortitude and the stamina to take what a term in the presidency involved.

The question of a barnstorming tour or a front porch campaign thus settled, Hugh Johnson, Raymond Moley and myself were summoned to the governor's mansion to draft a speech. It was to be delivered at Columbus. Each of us had his manuscript with him. They were three great speeches: resounding, earnest, and affirmative. Johnson's product bristled with fulminations against the enemy and was dotted with fine wisecracks over the incompetence of the Hoover administration; Moley presented the economic and social issues, and that lad certainly knew his stuff. My contribution was straight politics with some covert digs and sly insinuations of which I was a trifle proud. Unfortunately none of those three speeches was delivered. Instead the Governor suggested each topic, and we three repaired to our respective typewriters and ground out our views of the proper presentation. A brief discussion of these, and the Governor stretched himself on a couch and with his eyes on the ceiling dictated his own version, occasionally using one of our phrases but generally culling the best ideas that had been submitted and putting them in his own way.

So far as I know, this was the practice with every speech.

Moley, Johnson, Stanley High, Tom Corcoran, and Judge Rosenman may sometime have fared better, but I was never present when a big speech was born that the President did not take the political viands offered and cook them in his individual way. Take it from one rather experienced in the formation and presentation of speeches: Franklin Roosevelt is a better phrase maker than anybody he ever had around him.

We were interrupted while the Columbus address was being brewed. Mayor Walker was undergoing a gubernatorial court-martial, the issue being whether the Governor should dismiss him from the mayoralty. Martin Conboy, who would have been judge advocate if the proceeding had employed military terms, came in in the midst of our eloquence. Something had developed at the hearing—I think it was a threat that Mayor Walker would appeal to the regular courts—on which Conboy felt he should consult the Governor. He recited some of Walker's testimony at the Seabury hearing.

"No," said the Governor, "this is what he said"; and he recited verbatim what must have been two pages of the transcript without referring to a note. Then he turned back to us and resumed his comment on the farm situation.

"I think we will put it this way," he said, and he re-embarked on his speech.

Conboy came in at intervals, and about midnight there was a graver interruption. A man in Sing Sing was due to go to the electric chair at midnight. The Warden phoned that the prisoner had made a last minute confession implicating two accomplices in the murder for which he had to die. The problem was whether to regard this confession as merely a bid for a few more days of life, or whether justice demanded a reprieve in order that the alleged accomplices should be investigated. This required long-distance calls to the district attorney in New York City, extensive communication with the two detectives who had worked on the case, and further talks with Sing Sing —and with only an hour to go. Between telephonings the Governor went on with his speech. By midnight he had finished it, settled the Sing Sing problem, and straightened out Attorney

Conboy. So the "Alice in Wonderland" speech was born. Everybody knew what the term meant then, but for the benefit of a new generation it is perhaps worth a few words to explain that in this address he discussed the Republican administration's handling of, and explanation of, the great depression, achieving deft and deadly raillery in the terms of Lewis Carroll's classic of the Mad Hatter, Humpty Dumpty, and so forth.

I had no further direct contact with the candidate until he returned from the great swing around the circle—an epic journey unmarred by fulfillment of any of the forebodings. Not only did his health hold up, but he made no bulls in rear-platform impromptu talks, and he slid through the ambuscades of conflicting local leaders uncommitted and unharmed. Where there were struggles going on as to which of two was the more loyal supporter, he had both aboard the train as his guests; and if he did not always succeed in reconciling the conflicting claims, he parted on the best of terms, each rival believing that he had won the royal countenance.

2. FOR A CUCKOO'S EGG

Being the narrative of the nest that was builded to hatch out a second nomination for Al Smith and that was to produce a very different bird.

JOHN J. RASKOB had only a vague hope of unhorsing Herbert Hoover, when he essayed the rehabilitation of the Democratic party after the overwhelming defeat of Alfred E. Smith in 1928.

In fact, at the very first conference I had with Jouett Shouse —who, as chairman of the Democratic Executive Committee, had been endowed with all Raskob's authority and power—he told me that the National Chairman would be quite satisfied if the party should be rebuilt into a strong fighting institution by the time the next election, that of 1932, came around. My deduction at the time was that the multimillionaire chairman rather believed that Hoover was most likely to succeed himself but that when his second term was over (there was no thought of third terms at that period!) there would be a fine opportunity for the Democrats to stage a comeback, with Al Smith—for the Republicans had no popular hero—as a possible successor for the big job. It may have been that Raskob thought the 1932 election would wipe Franklin Roosevelt off the political map, for he had no great opinion of the Governor of New York either as an executive or as a vote getter.

This, it must be remembered, was early in Hoover's term, in June of 1929, when the country was in the midst of a boom and the President was still the miracle man of the preceding campaign presentation.

Raskob was no tyro at long-range planning. His wealth, at that time, was reputed to be in the neighborhood of a half a billion dollars; and even allowing for the exaggerations of the Big Bulge Era, he had enough so that the pledge of a round million to finance the rejuvenation enterprise for three years was no great drain. When the stock market did its crash dive, it was another story. However, the little magnate never squealed, and the cash to keep the show going kept coming.

On the fifteenth day of June, 1929, Jouett Shouse and I confronted each other across his broad desk of curly maple and attempted to survey the job that lay ahead of us. About us was a fine suite of vacant offices; and that vacancy was, it seemed to me, reflected in our own mental attitude. I, at least, had not the slightest idea of how or where to begin my function of converting the country from a Republican to a Democratic frame of mind, and I thought that there was no more of definiteness in the face across the desk than on my side.

The conversation was desultory. We did not know each other particularly well. I remembered Shouse as one of McAdoo's

floor leaders in the ghastly Madison Square Garden suicide
pact, and with other newspaper correspondents I had been
entertained by him at Kansas City during the Republican convention of 1928. As one of the chief factors in bringing the
Republicans to his home city, Shouse was saddled with responsibility for making the reporters as happy as possible in
the nightmare that a national convention always is for the
writers who must, in millions of words, tell the country what is
being done, guess what is going to happen, and make the ordinarily dull sequence of events appear startling and picturesque.
I had also encountered him about Governor Smith's headquarters in New York. In short, during the 1928 campaign he was
to me merely one of the pleasant people from whom information was to be obtained during a political melee. Nor did he
know me any better than I knew him. He had offered me the
post of press agent to a forlorn hope because of some facility
I had in the use of words and my presumed knowledge of
politics and government resulting from many years' service as
a Washington correspondent. So we sat, comparative strangers,
plumbing each other's minds without much result. Shouse explained the situation. National Chairman John J. Raskob had
agreed to finance the organization through to the 1932 convention in pursuance of his idea that the great obstacle to Democratic success was the party's habit of lying dormant for three
years and a half and then attempting to effect a political revolution in the brief period between convention and election
day.

I had no personal acquaintance with Raskob. The only near
contact I had had with him was when I was one of a numerous
group of reporters who had audiences with the Democratic
chairman as part of the routine of reporting a campaign.
Shouse told me, as a diversion of our conference, that when he
notified Raskob he had appointed Charley Michelson as publicity director, the Chairman's response was, "Who in hell is
Charley Michelson?" It was not until weeks later that we met.
Then Shouse called me from my typewriter, where I was
pounding out a statement for some senator on the tariff, to

FOR A CUCKOO'S EGG   17

introduce me to the Chairman. The mimeographs were waiting
for the release, so the session was limited to an exchange of
greetings and I promptly went back to my job.

I am afraid that this drab recital does not fit into the picture
so industriously circulated later on, of a careful conspiracy,
worked out in its utmost details between the Democratic chairman and the publicity director, to "smear Hoover" and destroy
the President's prestige. Like many other picturesque myths of
politics this was purely imaginary.

Our enterprise had a gloomy launching. The country was
happy in the high tide of prosperity; the Republicans not only
had a President elected by a seven million majority but dominated the House of Representatives with more than a hundred
votes to spare and had the Senate fifty-five to thirty-nine, with
one Farmer-Laborite who voted their way. To most people
President Hoover was still the magician of the campaign picture, and there were few who doubted that he would make
good the extraordinary promises of his letter of acceptance and
his platform speeches.

True, there were premonitory indications of a falling away
of popularity. He had come to the White House with perhaps
the largest clientele among the newspaper correspondents of
any president in our history, but within three months he was
quarreling with them. He had outlined a blueprint of his
purposed relations with the press that sounded alluring, for he
meant, or said he meant, to continue the bi-weekly conferences
that Harding had inaugurated, and that Coolidge had continued though with progressive restrictions. President Hoover,
with engineer-like attention to detail, took steps to avoid the
rock that had so embarrassed Harding, of having his impromptu replies printed. Harding more than once had Secretary of State Charles Evans Hughes tearing his beard. The
mix-up over which islands in the Pacific had had their security
guaranteed is elaborated elsewhere in these pages. On another
occasion Harding got in trouble with the then politically
despotic Anti-Saloon League by announcing that there would
be no such nonsense about national prohibition as preventing

the transit of Canadian liquor on railroads through the United States to Mexico, for instance. Hughes could and did convene another session of the treaty commissioners to make the facts square with the President's offhand declaration about the Pacific islands, but even he could not change the law which expressly provided against liquor transportation in the United States.

Well, President Hoover had safeguarded against such troubles by an elaborate division of the tidings to be learned at the press conferences. First there would be direct quotations of the President on such subjects as he chose, and these were to be written so there could be no misquotation. Second there would be news that the correspondents might attribute to "a high White House authority" or preface with the comment that "it was learned at the White House"; and the material of the third division, while just as authentic, was to be presented only as background and could be credited to nobody, though it might be used as the reporter's own view or guess. It was not a bad solution; but as it worked out, the presidential handouts were of no consequence and never dealt even remotely with the written questions that had been handed in. In fact, it is not on record that the President ever replied to a single question. The background material was thin and did not always stand up, and gradually the correspondents were getting to feel that the Tuesday and Friday sessions at the White House were being used solely for the advantage of the President and not at all for the benefit of the newspapers.

Then the three-secretary system worked badly. One of the secretaries—they were George Akerson, a newspaperman, Lawrence Ritchie, an ex-secret-service-operative, and Walter Newton, an ex-Congressman—would step into the correspondents' room and pass out a story, presumably with the President's approval if not by his order. If the reaction was not satisfactory, or if the President changed his mind, or if somebody—a senator or member of his cabinet, for example—then advised him against that particular piece of publicity, one of the other secretaries would presently appear and contradict the tale. As

White House news is always telephoned immediately to the newspaper offices and press associations, the story had usually been printed before the denial was launched. Consequently the newsgatherers got reputations for inaccuracy in their own offices.

The Hiram Johnson incident was a case in point. There was a dinner to a visiting foreign statesman, and the members of the Senate Foreign Relations Committee were bidden to it. All but Hiram Johnson. When the guest list was handed out by the secretaries, the newspaper people instantly noted the omission and asked about it. A secretary took the word to the President and presently returned saying that there was no White House comment to be made on the subject. The reporters thought perhaps the hitch was at the other end: that the California Senator—whose feud with the President was notorious—had declined. They phoned the Senator and learned that he had never been invited. So the yarn was sent out. This was four hours before the dinner. It reached Senator Dave Reed of Pennsylvania, who hurried to the White House and protested that the President of the United States could not afford personal vendettas. But the invitation was never forthcoming, and the next day Senator Johnson received an apologetic note explaining that a telephone girl had overlooked his name. Of course, nobody believed that the White House entourage, inheritors of experts who had been conducting state dinners for a century and a quarter, had ever made such a blunder; and moreover there had been, in the four hours after attention had been called to the omission of the California senator from the list, ample opportunity to correct the mistake —if there had been a mistake.

These are, in restrospect, matters of little note; but in such a history as this they have their place, for they were the forerunners of the terrific fall from popularity of the thirty-first president of the United States. However, at the time the Democrats started organizing for the campaign, the President's peculiarities of this sort were appreciated only by the correspondent corps. As nine-tenths of the big newspapers of the country are

Republican, even comment on the subject from Washington got no great publicity. To the mass of the nation Herbert Hoover was still the infallible criterion for all that was expert, forthright, dignified in things great and small.

The Treasury could not recommend adjustments fast enough to avoid stupendous surpluses. So vast were these that it was usual for the government's income to exceed what the Treasury estimated by hundreds of millions of dollars. On one occasion—in 1929—it missed its guess by a billion. All of this was converted into payments of the national debt, and nobody found any fault except a few Democrats on Capitol Hill who grumbled that it would be better to give the taxpayers the benefit of these surpluses in lower income rates.

But who paid any attention to the Democrats in those days? The party itself was shattered. The Solid South had been split wide open. Virginia, North Carolina, Florida, and Texas had gone Republican. Alabama and Georgia had barely stuck to the Democratic side. All of the border states had gone for Hoover. The religious bitterness engendered by the campaign against Governor Smith was still aflame. The tottering minority organization had come out of the 1928 campaign a million and a half dollars in debt.

One of my first tasks as publicity director of the wreck was to prepare a reply to a scholarly, pontifical dissertation in *Scribner's* magazine which pointed out that twilight had come upon the party of Jefferson; that its end was upon us, and that it must forthwith give way to a new party. The obituary bristled with historical incidents cited to prove that it had reached the state of coma that must inevitably pass into death.

Perhaps our protest against the lethal sentence was none too confident; perhaps we were voicing our long-shot hope rather than our conviction when we wrote our declaration that we were not dead. Few people believed we had a chance.

Political publicity was a new field to me. My experience had been on the receiving end. As head of the New York *World* bureau in Washington I had been deluged through campaign after campaign with soggy bales of material from both Repub-

lican and Democratic headquarters, mostly consisting of interviews with visitors to headquarters who told how fine the
situation looked in Oregon or Arkansas or some other state,
diversified with biographies of the candidates and their
speeches. To begin with, Shouse and I agreed that all publicity
departments had, and ought to have, an adequate research
bureau. So I started out to engage a research director. I went
around among my newspaper friends bidding ten thousand
dollars a year and a cast-iron, guaranteed three-year contract,
and I failed to find one of them I deemed up to the job who
had enough faith in Democratic prospects to take the chance.
Two good old stand-bys of the Democratic organization, veterans of previous publicities, remained to help us out; and it
is with rather a shock that I recount that, so far as I have been
able to notice, we never missed a research director—that indispensable first concern of the business, as we had supposed.
Somehow we scrambled out of the records we had inherited
from the Smith campaign committee what was called for, or
dug it up afresh between times.

I did not know, never have known, and do not know now
who composed the National Executive Committee of which I
was reputed to be the employee. Former Governor of Wyoming
Nellie Tayloe Ross, who came to us to take care of the Democratic women, ranked as Vice-Chairman, and churned among
women's clubs almost as vehemently as did the Chairman
before general audiences. When she joined up, she was the
leading figure among Democratic women by virtue of her governorship. Since then women in high office have ceased to be
remarkable, thanks to the custom that grew up of making an
officeholder's widow his successor; but she was almost unique
early in 1929, and had she been triplets she could not have
responded to all the calls that were made on her for speeches.

Slowly we felt our way. The private organ of the Republican
National Committee came out with a clarion cry to enlist all
good citizens in a crusade against the "Reds." There was no
particular Communist activity visible on our horizon; it was
simply a specialty of the organization functionary who hap-

pened to be running the paper. This gave us the opportunity
to talk about a red herring drawn across the trail and otherwise
to jeer at the windmill jousting.

We had difficulty in getting anybody to pay attention to the
Democratic efforts. The country was not interested politically,
so soon after election, and we had small pickings on which to
base our campaign. Fate, however, which it seems to me always
has come to the aid of the Democrats during the past dozen
years, took care of us. President Hoover had called a special
session to mitigate the woes of the farmer, suggesting, among
other things, some tariff raises on agricultural products. There
never was and never will be an administration that doesn't
want to make the vast vote represented by the grangers happy.
This goes likewise for labor and for war veterans. Wartimes
interrupt this procedure somewhat, but there was no war in
the offing then. The projected farmer's relief measure crystallized as the hugest tariff bill in the country's history.

The House of Representatives majority—functioning beau-
tifully under the great triumvirate, Longworth, Snell, and
Tilson—crowded the initial bill through with a minimum of
trouble, carefully safeguarding against debate, which was not
difficult when they made the rules. They made of the Ways and
Means Committee a Republican caucus, barring the Democratic members from the hearings and not letting them have a
look at the bill until it was ready to be reported out. There was
really little new in this star-chamber process of formulating
a tariff bill, but the secret sessions were made to order for a
hostile press bureau. It was easy to get before the country a picture of slavish legislators closeted with the representatives of
those industries whose owners had contributed most largely to
the Hoover campaign fund and fixing the rates as they were
told to do by Big Business. It was not such an erroneous picture
after all, as later developments before the Senate lobby investigation disclosed, when Grundy of Pennsylvania vaingloriously
told of his lobbying and it was revealed that Senator Bingham
of Connecticut had smuggled into the closed hearings of the

Senate committee an official of the Connecticut Manufacturers Association disguised by a fictitious senatorial clerkship.

Nor did the country accept the somewhat lurid picture of Congressional subserviency with any reluctance. The President's aura had already begun to fade, and it bleached out entirely under the criticism of his indecision about the tariff bill. Many of his own party, who were alarmed at the towering heights to which it was proposed to raise the rates, eagerly sought a sign from the White House and got none. For that matter, the embargo-raters sought with equal assiduity for a symbol of acquiescence with no better result. Every phase of tariff sentiment—the Old Guard, the Young Turks, the Progressives, and the Democrats—proclaimed with equal shrillness and equal authority that it represented the President's real view of what the bill should contain. The President explained his silence by a solemn assertion of his devotion to the principle of noninterference in a legislative function. Then, when it was proposed that the execution of the flexible tariff provisions be taken out of his hands, he poured forth a protesting message, as to whether the Tariff Commission, a creation of Congress, should report to the legislative or to the executive branch might be considered as much a congressional function as whether sugar should pay a toll.

The situation lent itself superlatively to caricature, and with our fertilizing processes the country blossomed with cartoons illustrating the presidential indecision. It became the general belief that the President did not have any tariff views, which is very probable. Tariff making is the most technical sort of legislation. That the more expensive foreign goods are made in the home market, the more money will be made by domestic producers, is obvious. The other side is just as plain: that the higher prices on imports are made, the more it is going to cost American consumers; and, as developed in the bitter sequel, it is equally true that tariff costs may be made so high as to provoke reprisals and so visit the sins of the profiteering domestic producer upon the head of the export business. Yet these simple truths are interwoven with all kinds of ifs and buts.

There are probably not half a dozen competent students of the subject—let alone experts—among the 531 members of the two houses of Congress, where tariffs are a recurring phenomenon on which they must debate and vote. Then what likelihood was there that a man like Herbert Hoover, whose whole life had been spent in a field far removed from such questions, should have been able to decide among conflicting opinions on the Smoot-Hawley tariff? But the psychology of our great country is that a president knows everything. Moreover, there is an echo of this thought in the White House itself. No president in my experience has ever admitted his incompetence in any respect or his ignorance of anything.

Least of all could one advertised as practically infallible if not omniscient, as Mr. Hoover had been previous to his advent as president, bring himself to such an admission. It would seem safe to guess that had Mr. Hoover not been a candidate for re-election, he would have endorsed the verdict of the one thousand and thirty-nine economic experts who warned him what the Smoot-Hawley—or, as it had come to be called, the Grundy—Tariff would do to business. But the men on whom he must depend for re-election wanted that bill, so he signed it, with apologies and promises of bettering it through flexible administration; and the whole press of the country became reminiscent of what had happened to Taft in a similar situation twenty years before.

Naturally we in Democratic headquarters helped the chorus of protest along in every way we could. The "Grundy Bill" was of our christening. The Grundy-bund took its place among cartoon characters, and so the President's prestige dwindled.

The advent of the panic made certain the doom of everybody associated in the public mind with the Smoot-Hawley Tariff. In vain did administration supporters talk about the aftereffects of the war, the world-wide poverty, to explain the destruction of our foreign business. All the people considered was that our factories were closing for lack of orders, the companies laying off men while they were establishing branch plants abroad to manufacture the products whose purchase

Charley's utterances began to command attention for their own sake; his name became more important than that of his average dummy.

(Herbert Johnson in *The Saturday Evening Post*)

The awe in which Michelson is held by Republicans is almost comic.

(Herbert Johnson in *The Saturday Evening Post*)

price formerly swelled American payrolls but now was going to foreign workmen. In the first place the public was reluctant to accept oblique and intangible causations of their misery. In the second place they had lost faith in the authors of the international explanations. Mr. Hoover in every campaign speech in 1928 had promised complete, continuous, and progressive prosperity. Moreover he and his orators, in their eagerness to impress on the country the axiom that Republicans alone knew how to govern, had proclaimed that after the Democrats had wrecked the country with the war, they had come along and restored it—not temporarily but permanently—and had in fact solved every problem resulting from the war.

In his political amateurism Mr. Hoover made no provision for anything but the uninterrupted current of a booming market. More experienced practitioners of the craft, like George Moses of New Hampshire, for example, or Jim Watson of Indiana, would have provided safety fields in the event of a forced landing; but the soaring candidate flew without even a parachute to ease his fall when the plane took a dive. We did not have to emphasize the gap between the promise and the reality. Whenever the stock exchange recorded a drop, the cartoonists and columnists of the nation's press did our work for us. The bewilderment of the White House was apparent almost from the day of the initial disaster. First the instinct of the well-wisher asserted itself. The President thought it his function to reassure the country by deprecating the intensity of the calamity. The stock crash "did not affect the business structure of the nation." It was a passing even though an unwelcome phenomenon. Then came the prophecies so reminiscent of the 1928 campaign. The upturn was imminent; it was just around the corner; and finally he ventured even to set a limit to the depression. It was to be over in sixty days. Unfortunately those cold-nosed fellows with lifetime experience in Wall Street did not accept the presidential cheer as real currency. They are gamblers, on either a rising or falling market. The bull of today is the bear of tomorrow, and they did not neglect this opportunity to ply their trade. Fate willed it that whenever the President issued a statement full of sunshine, the market found new and previously unsuspected depths. Then the conspiracy complex, which had always been a feature of this administration's psychology, asserted itself. It conceived a plot, fathered by the wicked Democrats, to discredit the President by timing bear raids so as to stultify the White House auguries. One day there came to our attention a handsome full-page newspaper advertisement, sponsored by the Republican National Committee, conveying the idea that John J. Raskob was selling the market short in order to destroy confidence in our Chief Executive. That was a simple thing to meet. Mr. Raskob merely issued a brief statement that he had never at any time during the depression sold a share of stock short, directly or indirectly. He further stated that while he was not particularly sensitive to the usual run of campaign abuse, he regarded the advertisement as a reflection on his business intelligence and integrity, and gave warning that he would hold any newspaper publishing the same responsible for it. The advertisement was not printed in a single newspaper, and the copy was hastily withdrawn by the Republican National Committee.

Undoubtedly there was a lot of short selling, not because of the President's promotional propaganda but in spite of it. There was nothing political about it. The men whose business it is to guess right on the market were pursuing their vocation. Their sources of information were better, apparently, than the government's.

Later on the Wall Street gossips reported that the President was promoting a Senate investigation of the bears, with the idea of catching some prominent Democrats engaged in the nefarious practice of bearing. The incident throws a curious light on the isolation of the White House incumbent and the inadequateness of his processes for getting information. The slightest competent investigation would have shown that as nonpartisan a flock of buzzards as ever swooped on a reeling market was fattening on the successive declines, and that the big Democrats for whom the trap was to be sprung were not in the market at all.

John Raskob informed a Congressional committee that his only stock market activity during the depression was the sale of some securities in order to take certain losses for income tax purposes. The transaction to which he referred was subsequently disclosed as the vending to Pierre S. Du Pont of six million two hundred thousand dollars' worth of shares at the market prices, which gave him a tax saving of approximately nine hundred thousand dollars. At the same time Pierre S. Du Pont sold to John Raskob an approximate of the same amount in shares, which netted him about six hundred thousand dollars. Each sold the other Baltimore & Ohio stock and Warner Brothers shares, but the other holdings traded were not identical. Du Pont sold General Motors, and Raskob sold National Cash Register. Du Pont unloaded Kennecot Copper, and Raskob yielded Anaconda Copper. Though the securities differed in name, the aggregate market value was about the same. It seemed as though the two wise plutocrats had found a flawless system of getting the tax benefits without having to part with their securities; but the best laid plans of mice and magnates "gang oft agley." The unemotional Revenue Bureau disallowed the reductions as an evasion of the law. The Board of Tax Appeals sustained the Treasury decision; a circuit court in turn sustained the tax appeals body, and the Supreme Court denied their application for certiorari.

For seven years Mr. Hoover had been enthroned in the Department of Commerce, supposedly with his finger on every financial wrist, and with twenty-nine thousand subordinates to count the pulse beats. This was while he was in his miracle-man stage, with his glamor still undimmed; when in the public estimation he was an almost supernatural figure whose wisdom encompassed all branches, whose judgment was never at fault, who knew the answers to all questions, and who could see in the dark. Yet the blow of October 29, 1929, took him with as complete surprise as it did any of the paper millionaires who had run a shoestring into a hypothetical fortune.

Of course, a man is not himself responsible for having such a reputation plastered on him. It undoubtedly had its part in making him president, for it was obvious that a country must be fortunate to obtain for its highest officer a universal genius, and that is what the American voters elected.

We in Washington did not wholly subscribe to the picture of the wonder worker. We knew him through his years in public office as a hard-driving, intelligent individual with a splendid capacity for handling a definite state of facts. Given a subject such as the soft-coal problem, for example, and a great deal of time, he would evolve a theory about its troubles and their remedies that to a lay mind seemed absolutely impregnable. He accumulated a roomful of data on this particular subject, and could and would talk by the hour about the wagon mines that could only operate at a profit when a strike paralyzed the larger enterprises or when such an emergency as war demanded the largest possible output from any and every source. He had the exact figures about the excess of miners beyond the industry's needs, and his solution was practically the delivering of the whole industry into a few strong hands—a settlement of the problem doubtless in perfect symmetry with advanced economics, but as inhuman as economics are prone to be. He made himself perhaps the greatest authority in the United States on soft coal, but no more came of it than of his elaborate plan for reorganizing the various government departments in order to eliminate duplication of effort and other waste. He used to deliver lectures to newspaper correspondents, at his well-attended conferences, on the number of bureaus having jurisdiction over bears—not the Wall Street kind, but the furred animals. So far ursus continues to get along, though the Kadiak kind is under one jurisdiction, the black bears under another, and the grizzlies under half a dozen. This may not be a strictly accurate tabulation of their distribution under the Interior Department, the Department of Commerce, the Department of Agriculture, the Forestry Bureau and the Park officials; but at any rate it used to be very interesting to see a great chart of the reconstructed government covering one of the walls of his spacious office.

I am aware of the controversy engendered by detractors of

Mr. Hoover as to whether he was not more a promoter of mining speculations than a mining engineer. But the fact remains: his is an engineering mind. Give him definite, concrete facts, and he is a master at arranging them and coordinating them in the form best calculated to produce the desired result. His analysis of the coal business was flawless. Had he been dictator, there would no longer be a coal problem. It was the same with his plan for government reorganization. To a layman it seemed perfect in its symmetry of structure, indisputable in its economical features. But when it came to the twin problem of getting it by a Congress swayed by the pressure of political friends whose patronage would be sadly mussed up, and of navigation amid the pride and personal concern of his cabinet-eers, he was helpless. The intangibles were beyond him. He did not know how to blueprint the processes of overcoming opposition. A stronger president could and would have browbeaten the political-minded Congress; would have issued orders to his cabinet officers; if necessary, would have carried his fight to the people; and with the clarity of his factual intellect would have won. But like all other amateurs at the art of politics he feared antagonisms for which he had no slide rule of calculations. His instinct in this untried field recoiled from conflict. This showed up during his 1928 campaign; it was responsible for much of his vacillation and all of his evasion on direct issues—notably the prohibition question.

Mr. Hoover had nothing to fear from the arid states; his problem was to hold in line the big commonwealths that had pronounced against the Anti-Saloon League and all its works. Every time Chairman Fess—a real and not merely a political dry—opened his mouth, he further alienated New York and Massachusetts, and Rhode Island, and even his own state of Ohio, which elected a wet Democratic senator and a Democratic governor who was dry only in a political sense and who was among the early ones of that persuasion who came out for the Democratic principle of a referendum.

It may have been because of the uncertainty of his views, and of his never having adapted a political policy, that Mr. Hoover

hesitated before coming to a conclusion on almost every problem presented to him. A story was told me by one of the research
men in the government. The occasion was a social gathering of
experts from the Commerce and Agriculture Departments.
Somebody told of a new wheat discovered in some remote section—the Sudan or northern Siberia—calculated either to resist
grain plagues or to withstand cold much more successfully than
the known varieties. Immediately it was suggested that an
expedition be started forthwith to explore and examine the new
discovery. Mr. Hoover expressed amazement at the celerity with
which the project was organized.

"Why not?" asked one of the experts.

"Well," commented the Secretary of Commerce, "you may
be able to do it, but for me, my idea of heaven is a place where
you do not have to make decisions."

The mass of standpat senators—the Old Guard that had borne
the brunt of innumerable battles—never did like their President. Most of the invidious and apochryphal stories that ran
the rounds about Mr. Hoover originated in the Senate cloakroom.

For example, there was that smoking-compartment yarn
about the President and Secretary of the Treasury Mellon walking together, when the President asked him for a five-cent piece
as he desired to telephone a friend. And Mellon replied: "Here's
a dime, telephone both of them."

Actually the attitude of the old-line senators chiefly reflected
their view, founded on long experience, that a president unfortunate enough to have hard times contemporaneous with his
term could not be re-elected. They were not unlike the Wall
Street gamblers. Congressmen make their political profits by
watching the trend of opinion.

Having concluded that Mr. Hoover's race was run, they became bears in Republican stock. Hence the dagger-tongued
Moses, the wholly opportune Watson, and a flock of other
formidable Republican stand-bys, including the most astute
politician of the lot, Vice-President Curtis, lent aid and comfort
to the enemy. Publicly, of course, they did lip service; but every

one of them let it be seen that they had not departed from the frame of mind they were in at the Kansas City convention of 1928, when most of them were assuring whatever audience would listen that Hoover could not be elected.

In fact the previous utterances of the President's spokesmen played no small part in what the administration supporters termed "smearing Hoover."

Officially, Mr. Hoover was ever a promoter. When he took over the Department of Commerce, it was a reasonably modest organization. He spread it all over the governmental map. He took the Bureau of Mines from the Interior. He dipped into the State Department when he realized his idea of commercial agents abroad and left the old commercial attachés of our legations jobless. He trenched on the Treasury, and when he was a member of the Debt Funding Commission not infrequently had Secretary Mellon appealing to President Coolidge, often futilely, for the acceptance of Treasury ideas in preference to those of the Secretary of Commerce.

It was not by accident that he builded for his department the hugest, at that time, and perhaps the most lavishly furnished palace that housed a branch of the government.

This, perhaps, sounds peculiar in view of what has been done under the Roosevelt Administration in the same direction. It should, however, be remembered that I am writing of things as they appeared fourteen years ago, and of the use we made of the material of that era.

I do not think I have exaggerated a single item in this survey of President Hoover's quality, character, and peculiarities. My acquaintance with him was, I assume, approximately the same as that of other correspondents of big newspapers.

Until he became president he was sometimes most cordial to me; at other times he snubbed me, which my newspaper colleagues inform me was likewise their experience. Perhaps the determinant of this mutability of disposition bore some relation to the character of their reports in their journals, for he was always notoriously the thinnest-skinned executive in Washington. Hardly a correspondent but has his stories of presidential complaints to his office concerning stories Mr. Hoover did not like, and the President's industry in ascertaining the authorship of the usually anonymous news articles was simply amazing.

This, then, was the picture we at Democratic headquarters thought it would be useful to our cause to impress upon the people. There was no occasion for billingsgate, no necessity for misrepresentation, no excuse for slander. A man sat in the president's chair who did not fit. His undoubted genius in certain directions did not run along the lines of the chief executive of a great nation. A successful president must be a great politician, using the term in its most complimentary sense. The ability to function along with parallel and equal partners in government is as much a requisite for adequate administration as any other branch of the science of statesmanship. The problem of an executive dealing with the legislative branch is nothing new. There are various formulae. Theodore Roosevelt bullied his Congresses, Wilson impressed them, Harding fraternized with them, Coolidge understood their political problems; but all of these had come up through the primary grades to the presidency, and moreover most of them were men of positive and even violent convictions. Mr. Hoover had no knack of dominating the Senate and House of Representatives. Uncertain of himself, he could not boss nor cajole, nor influence with his logic. He gave the impression of regarding Congress as a nuisance specially erected to worry him; he sulked when he should have fought, and personified into individual enmities any disagreements with his program.

All of which was water on the wheels of a hostile political publicity bureau.

When we of the Democratic organization published our assay of presidential shortcomings, usually in the form of a statement from some senator or representative, or when they were embodied in one of the innumerable speeches that were broadcasted, the President's defenders retorted that we were maligning the Chief Executive. When we pointed out his numerous mistakes as to the extent and acuteness of the financial depression, we were accused of reveling in the misfortunes of the people; of making political capital of distress, and even of prolonging and enhancing the panic.

This was so marked during the 1930 campaign that Senator Pat Harrison was able to pronounce his deadly aphorism that "the whispering campaign of 1928" had been succeeded by "the whimpering campaign of 1930"—a phrase that flowered into a multitude of cartoons depicting the G.O.P. elephant trumpeting his distress. Sometimes for the tearful elephant the classical figure of the Republican party was substituted as the whiner, and sometimes Mr. Hoover himself was the central figure.

Naturally we circulated these cartoons, with the newspapers' permission, of course, particularly featuring those from sources that had supported Mr. Hoover in 1928.

It was not surprising that the administration was indignant at such treatment. The presidential spokesmen took the extraordinary position that the President's performance was no legitimate element in a congressional campaign. The Columbia Broadcasting System conceived the idea that it would interest its auditors to hear a program of debates. The plan was that once a week a prominent Democrat or Republican would open in Washington with a twenty-minute speech presenting the issues from his side. An equally eminent opponent would take the air when he had concluded, answering from Chicago or wherever he happened to be. The first speaker would rebut the argument in a ten-minute close; and this privilege of opening and closing was to alternate between the parties.

There was a conference at the radio company's offices. The chiefs of the two political publicity bureaus were in attendance, and the details were in the course of arrangement.

In response to the radio officials' request I suggested as the opening topic, "The Hoover Administration: Has It Been a Success So Far or a Failure?"

My adversary demurred. He argued that the election of 1930 concerned, nationally, only senators and representatives, and therefore the President was in no way involved, nor could his acts be considered pertinent in any discussion as to whether the Congress to be chosen should be of his party or of the opposition. So the whole business died at that meeting. It was evident that the Republican press agent was acting under positive instructions. There could be only one source for such instructions.

It was at this stage of the political situation that *Scribner's* magazine published a delightfully written article purporting to reveal the true inwardness of our campaign. It was entitled: "Charley Michelson, Hoover's Gadfly." In the advance publicity for the magazine I was not the Gadfly but "Hoover's Nemesis." Between advertisement and publication some erudite person advised the magazine editor that Nemesis was a lady, and the substitution eventuated forthwith.

The theme of the article was the conspiracy between Chairman Raskob and his publicity director to break down the President's prestige, for which purpose the author, Mr. Frank Kent of the Baltimore *Sun*, explained that I had been retained at an inordinate, and presumably an extortionate, salary to plaster Herbert Hoover with mud. However accurate was the diagnosis that our object was to discredit the President—or, to put the matter in the Democratic form, to introduce the real Herbert Hoover to the people of the United States—his premise was all wrong.

The Republican National Committee distributed a million reprints of Mr. Kent's story (excising some personal compliments he had paid me), stressing the Democracy of the writer. They have been quoting him ever since. I wonder how valid is that Democracy in view of the fact that Kent was for Hoover in 1928 and 1932, for Landon in 1936, and for Willkie in 1940.

Meanwhile Governor Roosevelt at Albany was making hay in his own field. Shouse told me that the Governor had a spy in our office reporting to him on all we did. That sounds quite probable, for he never was a man to take chances.

Years later I was to be given a surprising example of the persistency of that particular form of vigilance. Farley was chairman, and the committee headquarters was, naturally, unqualifiedly the unquestioning supporter of President Roosevelt. I had, in order to meet the constant onslaughts of newspaper columnists, inaugurated a column of my own. This I called

"Dispelling the Fog." It made no pretense of nonpartisanship and was issued on the letterhead of the Democratic National Committee. It was widely used; it got a fair share of publicity even in the Republican press, which made its contents the target of denunciation. One day I wrote an issue devoted to Walter Lippmann. The proof of the article was on my desk for final inspection previous to mailing. I thought nobody had seen it except the printer and myself, and was electrified by a call from the White House mentioning that they were advised I was attacking Walter Lippmann. Actually what I had written was a somewhat whimsical reference to the philosopher-columnist. I held up the issue and sent my proof over to the White House, and presently got a phone call okaying the letter. I never asked, and do not know yet, how the White House got an advance tip on my production.

The information that Roosevelt had us under surveillance caused me no concern; for whatever we did we boomed in the newspapers, and if there was any real secret stuff, it was discussed among Raskob, Shouse, and myself, with no other present. In fact when I learned that the Republican National Committee had in mind planting an observer with us, I sent word to them that if they would give me the name of their spy, I'd send him a personal invitation and supply him with a desk adjoining my own.

Governor Roosevelt was making some resonant Democratic speeches, and it occurred to me that it would give a nonpartisan air to the Executive Committee's activities if we circulated those speeches. If we were going to stop Roosevelt—as my colleagues anticipated—it would be all to the good to insure party harmony after that event. That suggestion brought the only rebuff I had in my publicity efforts. The heavy foot of authority came down on my program, and the Governor of New York remained nonexistent in the output of the Democratic National Committee.

The hatching of a surprise egg in this well-built nest has been told in the opening chapter.

3. PIED PIPERS TO THE BALLOT BOX

Those who composed in a Democratic key: their hopes, talents, troubles, and performances.

WHILE the presidential candidate was barnstorming, we at headquarters at the Biltmore Hotel in New York were putting into operation the whirlwind mechanics of a campaign.

Farley was king there. His immediate court consisted of Bob Jackson, W. Forbes Morgan, and Frank Walker, who alternately filled such offices as secretary and treasurer, with me as composer of the music for the distinguished trumpeters who proclaimed our activities. Senators and congressmen, actual or expectant, shifted in and out as visitor advisers.

In later campaigns Morgan and Jackson faded from the picture, being replaced by Lawrence W. (Chip) Robert and Walter Cummings. Bob Jackson had too many clients interested in legislation and Chip too many war contracts to fit in with political window dressing—but that is getting ahead of my story. Walter Cummings, Treasurer, gave place to Oliver Quayle, Jr., who functioned during the hectic period of the campaign books, of which more hereafter.

In 1940 two amiable, efficient, and altruistic millionaires, Edwin W. W. Pauley (oil) and Dick Reynolds (tobacco), became respectively secretary and treasurer under Chairman Ed Flynn, with Oscar Ewing and Mrs. Gladys A. Tillett as vice-chairmen. In the '32 setup there was Molly Dewson, the greatest she-politician of my term, who retired after Roosevelt's second election. Two charming ladies, Mrs. Thomas F. McAllister of Grand Rapids, and Mrs. May Thompson, afterward took over, giving place to Mrs. Tillett for the '40 campaign.

Close by, in '32 Louis Howe burrowed in the most disorderly cubbyhole I ever saw. He rarely attended conferences, but he knew all that was going on and, I suppose, really had a veto power if he cared to exercise it. He was the merest wisp of a man, with a ghastly complexion and an asthmatic cough that prostrated him now and then; but back of his gasping, tremulous personality was a brain that never ceased working and an intensity that kept him planning, efficiently, and directing the strategy of the campaign. He knew as intimately the political situation and its crosscurrents as did Farley, who seemingly could call every leader, high and low, from Maine to California, by his first name and had that man's history, his loyalties, and his shortcomings, at his fingertips. Farley was inclined to deprecate his reputation for never forgetting a name or a face, saying that while he kept an acquaintance with at least one man in every important political division, he did not pretend to remember all the others. However, I recall that on one trip our train stopped at Laramie, Wyoming, and a group of seven or eight came aboard. I think it was Joe O'Mahoney, now senator, who performed the introductions in the course of which Farley extracted personal information about each of the greeters. Four years later we stopped at the same point for a few minutes, and Farley went to the platform and waved to the people.

"Hello, Jim," came a voice from the crowd.

"Hello, Sam," replied the Chairman, "How did your boy get along at West Point?"

This was one of the men who had come aboard four years earlier. I am quite sure that was the first time the two had met, and am equally sure Farley had not seen him again.

Farley was boiling with enthusiasm and confidence in every campaign. Howe was, or pretended to be, the gloomy pessimist. At the 1932 convention he doubted that Garner could possibly be induced to take the vice-presidential nomination and thought it was a better bet to work through Mayor Cermak on Senator J. Ham Lewis, Illinois' favorite son, as a candidate and, later, on Banker Mel Trayler, who had the Illinois votes when Senator Lewis was through with them. He refused to accept anybody's statement that such and such a state was safe but went on the principle that every Northern state must be handled as a battleground. He even insisted on making a try at Maine, though the general view of the strategists at the Biltmore was that such an effort would be simply money thrown away.

His ultimate ambition was to be the President's secretary, and he thought that later he could be appointed to some sort of commissionership, if Roosevelt were elected, but was a trifle pessimistic even about that. Roosevelt liked President Hoover's three-secretary system, which naturally Howe did not care for, as it challenged his status as the number one man. In one of the talks I pointed out to the President-elect some of the disadvantages of the three-secretarial program. My contention was that the President was not going to have time to see all the dignitaries who would come to the White House, and that while a senator, for example, could be pacified if he had his approach through *the* secretary, he would not be happy at being permitted to confer with merely *a* secretary. Whether it was because of my argument, or simply because the President became aware of Louie's anxiety and would not disappoint the oldest and most consistent of his friends, he did give Howe the seniority, though there was no disparity in salaries. That arrangement prevailed until Howe's death, when President Roosevelt reverted to the other system, dividing the work and responsibility, with Marvin McIntyre directing the political phases, Steve Early in charge of the press and related activities, and Colonel —later General—Watson, who had been his military aide, taking care of appointments.

My work during the first campaign consisted principally of writing speeches, getting out pamphlets, inciting eminent citizens to make statements in our favor, circulating cartoons and editorials, supervising the output of the various divisions of the headquarters force, and keeping the newspapers supplied with articles, with names attached of such importance that they could not afford to omit them. Then to me fell all the mail the busy executives did not have time to answer, particularly the suggestions for plans that would make Democratic victory certain. I shall always remember one.

A gentleman sent in this:

Wearing Out the Microphone
(T. E. Powers in the *New York Journal*)

> F—Farsightedness
> D—Democracy
> R—Recovery

He offered us the use of the masterpiece for five hundred dollars. I wrote him thanking him for the offer and explaining that I had no funds, etc. We answered every letter as politely as we could.

Some week later I received his bill for the five hundred dollars, with a covering note reciting that he had seen on a banner in St. Louis this legend:

> F—Faith in his fellow citizens
> D—Devotion to duty and the public welfare
> R—Repeal of the 18th Amendment

This he considered a base infringement of his patent. Of course there were hundreds of such anagrams displayed at local meetings, but none of them came from my shop.

There was unlimited material for publicity. Everybody apparently had come into camp. Al Smith made speeches for Roosevelt. So did John Raskob and Jouett Shouse. Frank Hague, who had been conspicuous on the other side of the fence, threw a huge demonstration for the candidate at Sea Girt, where a hundred thousand people listened to F.D.R.'s speech. So far as could be counted, every soreness of the convention was forgotten. John Raskob testified to his enthusiasm for the cause by knocking off from the debt owed him by the National Committee the sizable sum already referred to. This was, of course, before the days of the Hatch Act.

Later on these gentlemen switched again, and some of the most poignant days of the committee came during the 1936 campaign when the ex-Chairman was insisting on payment of the rest of the debt and we had no means of meeting the demand.

"John Raskob has served notice," phoned Forbes Morgan, then acting treasurer, "that he is going to impound our funds."

"Do you mean to say," was my response, "that he is going to impound our deficit?"

That was good enough for a laugh, but it did not solve our problem. It would have been uncomfortable for the Democratic National Committee to go into bankruptcy or to have a judgment against it that would have involved our desks, typewriters, and other paraphernalia for which the magnate had paid. Raskob is one of the gentlest, kindest men in the world, but we really thought that, in those days of Liberty League bitterness, he would push us to the limit. Ultimately Forbes Morgan dug up the money, and Raskob was so happy over the whole episode that he had photostats made of the check and sent them to the newspapers. I never asked where the ransom money came from but believe some of the labor organizations lifted us out of our peril.

For the time being, those who had fought Roosevelt's nomination most fiercely in 1932 did yeoman service. We were mighty glad to have these folks with us, and we played them up on every occasion. We took particular care to see that Al Smith's speeches were circulated to the voters of New York, Massachusetts, and Pennsylvania, and in other states where the Happy Warrior was strongest; that Raskob's words reached Wall Street, and that Jouett Shouse's orations were delivered to the same people he had addressed in the preconvention campaign. Raskob and Shouse were Democratic heroes when they were rebuilding the party from the ruin in which the election of 1928 had left it.

Naturally these important Democrats did not refer to the episodes of the period when they thought their work of reconstruction would culminate in the renomination of ex-Governor Smith. Their speeches dealt more with a comparison of Roosevelt and Hoover: the contrast between the gloomy occupant of the White House whom we referred to as the author of the depression, and the vibrant Democratic candidate with his words of hope and cheer.

Mr. Hoover's speeches were largely statistical, the theme being that the depression was licked and the only thing that could stop the upward movement was the election of Roosevelt.

In his final speech at Madison Garden he used a phrase that plagued him for a long time: "The grass will grow in the streets of a hundred cities, a thousand towns; the weeds will overrun the fields of millions of farms." He was referring specifically to the Democratic purpose of repealing the Smoot-Hawley Tariff, but the *New York Times* next morning carried as its headline: "Hoover Charges Roosevelt New Deal Would Destroy Foundation of the Nation." We used the grass quotation many times in subsequent campaigns. In 1936 we had a huge harvester machine threading the thoroughfares of Philadelphia with labels proclaiming it was out to mow the Hoover grass from the streets. This was at the period when our country was leaping to prosperity. I doubt if our horseplay influenced many votes, but we were at that time engrossed with the far from easy task of keeping the Philadelphia convention going for a long enough period to give the merchants and hotelkeepers of the City of Brotherly Love a decent chance of recouping, from the convention crowds, the money they had raised to bring the convention to them. They had bid, I think, two hundred thousand dollars for the privilege.

The battle of 1932 has frequently been referred to as a smear campaign. In looking back over the files, I find little of personal attack on President Hoover. The pamphlets and speeches that emanated from headquarters at the Biltmore Hotel in New York were practically all devoted to the various acts and omissions of his administration to which we traced the causes of the depression, the Smoot-Hawley Bill among others.

There had been published a series of books dealing viciously with Mr. Hoover's business career as a mine promoter. They were brought to me—by whom, I have forgotten—with the idea that they constituted an almost priceless arsenal of anti-Hoover ammunition. I turned them down—not because of any conscientious scruple against using any effective weapon against the Republican nominee, but simply because there was not time to investigate adequately the alleged facts in the books, and I did not feel I could take any chances of being confronted with disproof of the narratives. Nor did I permit use of any of the material during the campaign. There was a single slip-up. It occurred during one of my absences at Washington. I commuted between the New York headquarters and my shop at the Capitol, which was manned by veterans of the politico-publicity game: Dick Linthecum and Colonel Bob Gates and Buck Hayden, all newspapermen, and ex-Governor Cooper of South Carolina, now a judge in Puerto Rico.

The Women's Division made reference in one of their famous "fliers" to the employment in one of Hoover's African mining adventures of something approaching slave labor. The Hoover people cried out, and I was really as much disturbed as they, until we found reference to the incident in one of the counter-propaganda books written by a Hoover admirer. At all events, that was the only time the books on Hoover's business career figured in the campaign.

My second-in-command of the publicity division was Norman Baxter, who, after a notable newspaper career, took the desperate job of press-agenting Ritchie's presidential aspirations. Bert Ritchie's fate was queer. Extremely popular, with repeated successes as Maryland's governor, with the prestige of having come out for prohibition repeal when nearly all the other prominent political figures were pussyfooting, he never got farther in national affairs than becoming a possible second choice. He might have been Roosevelt's running mate if it had not been that the vice-presidency was part of the price of Garner's turning his votes to the New Yorker. Ritchie's publicity man was my first recruit when the campaign got under way, and no political press agent ever had a finer lieutenant. Many of the speeches for which I was given credit were his product. The determination to go after Maine in 1936 cost me his services for a time. We got for him a moribund newspaper, and he whooped it up for Roosevelt and was perhaps responsible for the cutting down of the Pine Tree State's usual Republican majority.

It was obviously going to be impossible for us to afford the retention of our big campaign staff after election day, and I had a tentative arrangement by which our most competent people would be taken into government service—with the proviso that I could reclaim them when another campaign came around.

Baxter went with Jesse Jones in the R.F.C. When I wanted him back, Jesse Jones demurred.

"You remind me of my father," protested Jesse. "When I was a boy, if there was a sorry piglet he gave him to me; and when I had nursed the animal into a fine, fat marketable animal, he'd take him back."

Jones finally loaned him to me for a time in '36. Ultimately he was lured away by the distillers at a grand salary. Forbes Morgan had quit the committee to be the czar of the liquor business, and his untimely death gave an opening for Norman Baxter. When the latter's hitch with the whiskey business was over, I reclaimed him for a while; but Jesse Jones soon took him away from me permanently. I was fortunate in being able to replace him with Eddie Roddan, a veteran White House correspondent, another fine lieutenant who made my work easy. Roddan refused to go into the government and ultimately enlisted in the army as a private. The army, promptly yanked him out of the ranks and made him an officer. Another of the fine fellows I had with me was Ed Brown, who did a term for us on the forlorn Maine front and later had charge of our reference room and got out my clipsheet, which supplied eight or ten thousand newspapers with Democratic news. I meant to groom him for my successor, but in one of our recurring financial doldrums he left to take a soldier job with an advertising agency. Among my efficient staff was Lorena Hickok, formerly of the Associated Press. She was taken away and made executive secretary of the distaff branch of the National Committee, which in wartime assumes greater importance than ever. With millions of men in foreign service, the women's vote may be the determining factor in the '44 elections; for however earnest may be the effort to get in the soldier vote, it is inevitable that many of the men in uniform will fail to record their preference with ballots.

The Washington office got out most of the pamphlets, because the statistics were in that city, and attended to the mechanics of printing and of circulating what we mimeographed from New York.

Looking back on that campaign and comparing it with the corresponding periods of 1936 and 1940, it was evidently a fairly comfortable engagement. The whole country was so worried about its economic affairs and so eager to try anything that promised relief from the terrors of the depression that friends of the Roosevelt movement bobbed up in the most unexpected quarters. Our "Republican for Roosevelt" league, instead of being a mere gesture to scare the enemy, which is the usual measure of such bodies, was an actual fighting force, so extensive that the Democratic candidate delivered to it one of his big addresses. The meeting was presided over by Richard Washburn Child, President Harding's ambassador to Italy and representative during Republican administrations at many international conferences. Roosevelt opened his speech on that occasion with these words: "I am here tonight at the invitation of a group of public-minded citizens who have placed principle above party. These citizens, whose party affiliation has been Republican, have publicly declared that they consider a change in the administration of government is necessary; that it is, in fact, indispensable to a restoration to normal conditions. And so, on such an occasion, it is fitting for me to speak as a citizen rather than a partisan."

Then he went on to recite his adventures as governor with Republican legislatures, pointing out that cooperation between the executive and an opposition legislative branch was feasible, and instancing that though he had vetoed many bills, not one of his vetoes was overruled, and not one of his appointments met with rejection. His comments may have some significance now in view of the complexion of contemporary Congresses.

From newspapers, in 1932, he received generally either outright support or only mild opposition. It was very different in later campaigns when eighty-five per cent of the big journals reverted to their normal Republicanism and assailed him with all their fury. From the record we might figure that the newspaper support which we considered of prime importance in our first presidential campaign had really little significance in elections, for in '36 and in '40 nearly all papers were anti-Roosevelt.

The phenomena are in line with the inability of a political figure to swing the votes from himself to another individual in general elections (though it has been done at conventions). The big newspapers may have the favor of multitudes, as shown by their huge circulations, but the readers do not take their political faith from editorial columns or colored news stories. Perhaps the same thing may be true of political speeches. Nobody has as yet figured that a particular speech won an election; but the indications are that sometimes an ill-timed or inept speech may hinder or lose an election, and we do not have to go back to the "Rum, Romanism, and Rebellion" bull of the Blaine campaign for an example of this lethal effect.

It is with this thought in mind that political managers are uneasy when their candidate is on the hustings. That was worrying the general staff when we doubted the wisdom of F.D.R.'s taking the risks of impromptu rear-platform talks on his first western tour.

Once during the 1932 campaign we were really alarmed. The candidate in his "Four Horsemen" speech at Baltimore had used this expression:

"After March 4, 1929, the Republican party was in complete control of all branches of the federal government. The executive, the Senate, the House of Representative and, I might add for good measure, the Supreme Court as well."

This implication that the Supreme Court was under political influence raised a terrific hullabaloo on the opposition side. Our candidate was arraigned for everything from irreverence, almost sacrilege, to an instinct to center all power in the executive branch in the event of his election. The Republican newspapers editorialized on the peril of having a man of such destructive views at the head of the government; the Republican orators went to town on Roosevelt's irresponsibility, and some implied that his mind was affected.

There were several conferences at Democratic headquarters, before the candidate got back, as to what should be done. When he arrived on the scene, he took the "let-the-heathen-rage" attitude. Actually that was all that could be done. To attempt to explain that he only meant that the justices had been appointed by Republican presidents and confirmed by a Republican Senate, or otherwise soften the expression, would have made matters worse; for it would have been backtracking and so would have weakened Roosevelt's stand before the people as a forthright, fearless man and no shuffler. Moreover, we knew that the candidate meant just what he said.

This gust blew itself out and evidently caused not the slightest difference in the result of the election a week later.

We saw his words turned into action when the time came.

4. THE MORNING AFTER VICTORY

Newsmen grant the winner a holiday, and he administers one to the banks.

WE HAD BARELY TIME to realize our victory when the job hunters were on our necks. The letters and personal calls almost overwhelmed us. I shared the burden of answering candidates for places. Later on, the flood of applications became so vast that we had to set up a regular bureau to handle it. As a preliminary we had a flock of girls making a first classification of the list. The "A" list comprised those who had all the endorsements—those of the senators, representatives, national committeemen, and state and county chairmen. The "B" list was those who had a sizable string of sponsors but fell short of completeness, and the "C" list took in the thousands who had a single endorsement. It worked pretty well until one day I got a rather petulant inquiry as to what was being done about the application of John Doe—I have forgotten the actual name —for a minor post in the Customs Division. Having in mind the source of the inquiry, we waded through the "A" classification. Nothing there. Then we went through the second division with no better results. Finally we turned the whole force loose on the mountain of "C" applications, and there we found it. The girls had done their work according to directions. The object of the inquiry had but one endorsement—that of Franklin D. Roosevelt.

The President-elect wanted to go away on a sea trip with his friend Vincent Astor but was fearful that this would be anything but a vacation if the yacht were trailed by newspaper boats. It is a newspaper tradition that an incoming president must be kept under journalistic surveillance every day and every hour of the day, for with a cabinet to be named, and such matters, wherever the new man is becomes a source of important news. Some tentative inquiries had been made, but the publishers were cold to relieving the incoming president from surveillance; and rather than head a marine parade, Roosevelt thought he must abandon the trip. I volunteered to see if I could not arrange matters, so I made the rounds, calling on the chiefs of the press associations and the editors of the big newspapers that would have chartered vessels to trail the Astor yacht. I knew them all and was sure, at least, of a hearing for my plea and argument. Generally they wanted to know how they would be protected in the event that anything exciting or untoward occurred on the yacht. Finally we came to this arrangement: The President-elect was to communicate with me daily by radio, and I pledged myself to call the newspapers and give them everything I got. They stipulated that I must be the medium, for they were suspicious that the vacation was a subterfuge for important conferences and decisions, and they were doubtful about the new secretariat.

So I waited at Washington until one morning I found that the messages were going to the secretariat at Miami and the news was coming from there. I was fearful that some of the papers that had been the hardest to placate might call this a breach of the agreement and put their men to sea; but nobody raised the question, and the President-elect had a pleasant and unwatched vacation. Some of the ship's company afterward told me that he throughly· enjoyed reporting his own doings; and the newspapers got all they wanted as to who caught a fish and who didn't, and equally vital happenings pertinent to the incoming administration. The episode is of no importance, but at the time it loomed big, for nobody wanted the new administration to make its start with a hostile press.

We learned, through the succeeding terms, that newspaper friendships were fragile. We had practically all of them in 1933. Like the rest of the country, even the largest journals were jittery. The New York *World* had folded up because of depression losses. Tremulous business firms could not face big advertising bills; the ten million, or was it sixteen million, unemployed bought no newspapers; the procession of falling banks made it difficult to meet payrolls and white paper invoices. Roosevelt appeared to be the only hope, and the journals whooped it up for the N.R.A., the P.W.A., the C.C.C., and the rest of the pioneers among the alphabetical projects that promised relief from the ghastly perils of the time.

A different situation in 1936 brought a different tune. By then business was well on its way up, and the large industries, no longer fleeing from possible collapse, were again thinking of bigger profits and looking askance at such legislation as the security measure and the Wagner Labor Act. Practically without exception the Republican press resumed its factional attitude. Even the Democratic line was seriously broken. The *New York Times* was cold, the *St. Louis Post Dispatch* was critical. All the so-called independents went with the tide. The Hearst papers were flagellating us, writing elaborately about dictatorship and dreamy-eyed brain trusters plunging the country into socialism, communism, collectivism and other isms that meant the destruction of the capitalistic system.

The Liberty League was in full swing, with Raskob and Shouse and a formidable roster of captains of industry bombarding the public with speeches, pamphlets, and proclamations all devoted to the weakness, recklessness, instability, stubbornness, indifference, fanaticism, etc., of the President. And the newspapers valiantly carried the whole of the barrage. Obviously no single individual could compass all these conflicting characteristics, but political wars involve neither consistency nor moderation. The basic strategy is to smash at every target, with the idea that by stressing absolutism as an issue there may be garnered liberal votes, and by emphasizing collectivism or paternalism the conservative element may be solidified. A vote is a vote, regardless of its parentage.

I do not subscribe to the doctrine that all newspapers are either sordid or self-righteous. Big business is big business, whether it is based on rolling mills or printing presses. The day of the Danas and Pulitzers who were capable of starting on a shoestring and an idea, and parleying it into a multimillionaire enterprise, passed with the advent of the trusts. Their present-day successors, perforce, subscribe to the philosophy of their associates and congeners in huge enterprise. Most of them believe that the thinking of a community should be in the hands of the successful; that happiness, in the economic field, can never be attained by way of the Jefferson hypothesis that prosperity should begin at the bottom and extend upward, but can only be reached via Hamilton's theory that the good and wise individuals—in the language of an industrial king of my earlier reporter days, the men "to whom God had entrusted the handling of resources of the country"—would always give the plain people steady work at wages proportionally commensurate with the profits.

It was no wonder that the owners of the metropolitan press should have exalted Governor Landon as a marvelous statesman and the white hope of America. From their point of view anybody was preferable to Roosevelt. Incidentally, our one headache during the 1936 campaign came about over Governor Landon. In one of his speeches Jim Farley referred to him as the governor of a "typical prairie state." There was nothing invidious about the phrase, any more than there would have been had he spoken of Pennsylvania as a typical manufacturing state or Idaho as a typical mountain state, but the Republican editors and orators read a sneer into it and charged us with insulting Kansas. They made so much noise that a ukase went forth eliminating the word "typical" from our political vocabulary forever. From that time on, every state mentioned was described as splendid or great or magnificent. Kansas, after all, cannot have been very deeply offended, for our candidate carried Kansas by about seventy thousand votes—which was certainly not typical of that particular prairie state.

In some respects the interval between our first Presidential election and inauguration was a busier period even than the campaign. We were in the midst of the depression, and the President-elect told me on one occasion that the bank crisis was due to culminate just about inauguration day. He outlined roughly his tentative program for dealing with that, and the other projects which finally crystallized as the "New Deal."

Due to my experiences as a reporter and editor I had a smattering of knowledge of these great questions, but told him that, like most newspaper people, I knew no subject thoroughly and did not feel competent to assay the wisdom of what he had in mind, though, as he presented the topics, they seemed the acme of logic. However, he persevered in his discussion of the fiscal problem, the farm problem, and the vast enigma of unemployment. He quoted from innumerable books and authorities, from Necker's effort to rehabilitate the finances of France in the day of the Louis' to the contemporary suggestion of the commodity dollar. He swung over to farm production and the dilemma of the agriculturalists, faced with mortgage foreclosures in a crushed market, which not only menaced the producers but carried with it a possible famine. I had known him as a young politician, as assistant secretary of the navy, and as governor of New York. Parenthetically, he was a lifesaver to the Washington correspondents during his naval incarnation, for in Woodrow Wilson's dour moments, when we had no access to the President, he was our great source of administration information, and he had shown an uncanny instinct for knowing what could be disclosed and what must be concealed.

Well, I had known him during these periods; I had heard his two speeches nominating Al Smith, the Happy Warrior, for the presidency, and had just seen him through a hot campaign; but this disclosure of his technological expertness was something new. Finally I burst out with:

"Governor, how on earth did you accumulate so much definite knowledge of so many things?"

"Well," he replied, and there was no suggestion of self-pity in his answer, "you fellows with two good legs spend your spare time playing golf, or shooting ducks and such things, while I have had to get all my exercise out of a book."

Just about that time, President Hoover invited him to collaborate in some holdover problems. The President-elect could not decline to discuss these things with the outgoing president, nor could he risk the almost certain clash between his own attitude and the reactionary philosophy of Herbert Hoover. Naturally Roosevelt did not care to have the dramatic effect of his intended proposals spoiled by a premature discussion of them in advance of their delivery. He saw no chance that the President would accept his philosophy, and it was equally certain that he was not going to alter it to conform to the Hoover thought.

On one occasion when F.D.R.'s personality was being analyzed for a newspaper article, I had ventured to tell the correspondent that we really had three Presidents: the fanatic idealist, the stubborn Dutchman, and the practical politician. The practical politician was on the job when the Hoover proposition was broached. The Hoover administration was winding up in a period of intense gloom, and Roosevelt's forecast was that things would be worse at its close. He had no mind to be identified with the crash, figuring correctly that only by a dramatic surprise could he restore the people's confidence and make them believe that better times were coming. So he and Professor Raymond Moley went to the White House, where Hoover had Ogden Mills as his second in what he apparently deemed a duel of wits. It was with the customary political habit of according no proper motive for anything the opposition had in mind that we interpreted, perhaps unjustly, President Hoover's purpose in extending the invitation. The prevalent theory around Democratic headquarters was that the passing president meant to embarrass his successor, either by making him a party to whatever expedient Hoover had in mind or by being able to present that the incoming president had refused to join in a program to stay the depression.

We were uneasy about the outcome of the White House conference, but it worked out all right. Roosevelt took the position that authority and responsibility had to go together, and therefore until he had assumed the office he could take no part in any decision from the White House.

Incidentally, I think we all underestimated Ray Moley, as we did the rest of the brain trust. They were about the offices, of course, but the practical politicians regarded them as more or less of a nuisance that had to be tolerated, and I do not recall a single instance in which they were consulted as to political strategies or policies.

Moley was the most effective of the lot. He not only seemed to have superb technical skill in economic matters, but he had a fairly hard-boiled attitude toward what was necessary in a campaign. In the retrospect it is evident that during the early development of the Roosevelt ascendency he was the most valuable contributor to the new president's success—except, perhaps, for Louis Howe. He had a fine gift for phrase making, and while it was part of our creed to attribute to him complete ignorance of political requirements and procedure, I believe that when the President occasionally disregarded the advice of his field officials, it was Moley's voice to which he listened.

Moley's view of the purely political entourage was as uncomplimentary as their appraisment of him. He had a truly professorial contempt for the people who managed the campaign, regarding them as an element that had to be endured but not encouraged.

Moley and Howe had a mutual detestation for each other. This was quite natural for men striving to be first in their relations to the President. Courts do not change, and neither do courtiers, and the White House circle differed little from the groups that make the history of the old French kings fascinating. Not all courtiers are sycophantic nor interested only in their own advancement. Loyal service is not incompatible with individual rivalry; and while these two were doing their best for their chief, they were eyeing each other askance.

The President could not have failed to note the feud, but there is an art in handling courtiers equal to the art of keeping in the good graces of the ruler. He was amiable to both. Louis was domiciled at the White House, and his illness kept him in his room most of the time, where both the President and Mrs. Roosevelt visited him frequently. Moley was with the President in his offices or in his chamber more than anybody else.

The value or detriment of sycophancy as an element in the success of those about the eminent or powerful is a moot question. Probably it depends on the personality of the magnate. I never knew a man close to the throne who did not claim to be independent and outspoken in his contacts with his chief, and I never knew a magnate who did not proclaim his desire that his people could contradict him whenever they thought he was wrong. But there are few among the dwellers in the shadow of the great who are self-assertive, and I am obliged to admit that in my intimacies there have been equally few of the dignitaries who relished either criticism or questioning of their judgment.

As a rough summary of my contemporaries, I should estimate Steve Early and Marvin McIntyre,* of the White House secretariat, as most likely to correct the chief; Harry Hopkins is reputed always to agree with him. I do not know, of course, what transpires when the President and his most consistent satellite have their confidential talks, but I recall that on one occasion, at least, Mr. Hopkins gave the friendly advice to a chairman of the Democratic National Committee to avoid differing from the President in the discussion of policies.

This condition prevailed until the preparations for the eco-

---

* McIntyre died in December, 1943.

nomic conference in London were imminent. By that time, so it appeared to an interested observer, the professor began to feel that he was deputy president and fated to run the show.

In the course of this rather random record I mean to tell the story of that historic conference—which got nowhere in its agenda objectives, but served to tumble from eminence a man of real ability. That story, of course, will be from the viewpoint of the United States delegation's official public relationship director, which was my title and job.

Almost immediately after Roosevelt's advent to the White House I was summoned there and told to report to the Treasury, where Will Woodin had just taken charge.

The Treasury job had been intended for Senator Carter Glass, who not only had been Woodrow Wilson's secretary of the treasury but had been the strong man of the administration in the financial committee of the Senate. Likewise he had made the great speech of the campaign which did much to alleviate the anxieties of the business world as to the prospective plans of the Democratic candidate in 1932. The Senator dallied with the treasuryship idea for many days but finally declined the appointment, doubtless because his conservative views on the money question did not quite square with the Rooseveltian program.

When Glass declared himself out of it, the natural choice was Woodin. Though he was a Republican, he had swung into the Roosevelt orbit and had been named by Roosevelt, early in the latter's first gubernatorial incumbency, as a member of the board to study and revise the banking laws of New York State. He had been president of the American Car & Foundry Company and a flock of other big corporations, and was an early and large contributor to the Roosevelt campaign funds. We knew him at campaign headquarters largely because of an amusing story told us by Jim Farley. One day Farley answered a telephone call. It was Woodin asking plaintively how a man with a fifty-thousand-dollar contribution could get in to see the chairman.

An overefficient doorman, deceived by the unobtrusiveness

of a visitor, had turned down the capitalist with the statement that Mr. Farley was too busy to see any salesman. At that time our Biltmore headquarters was a mecca for agents who wanted to supply us with campaign buttons, banners, advertising, and all the other paraphernalia a new political organization requires; and most of them knew Farley, or pretended to.

I never knew whether Woodin's self-effacement was real or whether it was a whimsical pose, for later I saw him stand up to some of the toughest fellows that ever bullied an adversary, with all the rasp in his normally ultrasoft voice the occasion required. He had inherited from Ogden Mills, his predecessor, a group of technical assistants, who stood by while he habituated himself to his job. Chief among these holdovers was Arthur Ballantine. Doubtless these men were conscientious in performing their functions under the new chief, but their philosophy was poles apart from the fiscal policies of the Roosevelt administration. They had constituted an hierarchy that entertained no doubts as to the sanctity of their methods and precedents; and in his daily dealings with them, the new Secretary was anything but the poet and dreamy musician pictured in contemporary estimates by writers who saw the dramatic possibilities of such a character in a hard-boiled job. There was a note of authority in his conversations with them that advised them he knew what he was about; and distasteful or not as was their office, they soon conformed.

The terrific responsibility of the task he had undertaken for a country in the midst of the most chaotic and disastrous economic condition it had ever known did not scare him; but he was gun-shy of newspaper reporters, and it was probably on this account that I had been assigned to take charge of his public relations.

I do not think I was very popular with the holdovers, who regarded me as a symbol of the changed, and to them deplorable, methods of the day. They hardly disguised their discomfort at having present at such conferences—they had come to regard them as cloistered mysteries—an outsider who did not even pretend to subscribe to the sacredness of the rituals. But as I had to handle the press reports on what was going on, I had to be among those present. My declaration (with no authority) that no statements should be issued that I could not understand almost provoked an earthquake.

I had one friend among the holdovers—Eugene Meyer, who was, I think, chairman of the Reconstruction Finance Corporation. This was before he bought the *Washington Post* and turned from banker to journalist. I had come to him (I was then on the *World*) with a story of the plight of a group of Western banks that I had been informed were about to fold up. I recited to him my information about their condition.

"Your information is absolutely correct," said Meyer. "Perhaps their situation is even worse than you describe. You are perfectly safe in printing your story. If you do, every one of those banks will close tomorrow. If you don't, we can save three-quarters of them. Now, damn you, it's up to you!"

Naturally the story was not printed.

Under Woodin's leadership the first thing they had to tackle was the problem of the banks. Roosevelt had already determined that, as a preliminary to the reform of the system that had the great financial institutions toppling like tenpins, a banking holiday was requisite, and so he issued his order closing all the banks until it could be determined which of them were solvent or susceptible to rehabilitation.

Technically these matters of deep finance were, of course, clear over my head, so I sat dumbly through the conferences that dealt with these propositions of tremendous import.

Presently I was told to prepare an address for the President. This was the foundation of his fireside talk which electrified the country. I told Woodin and the others that I would need somebody to keep me straight on fiscal nomenclature, etc., exaggerating my own deficiency by telling them I did not know a debenture from a due bill. So they assigned a young man to sit up with me while I batted out on the typewriter the first draft of the document. In a footnote in his volume published some time later, Professor Moley said the speech was entirely rewritten by Arthur Ballantine, which was my first information that that gentleman had ever seen the draft. It must have been handed him by Moley. The actual preparation of the speech followed the procedure I have described in regard to other speeches. I went over to the White House with my draft (I never saw or heard of any other) and the President lay on a couch and dictated his own speech.

Really my first job with the Treasury concerned the press conferences with the new secretary. I found that the establishment was plagued by a swarm of Wall Street touts who beat it to the telephone to convey their hints to stock operators and so forth. So we organized the Treasury Correspondence Press Association, and Woodin validated their decision that thereafter none but regular newspaper correspondents who had been accepted in the press galleries of the House and Senate were eligible to attend. This decision cost me many friends because magazine people and feature writers generally were debarred, but it did the job of cleaning house. The new secretary was a trifle shy at the initial conferences, but on my assurance that the regular correspondents there were absolutely trustworthy and that it would be perfectly safe to be frank with them and tell them what could and could not be published, he loosened up.

Within a fortnight Will Woodin was visiting the press headquarters, where he sat on a desk and regaled the correspondents with a mandolin recital of his new musical compositions. I even had some difficulty in persuading him against putting in a big refrigerator stocked with beer for his new friends—and they were his friends. Time after time in the conferences some member would speak up and suggest that something he had revealed had better be "off the record." They were as determined as I was that the novice in government should not make any mistakes.

The real stress of Woodin's job came with the separation of the financial sheep from the goats: the determination of which banks should be permitted to open, which should be aided to give them a chance for survival, and which should be eliminated permanently. In the end he had to make the decisions, under the bombardment of old financial associates bent on protecting institutions of doubtful solvency and in the face of the terrific responsibility of protecting or crippling millions of depositors. He was seriously ill when the burden was heaviest.

My order to go abroad with the delegates to the London Economic Conference came in the midst of this. I never saw Will Woodin again. He was practically on his deathbed when his advice was sought to influence the currency stabilization talks that aided in wrecking the ill-omened conference.

5. RAGS ARE ROYAL RAIMENT

. . . when worn for virtue's sake. The trials and tribulations of conducting political campaigns on a shoestring. High finance that by-passed the law.

THERE HAS HARDLY been a time since the Raskob regime that the Democratic National Committee has not been afflicted with money troubles.

We came out of each of the three national campaigns from $500,000 to $800,000 in debt.

Sometimes we were able to clear up these obligations promptly, but only to run into debt again. The first Roosevelt preconvention campaign was pulled through with the dollars of Frank Walker, now postmaster-general; Will Woodin; Ed Flynn, successor to Jim Farley as national chairman; Jesse Straus, and a few others. They continued to help after Roosevelt's nomination, with Henry Morgenthau, Sr., and James W. Gerard among the other contributors. Frank Walker had become treasurer, and his efforts among the wealthy were timely and effective. There were next to no general subscriptions. The Democratic party throughout the nation was demoralized and politically broke. The Hoover landslide of 1928 had dumped Democrats out of many state and municipal jobs. Three Republican terms had rid the national government of Democrats; so the usual reservoir of officeholders' money was empty so far as we were concerned.

But we, the practical politicians, saw a promised land ahead. There was no record of a party in power being hard up. Consequently our $600,000 deficit was regarded as a decoration rather than a calamity. But it turned out to be a long trek to that promised land. The big appointments, and presumably patronage jobs, were chiefly on relief measures; and though the other party called appropriations to W.P.A., P.W.A., N.R.A., etc., stupendous corruption funds, not even a trickle of money from these sources flowed into the National Committee's treasury. We plugged along with victory dinners and other conventional expedients, and it was five years before that debt was wiped out. By that time the 1938 deficit had been superimposed, and we had to climb up an even higher hill to get in sight of the horizon of solvency.

We were pretty pure in those days. The ukase went out that to avoid such scandals as had afflicted previous administrations, there should be no taint of lobbying about the National Committee. Bob Jackson, secretary, dropped out. Bruce Kremer resigned his national committeemanship. Forbes Morgan, garnering his whiskey czarship, was succeeded as treasurer by Oliver Quayle, Jr.; and Lawrence W. "Chip" Robert became secretary.

In 1936 the United Mine Workers came to our rescue with contributions of $100,000 to the National Committee and $50,000 to the "Nominators and Electors," a theoretically nonpartisan group like the Good Neighbor League.

In November of that year the mine workers came across with an additional loan of $50,000 to the National Committee. John Lewis was willing to forgive that debt, but we insisted on paying it, which we did with bittersweet consciousness of rectitude

and perhaps with more alacrity than if the enemy had not
constantly taunted us.

Meanwhile the Hatch Act had come along to plague us with
its various restrictions, prohibitions, and limitations. It took all
the ingenuity of the strategy board to evade these. Big contributions and loans now had to be made to state organizations
or else be attributed to individual names in amounts not in
excess of $5000. We had to vary the processes for our hundred-
dollar Washington, Jefferson, or Jackson Day dinners. It had
been the practice to charge the full amount for a ticket, though
the actual dinner costs were less than ten, it being understood
that the excess went to our treasury. Smaller dinners of the
same order were held in many cities, and usually, but by no
means invariably, the net proceeds came to us. The alteration
was to invite to our banquet those who contributed $100—
which produced the same return but brought us within the
law. Sad to relate, some states held out on us part or all of the
dinner proceeds.

Then the convention-book expedient was resorted to. The
souvenir volume for national conventions was an old institution. The book had been a relatively modest affair peddled
out for a quarter or some similar small change. We elaborated
it. We got out an impressive tome with full-page illustrations,
histories by eminent writers, and advertisements. Corporations
may not contribute to political organizations, but there is no
bar to their advertising their products in any publication they
choose. By guaranteeing a circulation of a hundred thousand
we were able to fix a high rate, with pleasurable results. We
got $2500 a page for some of this. Moreover, we charged $2.50
per copy for the paperbound edition, $5.00 for the clothbound,
and $100 for the de luxe limited edition, every copy of which
was autographed by the President.

I had some difficulty in convincing the President of the
righteousness of the procedure, or perhaps his hesitancy was
largely due to the drudgery of writing his signature so many
times, but he did it.

Hundred-Tongued Charley, the Great Silent Orator
(Herbert Johnson in *The Saturday Evening Post*)

"How do we get down?"
(Jim Berryman in the *Washington Star*)

After the convention we put the business in the hands of a sales agency—and they went to town.

Occasionally I would get an indignant protest from somebody who had been approached by a solicitor, charging that he had been threatened with some sort of reprisal if he failed to buy books or that he had been offered some advantage if he came in. I immediately called down the agency and invariably got back an abject apology stating that the solicitor had misrepresented his mission and had been discharged. However, the campaign went on. The opposition press and orators roared their indignation; speeches were made in Congress denouncing us as holdup men. We countered by presenting that the Republican convention book was on the same order, if on a much smaller scale.

We realized about a quarter of a million dollars by this advent into the publishing business, and cut our debts by that amount.

We did not take all the money that was offered us. For example, one day an eminent gentleman called on me and told me he would produce $200,000 for our campaign fund. Naturally the circumstance that he came to me instead of to the treasurer made me think that there was something in the background. I mentioned it to the President in the course of a conversation.

"You know," he said, "that that gentleman is a candidate for a high diplomatic position?"

"I believe he is."

"Well, you know he is not going to be appointed to that place?"

"I know it now."

"If the committee took that money he would have a right to assume that he had bought something; so you will have to get along without it."

I did not communicate any further with my $200,000 man.

On another occasion a friend came to me with a mass of figures and charts.

They concerned floor space and New York rents. He demonstrated to me that the government could save a huge amount in rentals by exchanging its various New York offices for a centralized headquarters in the big city, and he proposed that the government buy the Empire State Building, at a figure seven million dollars less than it had cost to erect that white elephant.

It sounded like a good business proposition, even though he offered me a $50,000 commission if the sale went through.

"Change that," I told him, "to have ten men contribute $5000 each to the Democratic campaign fund, and I'll see what I can do."

On that basis I went to Leo Crowley, then head of the Federal Deposit Insurance Corporation. He was intrigued by the prospect of a bargain, but negotiations there were barren of result; so I finally got to Jesse Jones and told him the story. He thought that in time something could be worked out, with mortgages or some other of the banker expedients, but time went by and nothing happened. Finally Al Smith came to Washington and had a talk with the President.

The government did not buy the Empire State Building but rented some acres of the vacant floor space—and our campaign fund did not get the $50,000.

Another time, with a $20,000 contribution to excite me, I nearly got into trouble. It concerned a tract of land in the Adirondacks, which I was told was the only remaining bit of virgin forest in the state. It had been leased to a hunting club that was breaking up, and the owner almost wept when he narrated to me that lumber interests were poised to move in and cut the timber. He wanted the tract to become a public park. A bill, introduced by Senator Wagner, had already passed the Senate. The House was on the eve of adjournment, and the bill was swamped in the rush of the closing session. It was represented that New York State could not get through a bond issue in time to save the timber, and the Wagner bill provided for the federal government to put up the money until such time as New York could do it.

I asked Speaker Bankhead to recognize Representative Merritt of New York in the midst of the hurly-burly of the session's ending. The Speaker consented, and the House passed the bill forthwith.

Kindly Fate and a vigilant Bureau of the Budget saved me, for the latter reported adversely and the President vetoed the measure. Not until that had happened did I discover that pretty nearly every lobbyist between Albany and Washington was in on the deal for a fat commission.

Thereupon I realized that the lobby sea was far too perilous for an unsophisticated publicity man; and since that narrow escape I would not embark on a similar enterprise—not even if it were a bill to validate the Ten Commandments.

A less definite proposition that came to my attention was the idea that if the State Department would relax its restrictions so as to admit some unnamed wealthy Jewish refugees from German persecution, we would not have to worry about a campaign fund. That one I did not go to work on; for though we were famine-stricken for campaign money, I did not see myself asking Cordell Hull to connive at the violation of the immigration law.

Actually ours was a hand-to-mouth existence most of the time. When the hunger became acute, you might hear Chip Robert on the transatlantic telephone calling on Ambassador Tony Biddle for a hurry-up check for a few thousand to tide us over. For the year previous to this writing I am sure that Secretary Edwin W. Pauley and Treasurer Dick Reynolds kept the establishment alive.

These two were the political heroes of 1941-1942. Their contribution had to come by a devious passage. It was on the same principle that our freight ships to the war fronts had to be routed around the Cape of Good Hope to avoid being torpedoed—which suggests that if the motive be virtuous and the desire intense, there can be no insurmountable obstacles.

Such a kind of navigation was necessitated by the magnificent radio program from the White House closing the 1940 campaign. That masterpiece set us back about $200,000. Rather, to be more accurate, it dumped an obligation of that amount on a sovereign state. Both New York and New Jersey composed the rescue corps—the Hatch Act does not forbid contributions to state organizations, so the desired result was achieved with scrupulous attention to the letter of the law. Oscar "Jack" Ewing, an eminent New York lawyer, was vice-chairman at the time and piloted the enterprise through the tortuous and perilous channels.

Chip Robert fell a victim to the puritanism of the White House on the subject of National Committee officials exploiting their posts for personal advantage. Robert was head of the biggest engineering company in the South, and naturally that company got a lot of big navy, and some army, contracts. His outfit had done considerable work for the services in prewar and presecretary days. There developed a perfect storm of criticism. In Congress, and in the anti-administration newspapers, the matter was heralded as a barefaced grab; a shocking example of favoritism, with more than a hint of some hidden corruption. The bombardment was so bitter that the War Department refused the Robert company some contracts in its own territory that would naturally have come to it. The pressure became so intense that Chairman Ed Flynn had to accept Chip's resignation from the secretaryship.

Then came the renegotiation commission charged with revising war contracts that gave inordinate profits. They swooped down on Robert with the avidity of a bomber on a surfaced U-boat, for he was a shining mark; his head would have been the greatest trophy of the game they were hunting. They turned his contracts inside out; they pored over his accounts and cost books—and gave him a clean bill of health. There was nothing to renegotiate. Morality aside, Chip was too smart an engineer to be so oblivious of the vulnerability of his position as to attempt any funny business, and he leaned over backwards in his dealings with the government.

I have had my share of bombardment. For a period I was a consultant on publicity for the Crosley Radio Corporation. That company was putting up a fight to retain its license for its five-hundred-thousand-watt station—incidentally, they lost that fight. The coincidence of my employment with them and of the proceedings before the F.C.C. was accentuated. My contract with the radio company specifically precluded any lobbying activities, or other activity except as to trade publicity; but that did not prevent a steady barrage about the nefariousness of my functions and my general iniquity. As a sample of what I really was engaged in: I suggested that the company seek, and endeavored to procure for them, the services of General Craig, former chief of staff of the army, to broadcast his analysis of the war moves in Europe. This was, of course, before we got into the war ourselves. President Roosevelt blocked the negotiations. In an effort to overcome his objections I cited that he, when assistant secretary of the navy, had drawn the contracts under which the New York *World* was to have the exclusive stories of aviators Reed, Towers, and Bellinger, who were sent on the first official transatlantic flight. The navy flyers were given all the profits of the syndication of these articles, among other considerations. Reed was the only one of the three to complete that flight; the planes of the others, after some great adventures, bogged down at or near the Azores.

The parallel did not impress the President; so Crosley lost a great feature, and the retired general lost a whopping salary.

To return to the National Committee's financial adventures: Twice we were clear of debt. Once was just before the 1940 convention, when we were able to report to the clerk of the House of Representatives that we had no outstanding obligations; and once just after the convention. Our freedom from money embarrassment in the latter case endured only twenty-four hours. Then we were back in the red.

Through the years occasionally a check for $1000 came from the President of the United States, but there were times when the White House connection was anything but helpful to our exchequer. For example, there was the time Frank Walker went among the President's friends to raise the fund required for completion of the library that was to house the Roosevelt records and other material appertaining to his history and incumbency. The President gave the land and the proceeds of the sale of his volumes of his speeches, messages, etc., but that did not nearly suffice for an adequate library, and Walker undertook to supply the deficiency. Naturally, Walker on such a mission went to our records, for that was the obvious source for the roster he sought. We were alarmed lest the appeal to our contributors might dampen their readiness to come across for campaign expenses. I don't know whether the library fund raising really interfered materially with our subsequent calls, but at the time it seemed dangerous to us at headquarters.

I do not recall seeing Jack Garner's name on any list of campaign contributors, though he probably was represented in the Texas quota, which came to us as a lump sum. Moreover, I cannot recall that anybody asked the Vice-President for financial help; which is rather remarkable, as he was reputed to be two times a millionaire, and I can't remember any other possibility who was overlooked by our dollar hunters.

Perhaps nobody thought of it; or it may be that our efforts to drag him into positive participation in the campaign made us forget him as a probable source of revenue.

PART TWO

HOW I GOT THAT WAY

6. FRONTIER BOYHOOD

The Comstock lode, Indian doings, highbrow influ-
ences, mining camp adventures and various vocations.

MY EARLIEST RECOLLECTION is that a milkman
picked me up way down on the road that led from Virginia City
to Six Mile Canyon, where water wheels of towering magnitude
operated the works in which the ores of the Comstock mines
were reduced. I was lost, but fortunately it was our own milkman, and he delivered me to our home on F Street, which the
whole family had deserted in search for me. They drifted back,
and I was washed and spanked and put to bed for violating the
parental law forbidding me to go beyond the street that went before our door. That birth site has been buried for forty years
under a mountain that was the waste dump of one of the big
mines.

Not a great while after my first adventure we moved to a more
pretentious house on aristocratic A Street, where we remained
until a fire devastated the town and we found refuge in a miner's
home far up on the slope of Mount Davidson. There were no
hardships; but the sister next to me—Miriam, a successful novel-
ist in later years—and I both felt it our patriotic duty to patron-
ize the relief stations. We gorged ourselves with their ham sand-
wiches regardless of the circumstance that we had to eat the

bountiful meals at home or make awkward explanations of our lack of appetite.

Virginia City was a booming town in those days, with a six-story hotel, a flamboyant red-light district, saloons and gambling places on almost every corner, business district, fashionable clubs, and a series of palaces belonging to the bonanza kings, Mackay, Fair, Sheron, and their immediate satellites.

We had our historical landmarks, like the old scaffolding over an abandoned shaft where the vigilantes had hanged a man named Larkin. We had our local feudists, like Crosby and Scanlon, who used to shoot it out occasionally; and I remember once trailing one of the wounded heroes who was being carried up to the doctor's office after one of these social events.

Occasionally some of the local sports, after a successful session at faro, would amuse themselves by tossing silver dollars into the streets, where small boys scrambled for them. I was too little to make much of a success in the melees, but I did manage to get pretty well bruised, and after one of the coin tossers had rescued me, he gave me a whole dollar for myself.

The saloons were out of bounds for the children, but I was told later on it had been a habit of the day that the first drink was always on the house.

My father was a rather prosperous storekeeper, my eldest sister a schoolteacher, and my oldest brother was an ensign at Annapolis—this was Albert, who became the first American to win the Nobel prize for physics, that award being made for his measurement of the velocity of light.

We were a bookish family, and I was spelling out the works of Dumas and Dickens when I should have been in the Horatio Alger period of literature. I regret to recall that the Miner's Union Library was responsible for many unlearned lessons that got me in trouble at school.

I had four sisters, all a trifle highbrow, and every one of them felt bound to do her full duty toward her youngest brother. Not only did they sternly supervise my homework on my lessons, but they purposed that I should not disgrace our musical family. If there was a more refined torture than keeping a small boy, with not a vestige of music in his soul, on a piano stool while his gang were yelling outside, I did not encounter it.

One incident rankles still. The circus had come to town, and I was given a quarter to pay my admittance. I was told to go with Mme. Bellmere, another cultured lady, whose two sons were my intimates. A "Washoe Zephyr" swept down Bullion Ravine and blew the big top down, but Mme. Bellmere had an alternative ready. There was a violin recital at National Guard Hall, and I saw my precious quarter go to the ticket taker, and for hours I watched a bald-headed man sawing a fiddle!

Those were the days before moral suasion had come into the scheme of education, Minor infractions were punished by the teacher, who slapped your hands with a black rubber ruler, while more serious offenders were sent up to the principal who presided at the high school and took care of the criminal with a strap applied to the appropriate place. One day I appeared in the little antechamber to the high school room. The executioner came out, turned me over his knee, and did his full duty. He had barely finished when another small boy oozed miserably into the room.

"Well?" asked the principal.

"Miss Simpson sent me up to be punished," replied the newcomer.

"Well, what about you?" said the educator, turning to me.

"My sister told me to come up and wait for her." (Miriam was one of his high school pupils.)

He was a just judge, at that, for when I appeared a few days later as an authentic malefactor, he let me off with a lecture, concluding with "Now our accounts are balanced."

My diversions outside of the regular street games were the excursions up Mount Davidson to gather burrs, which we burned in wonderful bonfires and then extracted the pine nuts. Another great source of entertainment was to go up to the big flats west of Mount Davidson and ride the Indian ponies. There was some technique about this. It appears that, years before, there had been a war between the Piute and Washoe Indians. I have forgotten which won the war, but the victors took all the

ponies, and thereafter none of the losing tribe was permitted
ownership of a horse. This situation involved our posting of
sentries. If a loser came along, we paid no attention; but if it was
a victor, we fled. Just how we distinguished a Piute from a
Washoe, I cannot now recall. Obviously the city and county
authorities respected the tribal edicts, for no Indian appealed to
the American courts when the enemy tribe seized his livestock.

Our Indians were an amiable set. Once—it must have been
during the Modoc war in California—a great swarm of the red
men rushed through the city yelling "Me heap Modoc," but
nobody paid any attention to the foray. The citizens regarded
it as merely one of the amusing antics of the aborigines, like the
fandango they used to stage for the entertainment of the whites,
passing the hat after what we were told was their war dance.
They were blanket Indians, who lived in wickiups made of junk
gathered from the mine dumps on the outskirts of the town. The
squaws were the white women's laundresses. When one of them
got a job, the males of her family and of other Piute families
moved to the nearest empty lot, spread their blankets, and
gambled for the funds the squaw would produce when the wash-
ing was done.

The losers of the session would appear at the door, and with
the explanation "Injun heap hogaday," which meant the ap-
plicant was very hungry, would stand expecting—usually with
success—whatever there was of leftovers in the householder's
larder. Sometimes the recipient of the food would consent to
split a little wood for the kitchen stove, but I regret to report
that the bucks were not all trustworthy and like as not, on these
occasions, faded away, carrying along the axe.

If the Piutes were the vanquished, nevertheless I know one
of them who was permitted on horseback. Captain Sam, chief of
the Piutes, was always pressed into service at our Fourth of July
parades and, mounted bareback on a charger from Mooney's
livery stable, swinging an old cavalry sabre, marched ahead of
the National Guard. It seems, now, there was some faulty
ideology in this, but it added to the picturesqueness of the procession. We were great on celebrations of the nation's birthday.

For weeks preceding the anniversary volunteers hauled wood to the top of Mount Davidson, and on the big night a pyre was lighted that we used to be told could be seen as far away as Utah.

Another feature of the parade was the ship of state, commanded by an ex-sailor who sang ditties, danced a hornpipe on the deck, and heaved a line. The patriotic saloonkeepers on C Street were supposed to hitch bottles of whiskey to the line, and the sailor heaved them aboard carefully. By the time the parade reached the Divide, the decorated mules that hauled the craft were the only effectives left standing.

Later on I got very well acquainted with Captain Sam. It was when I joined the staff of the *Virginia City Chronicle,* where I was bookkeeper and assistant reporter. I wrote a glowing story about the Chief's killing a timber wolf near Lake Tahoe. I do not know what literate native read it to him, but the following day he appeared at the newspaper office with his return courtesy —a big string of mountain trout. That established a valuable precedent, for my colleagues developed the lead to our profit in game, pine nuts, and other sagebrush products. It worked very well for a time. Somewhere I learned that our enterprise was not original but was merely a revival of an old *Chronicle* custom. The failure of the previous entente was charged to an oversmart San Francisco reporter who dropped in. He wrote a story that Captain Sam's wife had presented him with twins—and the Chief threatened to wreck the office. The palefaces did not know that, according to Piute lore, each twin implied a separate father.

The early-childhood, peaceful phase of my career terminated when I was thirteen and went to the Territory of Arizona. This was not with the object of running away which has been reported, for my brother—not the Annapolis man—had got a job in Arizona with a copper company, and I wanted to join him.

By this time stock market misadventures and decline of the big mines had blasted the family fortunes.

I reached Lordsburg, New Mexico, without serious adventures. Everybody along the way was kind to an undersized boy traveling alone.

The camp was eighty miles by stage from Lordsburg. This was, of course, long before the railroad came in, and all the traffic was by prairie schooner hauled by from twelve to twenty yoke of oxen. Obviously ox teams furnished the cheapest form of transportation, so I applied to one of the outfits to be allowed to work my way to the copper camp. The old Mexican boss seemed rather amused at the request but cheerfully granted it. They gave me a goad, and I had the proud privilege of walking those eighty miles prodding the reluctant cattle. When it was evident that my short legs were giving out, I was hoisted to the top of the leading wagon piled high with boxes of goods and told that I was to watch for Indians. The Apaches were raiding all through that section, with Geronimo and Juh and the Apache Kid all on the warpath. We encountered no Indians on that trip. Later, around Clifton, I frequently saw the signal smokes of the raiders and once or twice witnessed the sad procession of burros bringing the bodies of prospectors who had been slaughtered in their isolated camps.

In Clifton I also encountered my first hero. The Apaches had attacked one of the ox trains, but the teamsters had stood them off and had killed one. The proud slayer had heard of scalping, though the Apaches did not scalp. Naturally he was not an adept of the art, so instead of merely taking the scalp lock as a trophy, he brought into Clifton the whole skin of the Indian's head, including the ears.

Clifton did itself proud in recognition of this gallant exploit. The hero was given the freedom of Dave Soloman's bar; a ball in his honor was given in the adjoining ballroom, and a collection was taken up to buy him a new Winchester rifle, a frontier six-shooter of the same calibre, and a cartridge belt. Little Pete, the carpenter, built a stadium for the presentation by Senorita Juana Vaquera, who was the nearest thing we had to a glamour girl. The program was not carried out fully, for when it came time for the presentation, the hero and Juana were fast asleep at the table in the little room behind the bar, so the ball went on without them, and the tokens were deposited with Dave Soloman and were presented privately next day.

Popular report had it that a month later the hero hocked the whole outfit in a monte game at Tombstone.

I was given a job as a clerk in the company store. That position lasted until another happening brought me back to the road to Lordsburg.

The stage between the two places was always being held up, for rustlers were active through that section. So the payroll used to be brought in wrapped up in bales of blankets or disguised in boxes containing canned goods, the freighters being in total ignorance of the specie cargo. Once one of these treasure vans was overdue, and after a reasonable time for possible breakdowns had passed, I was put on a horse and told to go down the road and see if I could find the missing freighter. I covered the entire distance to Lordsburg with one stop at the Yorke ranch and then rode back to Clifton, reporting that I had seen nothing of the missing ox train. The obvious conclusion we reached was that the freight crew had discovered the treasure and carried it off to Mexico. There were no telegraph lines in that part of the country. I don't think anything was done to head off the supposed defaulters. However, the sequel shows the fallaciousness of circumstantial evidence, for one day in the fall the missing freighter showed up with everything intact. The boss freighter had remembered that he had a ranch somewhere on the Gila River and headed up there to use his cattle for plowing. So my term as an ostensible mail carrier, with its concomitant avocation of watcher of the treasure train, came to an end.

The payroll money, by the way, was always in Mexican dollars, which could be purchased at a considerable discount but could be paid to Mexican and Chinese miners at face value. There was another little quirk to this. The only place where anything could be bought was at the company's store. Wages were paid half in silver and half in boletos—merchandise script. We had two prices in the store. One was for Americans with cash, and the other one—higher prices—for those who paid with the merchandise script. This, please remember, was sixty years ago.

The outfit that owned the mine, distant relatives of mine, sold out to the Arizona Copper Company, which effected a lot of improvements. They supplanted homemade smelters, built of blocks of copper, with modern blast furnaces and brought out an efficient crew of technical men from Scotland.

In the service of the Arizona Copper Company I was advanced to charge of the butcher shop. That required no very elaborate mercantile training, because we had one price for meat—twelve and a half cents a pound. We had a huge Mexican to cut up the meat. There was no picking and choosing of the cuts. The first customer got a chunk off the neck, the second customer the next piece, and so on. Economists might figure that this would result in people's waiting until the roast-and-steaks section was reached, but that difficulty was met by limiting the supply so that the fellow who waited might find the carcass exhausted before he got there. We had beef about once a week, and the rest of the time we fed our population on mutton. The company would bring in about three thousand sheep. The expert accountant would charge me with three thousand sheep at three dollars a head. When the butchers' report came in of so many sheep slaughtered per day, I would be credited with that number at the same price. Before that accounting system was in vogue, nobody knew how many sheep were being stolen or taken by the wolves or coyotes.

Presently I lost my job. I always attributed it to the pique of the superintendent, because I invariably beat him at chess. But I suppose the real reason was that I was a poor clerk, more interested in what was going on around me than in my business. I have told the story so often that now I almost believe it, that when I went up to the bookkeeper's office to get the pay that was coming to me—about seventy dollars—the bookkeeper, after scanning his accounts, kept on dishing twenty-dollar bills until he had reached more than two hundred dollars. When I mildly suggested to him that he was making a mistake, he retorted with the most scornful Scottish inflection:

"Well, if you knew as much about your own business as you think you do about mine, perhaps you wouldn't have lost your job."

Naturally my expostulation ceased. What had happened was that the fiscal expert had not taken note of the circumstance that three thousand sheep left to their own devices would multiply, so consequently I got credit of three dollars for every lamb born.

Then began the most perfect period of my life. I really became a frontier tramp. I had a horse and a gun, and I made my headquarters with an old prospector and friend. The country was full of game—deer in the hills, turkeys in the valleys, antelope on the plains; and when I needed money and did not care to fall back on my industrious, commercial-minded brother, I had only to appear with my products of the chase to find a welcome market. The isolated prospectors, working their claims, had neither time nor opportunity to vary their diet of salt meat, beans, and canned stuff. I did not loaf all the time. Whenever an American felt the urge for a vacation, or was ill, or for any reason vacated his job, I would fill in. Sometimes I was a clerk, sometimes a bartender. I also was available as a helper with cattle and mules.

When I threw my diamond hitch over the pack on my sumpter burro, there was always a book or two in the cargo. I still recall, with a feeling of remorseful guilt, poring over Winwood Reede's *Martyrdom of Man* by the light of a gorgeous campfire when I should have been reporting in town to substitute for the assistant barkeeper at Church's Camp.

My idyllic life terminated when my family finally rounded me up, shipped me back to Virginia City, and sent me to high school.

Presiding over this acme of Comstock academic effort was Professor H. F. Baker, a dignified and scholarly gentleman, who, however, was addicted to the habit of interspersing his class lectures with incidents of his experience and habits. One day he came to the recitation room to find chalked on the blackboard this bit of doggerel:

> Hezekiah Festus B.
> Went to school in Tennessee,
> Ate two meals instead of three,

Used no sugar in his tea!
Isn't he a marvel? Whee!
Hezekiah Festus B.

By some process of deduction he arrived at the conclusion
that I was the author and bade me stay after school. My frontier
life had left me hard as nails physically, and he was not much
bigger than I, so I debated in my mind whether to submit to
or resist a thrashing. He began to talk—not a word of reproof,
not an accent of resentment. Instead, an amiable, courteous les-
son in the duty of boys approaching manhood to co-operate in
the effort to fit them for their future life, and to set an example
for younger boys in respecting their teachers. He left me suf-
ficiently ashamed to insure decent behavior on my part thereafter.

I graduated at the Fourth Ward School with passable credit.
The graduation ceremonies were at Piper's Opera House, and I
delivered an address. That was my first experience with ghost
writing, for Sister Miriam, disgusted with my own production,
spangled with frontierisms, wrote that address for me.

But, I think our class song was mine. It was in the meter of
"The Cowboy's Lament."

7. MY RINGSIDE SEAT

*Half a century at close-ups of the big news. Journal-
istic ups and downs in the most fascinating of all pro-
fessions.*

DENNIS McCARTHY, who owned the *Virginia City
Chronicle,* gave me the job of bookkeeper and assistant reporter.
Our main source of income was the list of assessment sales of the

stock in the declining mines. The magnate of the shop, apart from the proprietor, was the composing-room foreman, who got thirty-five dollars a week. That is, I handed him his pay envelope with that amount, which he never opened. Instead he dropped into the Delta Saloon after the paper was out and tossed the envelope on the faro table. His theory was that thirty-five dollars was no better than nothing for a gentleman with his tastes. If his initial bet lost, he became a strict economist until next payday.

The mines were dropping back daily, payrolls became uncertain, and presently I get a chance to go to San Francisco. After a brief term in an insurance office, where I am sure I was not of the least use, Arthur McEwen, my brother-in-law, took me on the *San Francisco Evening Post*, of which he was the editor, at seven dollars a week. I found a joint on the water front where you got chops and coffee for fifteen cents; and my breakfast, coffee and doughnuts, was a dime. I shared an alley room with a Virginia City classmate, David G. Davis, who was doing about as well in the White House department store. Now he is George Davis, director of banks, president of the White House Corporation, patron of the arts, and generally a member in good standing of the order of California millionaires.

William Randolph Hearst, fresh from Harvard, had taken over the *San Francisco Examiner* and begun a whirlwind campaign to lift the paper from the sombre stodginess of a party organ—his father, Senator George Hearst, had got it in a political deal. That looked like the Promised Land, and I promptly became a sooner in the journalistic Oklahoma rush to join the new outfit. Joe Ward, the city editor, took me on as an extra man. I got two dollars for afternoon assignments and one dollar if they used me at night. My early run was the police courts, where a thousand interesting incidents, some of which really happened, brought me promotion to the regular staff at eighteen dollars a week.

One day I was covering the water front and ran into a story no reporter could resist. Henry Norman, a distinguished British journalist, afterward Sir Henry, was out with a society yachting party and leaped into the bay to rescue his hostess' handkerchief, which she had tossed overboard daring him to show his gallantry. The gentleman happened to be Mr. Hearst's house guest, which circumstance I ignored. I wrote the tale with all the embellishments an irresponsible youngster could put pen to—including his being hauled back on board with a boat hook through his pants; and the *Examiner* printed the story.

Next day there was a riot in the office. Mr. Norman published Hearst's apology in the opposition paper. Hearst fired his managing editor and put in his place McEwen, who, like practically every conspicuous journalist in town, had been gathered into the *Examiner's* fold. Nothing happened to me.

San Francisco at that period was the most wonderful city, journalistically speaking, in the world. The old bonanza kings and railroad millionaires, as tough an aggregation as ever hacked their way to fortune, were still alive. Their sons were figuring in all the fights and scandals that the community enjoyed. The mines were still pouring in their millions, the ships from Australia and Hawaii and China were bringing in the romance of the Orient, the cattle ranchers were supplying their stint of picturesque news, and politics were raging furiously.

Where else but in such a commonwealth could a reporter have the opportunity to write about a former supreme court justice of the state climbing over the bench of a presiding federal justice in his efforts to knife him for a distasteful decision or an affront?

That was David S. Terry—survivor of vigilante times—who had killed Senator Broderick in a duel just outside the city limits. The case was the divorce suit of Senator Sheron of Nevada. Sheron lost in the state courts, but in some mysterious way the people of high influence managed to get the case into the federal courts, which granted the Senator's divorce. Terry, the attorney for the divorced woman, married her. For his exhibition with the bowie knife Justice Field sentenced Terry to six months in jail for contempt of court. Terry served that sentence sullenly. Not a great while later he encountered Field in the Southern Pacific eating station at Lathrop and started around the table for the judge. Then up rose Dave Nagel, an Arizona desperado who had been secretly appointed deputy United States marshal and made Field's bodyguard. Deadshot Nagel killed Terry on the spot. I remember the simple headline we put on the story, to wit:

"They Have Met."

Then we had the famous story of Senator Fair's will. He had divorced his wife, quarreled with his children, and written a will leaving forty million dollars in trust so tied up that his natural heirs could not get hold of any appreciable amount of it for many years. He had included in that will what is now known in law as the California provision. It runs something like this: "I have had no wife but Teresa Rooney Fair. I have had no children but James G. Fair, Jr., Charles Fair, Teresa Fair, and Virginia Fair; but if any competent court decides that any other woman is my widow or any other child my child, I hereby set aside one hundred dollars as the share of the said alleged wife or child from my estate."

That provision was deemed necessary because we had in San Francisco a rather famous lawyer whose specialty it was to dig up illegitimate heirs to the big estates of rich men. Senator Fair, as an additional precaution, had convened a congress of the leading alienists of the state to pass on his sanity, so that no attack could be made on the will on the ground that he was crazy.

The estate was left in trust, with fees for the trustees of such magnitude as to insure against their being influenced by blandishments—or other considerations—to surrender their trust.

The resulting litigation seemed to furnish meal tickets for half the San Francisco bar. It might have gone on indefinitely had it not been for the advent of a lady altruist who produced a penciled document which was presented as a later will. That made things fine—until the lady also presented alleged evidence of her marriage to the Senator. She did not ask dower rights, for then she could have claimed no more than the paltry hundred-dollar bequest, but she did file deeds for some millions of dollars worth of San Francisco real estate, in the same penciled handwriting. Ultimately the children who survived got the fortune, and the altruist did not get the real estate, which suggests that California law has a full place among the wonders of the golden state.

Senator Fair was a marvelous old pirate remembered largely for his wisecracks. For example, when John W. Mackay, his old-time partner, came a terrific cropper in an effort to corner the wheat supply of the world—which effort, according to reports, was that of his wife without his knowledge—he had to turn over the Nevada bank to Fair; and when Fair was interviewed about the episode, he affected complete surprise and said:

"Poor old John, and all his money at the bottom of the sea." His old partner had financed the laying of the Mackay-Bennett Atlantic cable.

It fell to me to cover nearly all of these trials. I remember one in particular. A mousy old gentleman named Blythe had amassed a fortune of several millions and suddenly died. Nobody knew where he came from or anything about him, but claimants soon appeared from all over the world. They were the "gypsy Blythes," and another Blythe who cut his mustache and by other devices enhanced his resemblance to the dead millionaire. There were forty claimants. Among them was a little fourteen-year-old girl who appeared with her mother. The mother testified that in London Blythe had picked her up and that they had lived together for a time, this child being his progeny. Moreover she had communicated with him, and he had sent letters to her and money to the child. This was the only thing approaching direct evidence that was brought out, and the little girl was awarded the whole fortune.

The *San Francisco Examiner*, as young Mr. Hearst made it, was a newspaperman's dream come true. It gathered under one roof practically all the talent of the Pacific Coast. He had as his columnist Ambrose Bierce, whose short stories, now forgotten except by collectors, were the masterpieces of their day. Bierce was a queer, sour old man with a background of service as an engineer in the Civil War. His assaults on local celebrities who had incurred his or Hearst's disesteem are still classics. He finally embodied them in a book, the title of which alone—*Black Beetles in Amber*—ought to give them immortality. His end was a mystery. He disappeared from the newspaper world and was never heard of again. Tradition says that he wandered in Mexico, was caught by one of the raiding bands of Villa or some other rebel captain, refused to explain himself on the ground that it was not worth while, and was shot by a firing squad. Bierce was a poet and a good one. One of his at that time famous versifications might have been called "Gloom." I remember it began: "The world's a hell and my heart's a hell and I hate all men and all women as well"; and, if I recall correctly, it wound up with this: "And in the gathering gloom a wolf sits howling on a broken tomb." He was great on titles. For example, one book was labeled *The Monk and the Hangman's Daughter*.

Somebody said, in contrasting his literary fate with that of Kipling, "If you publish a book in London, it blows across the whole civilized world; if you publish a book in San Francisco, it blows across the Pacific Ocean."

Hearst imported from the East "Phiny" Thair, who gave to the world "Casey at the Bat." He developed on the art department side such cartoonists as Homer Davenport and the best of the comic-strip artists: Rube Goldberg, Bud Fisher (Mutt and Jeff), Tad Dorgan, who brought the sports world to the comic page, and a flock of others. You may like or dislike William Randolph Hearst, but he was the nearest thing to a genius as an editor and publisher that I encountered during my half a lifetime in the field of journalism. It might be said of him that he never was a young man mentally. In those days he was a tall, horse-faced fellow with a pair of pale bluish gray eyes. The only animals I know of that have that particular ocular coloring are the coyote and the shark.

Naturally, under such leadership, there were many startling newspaper assignments. For example, I was once detailed with Allen Kelly to go out and capture a grizzly bear, as Hearst wanted a good specimen of the state's emblem as the foundation feature of a San Francisco zoo. We found that there was no such animal available for purchase, so we went to the mountains.

Down in the Bakersfield region we learned of a monster bear that pretty well terrorized his part of the world. The superintendent of the Beale ranch, over which the animal ranged, told us that they calculated the Castac bear cost the outfit, on an average, three steers every two weeks. There was an outstanding reward of two hundred dollars for anybody who captured or killed the animal. We heard a hundred stories of his ferocity. The Mexican herdsmen spoke of him as *El Diablo,* the devil.

Well, we built a multitude of traps and spent weary weeks dragging quarters of beef over the trails that were marked by the fourteen-inch footprints of the monster. We baited our traps with honey and sheep, etc., but never got sight of him. We had camped at the last waterhole in that desert country. The water was foul and almost gagged us, but there was no alternative. We finally gave up the Castac bear and I went back to do some other job, but Kelly persevered and in some other section really caught a huge grizzly, not as big or famed as the Castac bear but a gorgeous specimen, and I helped bring him in. They called him Monarch; Hearst had christened his paper "The Monarch of the Dailies." Monarch lived a long time in his enclosure in Golden Gate Park, and got over his ferocity to the point of graciously accepting the peanuts and things the children would toss him.

After I had gone East, when Hearst started his ventures there, I got an order to find a mate for Monarch. The Eaton ranch people up in the Northwest said they had a female grizzly, and we bought her. She had only one eye and was a silvertip, not more than half the size of the big black brute she was to companion; but they got along well, and their descendants are still featured at Golden Gate Park.

To get back to that foul drinking pool on the Castac range: I resolved to get that bear and squandered every vacation for years haunting the old trails to get a shot at the beast, always cursing that foul, smelly, acrid water. Many years later a wiser man camped at that pool and recognized the taste. It was just oil, and in that section now are some of the most wonderful wells in the country.

Another assignment I will never forget was that of an interview with Black Bart on his release from San Quentin penitentary, where he had served fourteen years. His specialty had been holding up stages that were bringing back gold from the mines in the High Sierra. He followed this lucrative pursuit for many years. His procedure was to cover the driver and the Wells Fargo with a shotgun and make them throw out the strongbox. He never had to shoot, and the posses that went back after him would find the broken box by the roadside with an obscene poem enclosed and signed, "Black Bart, the Po8." Finally somebody did take a shot at him. They didn't hit him but shot off a cuff, those being the days of the detachable cuff. On this they found a Chinese laundry mark, and so they backtracked to a quiet little man with an office in a Nevada bank on the door of which was lettered "Charles J. Bolton, Mining." This quiet individual was appearing every now and then at the U. S. Mint with a small bar of gold and getting currency for it. This was Black Bart.

He came out of a long imprisonment quiet and amiable. He told me in the course of the interview that he broke his shotgun a dozen times before every holdup to make sure it was not loaded, for it was the dread of his life that he might have to hurt somebody. Of course he insisted the holdups were youthful indiscretions and that he was definitely through with anything of that kind. The story persisted in San Francisco that Wells Fargo & Co. put him on a pension list on his promise not to hold up any more stages.

While on the subject of holdups, I come to the Evans and Sontag gang. They held up Southern Pacific trains, and when their identity had been learned—they were apparently quiet country people living in Bakersfield—they took to the mountains. Their chase through the High Sierra was a never-ending series of thrills. Hearst delegated "Petey" Biglow to join the outlaws. My job was with the posses, but I did manage some contact with the fugitives. There were several battles in which officers were killed or wounded, but finally the outlaws were ambushed at what they called the Stone Corral.

Accompanying me with the posses was Jimmy Swinnerton to do the art work. It was bitterly cold treking through the snow, and we each had on two of the heaviest suits of underclothes we could find. One night I woke up in camp pretty cold and discovered that I had only one suit of underwear on. Jimmy was sleeping peacefully in the blankets beside me. I investigated and found that my sleeping partner had on three suits of underwear. How or where the shift occurred I will never find out.

I read not long ago of the release of Chris Evans from the penitentiary after having served forty years on a life sentence.

I had another adventure which will be appreciated by people of my own craft. I was in Fresno reporting for the *Examiner* the trial of a society murder case. Covering it for the *San Francisco Chronicle* was my intimate friend, Fred Lawrence. The trial was of sufficient newspaper importance to bring to Fresno practically all the leaders of the San Francisco bar either for the prosecution or for the defense. Among them was Billy Foote, who was not only eminent in the law but a powerful politician. During some of the dry periods Fred Lawrence and I arranged a wicked compact. We had made some delightful acquaintances, and the deal was that I was to cover the trial for both while he disported himself at house parties. The next day he would take the burden while I enjoyed myself. It worked well until one day something catastrophic in politics happened in San Francisco and I got a hurry-up order to interview Billy Foote on political developments. I dug him out of a dinner party and presented my request. Foote was feuding with Hearst and responded, "I'll be damned if I'll give any interview to a Hearst newspaper. Tell him for me to go to hell."

I reported by telegraph that the eminent attorney refused to be interviewed, whereupon the operator handed me a telegram for Fred Lawrence asking the same thing. So again I dragged Foote out and explained the situation. He grinned knowingly and proceeded to give me a splendid two-column interview which, of course, I sent to the *Chronicle* with Lawrence's name attached. The next day Lawrence got a fine bonus, and I was recalled in disgrace.

About the turn of the century Hearst went to New York and started the *New York Journal*. At that time I was assistant Sunday editor of the *San Francisco Examiner*. He took the Sunday editor along and appointed somebody else to that job. I announced that I was tired of being an assistant and moved over to the *San Francisco Call*. I was fortunate enough to get one or two big exclusive stories in my new job, which probably motivated my old boss to send me a proposition that I go to Cuba and cover the revolution. That was bait I could not resist. And so presently I was in Havana with five thousand dollars in my money belt and all the credentials and paraphernalia of a full-fledged war correspondent.

Havana was the center of the world's biggest news just then, and among the people I encountered was a roly-poly little Englishman, whose distinguished lineage brought him especial attention by the Spanish authorities. The young man had with him as bear leader one Lieutenant Barnes. We case-hardened correspondents agreed that he needed a chaperone. Because of his name and descent my paper wanted an article from him on the Spanish-Cuban situation, and, to my surprise, he really showed himself capable of writing one. Not only was he a handler of words, but he showed the professional touch by charging me a shilling a word for the production. He was anything but a spendthrift. For example, he had a number of the correspondent corps up to his room for a session of poker. As the cards were being dealt, he ordered "a bottle of champagne and one glass." His American guests blinked, but conformed, and so we sat through the evening, every man with his own bottle and glass. I don't think he was more than a guinea ahead when he adjourned the session.

His name was Winston Churchill.

All this time Hearst was plugging for a war to free Cuba from the Spaniards. Fiery editorials and flaming cartoons came out daily picturing Weyler the Butcher, Weyler being the new governor-general of the island. One day the paper came in with a two-page illustration of Weyler flourishing a blood-dripping sword over the female figure supposed to represent Cuba. Just before this I had gone to a little town in western Cuba where a battle was being fought, according to reports. There wasn't any battle. A rebel troop had marched in, had drilled in the public square, and the men had marched away again. A couple of hours later Spanish troops appeared, and there was some shooting; but as far as I could learn, the casualties were only among the civilian population. I had had to show my credentials to the Spanish authorities, so they knew of my identity. The night of the day on which that ghastly picture appeared, my door flew open and a Spanish secret service official told me that I was under arrest. They marched me down to the water's edge, put me in a boat, and took me over to Morro Castle, where I was locked up. There I stayed for ten days, incommunicado. I was fairly athletic and was able to climb up to an embrasure in which I could look over the city. The patrolling sentinels would catch me there and poke a bayonet at me so that I would have to drop back to the cell floor. The furniture of the cell consisted of a large can. Twice a day when the guard was changed, my cell door would fly open and a ration of bean soup would be left. At first the guards would not speak to me, but before a great many days I had managed to arrange to have meals sent over from the Inglaterra Hotel and even had a hammock smuggled in. With each meal came a bottle of red wine, which I gave to the guards. This and the circumstance that I had a pocket full of money mitigated the horrors of confinement.

After ten days of this the guard came in and told me to put on my clothes. I asked him what for. He said to go out. I said, "Out where?"

"Out on the street."

Then he left me, and with many misgivings I went down a long corridor to the front office of the prison, which I found deserted. The entrance to Morro Castle is a great archway. Across this were a file of Spanish soldiers, who ignored me. Finally I figured that if the *ley de fuga* was going to be used on me, it didn't make much difference what I did, so with a *"dispense mi"* I elbowed my way through the file of soldiers and down the long roadway to the landing place. My fears had no foundation. Nobody paid any attention to me, and I was able to hire a boat to take me back to Havana. People that I knew came rushing up to greet me, and I had to gesture them back because that cell of mine had been full of vermin.

I learned that I had been provisionally released, but I was watched closely even to the extent that a guard was posted at my bedroom door at night.

What had happened was that Murat Halstead had been tipped off to my arrest, and so the people in New York were advised and began operations in my behalf. The U. S. Government had stopped a filibustering expedition which was the courteous excuse for the clemency extended to me.

Presently I was summoned to appear before a colonel at Atares fortress, for examination; the message commanded me to bring seven sheets of hotel stationery, thirty sheets of copy paper, and four envelopes. The colonel greeted me cordially and told me to write ten lines in Spanish on the hotel stationery. I complied, and he compared it with a paper he had in his hand. Then he asked me to write five lines in English.

"What about?" I asked. He said, "Anything you like." Then, counting again, he asked for ten lines in English on hotel paper. Then for four lines on one of the envelopes. "Pardon me," I said; "if it is not against the rules, am I permitted to ask what this is for?"

"Why," he said, lapsing into English, "I was once an attaché of the Spanish embassy in Washington. I know newspapermen, and I know that you are not a spy but a correspondent—might I add, a very indiscreet correspondent? You gathered these notices while hunting for news—but I likewise know that if I presented to a court-martial the documents taken by the police in your room, you very likely would be shot." To emphasize his comment he held up several lines of Spanish which made me a complimentary major in the rebel army. The police report had merely turned over to the military authorities a report of so many lines in Spanish on one kind of paper and so many lines of English on some other kind of paper and so forth. So he destroyed all the incriminating documents and put in their places the innocuous stuff I wrote for him. He stopped my expressions of thanks by saying, "Don't thank me—I am doing this under orders." Whereupon he congratulated me, gave me a cigarette, and hoped we'd meet again. And I took the first boat I could get to Key West.

Later I was sent back to the Caribbean with Richard Harding Davis and Frederick Remington to join the rebels. Mr. Hearst kindly furnished us with his yacht *Vamoose*. That craft was a hundred and ten feet long with a ten-foot beam. It was a grand thing in the Hudson River, but I never could find a captain who would take us across the Gulf Stream to Cuba. Whenever we got to the turbulent current, something would go wrong with the machinery and the captain would insist that we go back limping to Key West. So the jeweled sword I was to present to General Maxime Gormez of the rebel forces was not delivered. It was in the course of this incident that a famous telegraphed correspondence between Remington and Mr. Hearst was supposed to have taken place. According to the story, Remington wired that he was returning, as he did not think there was going to be any war involving the United States; and Hearst is reported to have replied, "Go ahead, you furnish the pictures and I'll furnish the war."

Simple war horror stories, with Weyler the Butcher as the main theme, did not seem enough for the campaign. So we brought out Evangelina Cisneros, a beautiful Cuban girl who was in prison in Havana as a Cuban rebel agent. We pictured all the terrible things we could think of, with the possibility of her execution as an undertone to all our sympathetic concern. Looking back, it seems to me that we pictured the brutal Captain-General as giving more attention to persecuting the heroine than to coping with a revolution. When we had the country adequately worked up, Mr. Hearst organized a rescue squad. Much to my disgust they refused to give me the assignment and sent Karl Decker. In due course he returned to New York, bringing with him the young lady and a fitting story of a thrilling jail break.

The Hearst papers went to town on the scoop. We quartered

her at the Waldorf; we had receptions, enlisting all the society folks as well as all the officials we could gather, to hail and greet her.

Actually she was not only beautiful but intelligent. Doubtless she realized that she was being exploited, but she went through with it all quite self-possessed, with a proper modesty but no embarrassment. She showed no signs of ill-treatment, despite the awful stories of her misery we had published. Altogether she seemed just a nice girl, of fair education, glad to be through with her jailing, but not hysterical over it. There were no movies in those days, otherwise Hollywood must have beckoned her. As it was, after the war she disappeared from the front pages, married a Cuban banker, and, it must be assumed, lived happily ever after.

When hostilities between U.S. and Spain actually began, I was put on a Norwegian freighter with George Coffin, a famous marine artist, to catch up with the American fleet and report the expected naval battle. We were given a cabin that had been used as a storeroom for cheese, the redolence of which was so permanent that we mostly slept on deck. Poor Coffin was a bad sailor and almost collapsed when the Scandinavian captain assured him that bean soup with prunes was the best remedy for seasickness.

As we approached the Caribbean, the captain informed me that regardless of the purpose of the voyage he would not take his ship nearer than three Norwegian leagues to any hostilities. I believe a Norwegian league is nine miles. A correspondent twenty-five or thirty miles away from action is of no particular use, so I gave up my command at St. Thomas and went back to the New York office.

My next dispatch was with quite a crew of Hearst people, including Stephen Crane. By that time Porto Rico was the focal point, and we took a tugboat out of Pensacola and had a pleasant but rather tumultuous voyage to Ponce, a port on the southern coast where General Miles was landing his army. The only thing savoring of adventure occurred when we were off San Juan and Porto Rico, where we encountered the cruiser

Prairie. Way off, in shore, you could see a couple of Spanish gunboats. The *Prairie* suggested that we run in fairly close so as to coax the gunboats out to where they could get a shot at them. The Spanish craft evidently realized the strategy, because as we turned toward them they scuttled into San Juan harbor. We landed at Ponce and participated in a parade across the island of San Juan. The road winds through the hills, and the Spaniards had established machine-gun nests, etc., on the high spots commanding the road. Our troops naturally did not go up the road until flanking parties had cleaned out the machine-gun nests, which were abandoned as they were flanked. The only battle I reported was a skirmish east of Ponce, and as I could not find the censor I had to go aboard one of the battleships and wake up General Miles and get him to okay the story, and that was about all of my experience in that war. I joined Mr. Hearst off Charleston, S. C., on a steamer he had chartered. The Battle of Santiago had been fought and he was returning from it. The idea was that I was to follow Admiral Schley's fleet to the Mediterranean and report him heading off the Spanish flotilla that was about to go after Dewey in Manila. The Spanish fleet did not go, so Schley's assignment was vacated and I went home.

Incidentally, Ned Hamilton and I reported the Battle of Manila—from our desks in the *New York American* office. We blew up the short official bulletin of that engagement into pages. During my stay at Key West I had been on board our cruiser the *Raleigh,* and had become well acquainted with the personnel; consequently our stories purported to emanate from the vantage point of the *Raleigh* deck. I think we made only one bull. I had Paymaster Key making some brilliant comment during the battle, but he, unfortunately, had been transferred to another ship months before.

It was a shameless bit of faking, but all the newspapers were doing it—so much so that one day the *World* copied, as a special signed dispatch, a story that appeared in the *American* narrating the comments of Colonel Reflipe W. Thenuz, eminent Austrian artillery expert observing the work of the American cannoneers in Cuba. In our next issue we gleefully published that a little transposition made this read "We pilfer the news."

After the war the Hearst papers engaged in a terrific bombardment of President McKinley. All the cartoonists and columnists were put to work on this detraction. Fred Opper's mischievous cartoon series on "Little Willie and his Papa" (William McKinley and the trusts) was one feature. Another one was a quatrain from Bierce to this effect:

> The bullet that pierced Goebel's chest
> Will not be found in all the West.
> Good reason. It is speeding here
> To stretch McKinley on his bier.

The reference was to the assassination of Governor Goebel of Kentucky. What Bierce meant was that the political implication of the Goebel murder had destroyed McKinley politically; but when the anarchist Czolgosz soon thereafter assassinated McKinley at Buffalo, the Republican press interpreted the verse as a direct invitation for the killing of the President.

That episode was, I think, the most critical crisis in Mr. Hearst's career. The story was broadcast that Czolgosz had in his pocket, when he was searched, a Hearst paper in which the President was violently assailed.

I was hurried off to Buffalo and was able to learn that Czolgosz never had read a Hearst paper. He said he read nothing but communistic literature.

However, the anti-Hearst crusade went on in full force. Newsstands displaying the Hearst papers were kicked into the streets. The papers were barred from numerous clubs and hotels. Our circulation went down and down, and at one time it appeared not impossible that the Hearst press empire was on the verge of destruction.

Gradually we weathered the storm. I remained in Buffalo and covered the Czolgosz trial, and accompanied the assassin on his last journey—to the penitentiary where he was executed. As we were leaving Buffalo, the assembled crowd were shrieking denunciations of the murderer and even sought to break the windows to reach him. The assassin seemed unperturbed.

"Don't you realize," I asked him, "that you were wrong?" He shrugged his shoulders and replied:

"They'll be putting up a monument for me in a couple of hundred years."

No Hearst reporter was permitted to be present at the execution. Our purpose was to have it reported by a professor of history from one of the great universities—but even that was refused.

I continued on the Hearst staff reporting practically every big trial, such as that of Harry Thaw for killing Stanford White, with an occasional lapse into editorial writing.

The advent of Charles Evans Hughes when he conducted the insurance investigation was an early assignment. The inquisition involved mainly the Equitable Life Insurance Company; and the president of another great insurance institution, thinking he saw an opportunity to show how good his company was in comparison, insisted on getting on to the witness chair. Within fifteen minutes Hughes demonstrated that he knew more about that fellow's business than did the witness, and, apparently, had him fighting to keep out of jail.

I accompanied William Jennings Bryan to London on his first trip abroad. I cabled a story from the British capital, a column long, on Bryan's shopping and his purchase of his first top hat, a necessary part of his equipment for his audiences with kings and czars and emperors as he went around the world.

My assignment took me only as far as London. The rest of the global circumnavigation was chaperoned by Eddie Flynn, Hearst's London correspondent.

Hearst had supported Bryan for the presidency when the other New York papers had bolted because of Bryan's stand for silver. It was really a great boost for the then new Hearst enterprise, for the dyed-in-the-wool Democrats naturally flocked to the newspaper which had stood loyal to the party. I had gotten to know Bryan very well, and our friendship continued until the Scopes "monkey trial" in Kentucky. He was always the serious politician and humanitarian. We went to Westminster Abbey, and while I was awed by the overpowering historical effect of the tombs and statues, Bryan's comment was, "It is terrible to think of all these things commemorating war and bloodshed."

I recall interviewing him at the convention in San Francisco in which Cox was nominated to run against Harding. All the other Democrats there expressed their enthusiasm at the nomination, but Bryan said, "My heart is buried in the grave." His disappointment and sadness was on account of the convention's failure to stand by prohibition.

The highlight of the Kentucky trial was the cross-examination of Bryan by Clarence Darrow.

The defendant was on trial for violating a state law by teaching the doctrine of evolution to his class in the university. Bryan, who came in as an attorney for the prosecution, finally took the witness stand.

The atmosphere of that remote village could not, I think, be duplicated in any other American community. The people used to assemble on a hillock opposite the house in which the attorneys for the defense were housed, expecting momentarily the bolt from heaven that would destroy the "blasphemers of religion."

Prohibition was a cardinal tenet of the town's creed, though some of the reckless natives did take us up in the mountains to visit a moonshiner's still—sending scouts ahead to tell the distiller that it was not a revenue officers' raid. That was a picture! A wild glen illuminated by a bright shining moon, with an old mountaineer, whose white tobacco-stained beard came to his waist, stirring a hell broth in a huge kettle, while on a boulder alongside of him rested a radio from which was emanating a sermon speech by William Jennings Bryan in town.

Darrow's cross-examination of the great commoner who had testified eloquently to the viciousness and falsity of Darwin's evolutionary theory ran along in this fashion:

"Colonel Bryan, do you believe in the story of Genesis and the fall of man and the garden of Eden?"

"I certainly do, Mr. Darrow."

"Do you, then, accept the biblical story that after that fall of man the serpent crawled on his belly and the foot of man trod his head?"

"I certainly do."

"Then, Colonel Bryan, would you mind telling this jury, what is your idea of how the serpent progressed before the fall of man?"

The lawyer finally had the evangelistic politician breathless and indignant, and he could only voice his sentiments by shrieking, "Infidel, blasphemer!"

In the midst of the trial I got a telegram from Herbert Bayard Swope, my executive editor (I was then on the New York *World*), directing me to ask Mr. Bryan if he thought the world was flat.

Bryan exploded when I transmitted the question.

"I'll have you know, sir," he stormed, "that I am a classical scholar and will not stand for any of this impertinence."

"Just wait a minute, Colonel," I expostulated. "There's nothing personal in this. I am merely delivering a message."

"I choose to make it personal," was his retort, "and I will not be insulted."

No effort of mine could smooth his feathers. He never spoke to me thereafter.

But to get back to my Hearst service. I was shipped off in 1913 on the tugboat *Senator Joe Bailey,* in which circumstances there is some kind of a wheeze, as Hearst crusaded against Bailey and credited himself with having driven him out of politics. This was to cover our occupation of Vera Cruz. There the American correspondents bumped into a paralyzing censorship, which was particularly sad since the direct line to Mexico City was unvexed and so it was our grief to be scooped on our own stories by the correspondents in the Mexican capital.

One fine memory is the celerity with which young army and navy officers took over the administration of the city government. One day a Mexican appeared at the office of the young American lieutenant who had become chief of police. He brought with him a large sack of Mexican dollars, explaining that this was the usual contribution from the gamblers and houses of prostitution. When the payment was refused, the envoy of sin demanded that he be told where it should be delivered. I think it finally was handed to the Mexican authorities with the customs funds, etc. when the occupation was over.

I got one good story out of the show when on a stormy rainy night a tanker arrived from Tampico. One of my naval friends was kind enough to tell me about it, and I boarded the vessel and obtained the first detailed story of the taking of Tampico by Mexican rebels.

At one time I was shifted from the writing end to the administrative end of the business. After a term as city editor of the *American* I was shipped to San Francisco to be managing editor of my old paper there. I got there just in time for the fire and earthquake. The publisher, the late Dent Robert, was away at Los Angeles so it was my job to handle the wreck. I was able to arrange with Bill Dargie, owner of the *Oakland Tribune,* to use his plant in Oakland, and there we got out the combined *Call-Chronicle-Examiner.* A banker friend took me down to his vaults and let me have money enough to tide us over the first period although the banks were all officially closed.

Incidentally, those combination papers became valued souvenirs in later years. Some thrifty person in the *Oakland Tribune* office preserved the plates and for years garnered a moderate income by selling copies at a dollar apiece.

Hearst shipped Bill Leach, his Chicago publisher, to San Francisco with a load of presses, etc., and we set up a shack office on the water front opposite a power plant the front wall of which had been knocked down by the earthquake but whose machinery had not been seriously damaged. There we got our light and power—sometimes. When the patched-up power plant failed us, we geared up automobiles to furnish power for the presses and did our printing by candlelight. There were two miles of ruins between us and the habitable San Francisco, but we functioned pretty well.

During this period I had one hideous hour when I thought I had sent Harry Coleman, the ace of all newspaper photographers, to his death. I was anxious to get a bird's-eye picture of the ruins of San Francisco, and having learned that an itinerant balloonist had salvaged his gas bag, I ordered Coleman to charter it and do the pictures from the skies. Word came that the balloon had collapsed in mid-air. When Coleman appeared at the office, I lived again. The balloon had not collapsed; it had merely leaked in so many places as to ease itself back to earth. Coleman, in the intervals between coughing because of the amount of illuminating gas he had inhaled, told me he had heard of another balloon, in Ogden, I believe, and wanted me to charter that so as to complete his assignment.

The big graft exposures came along while we were still in the water-front shack. The Mayor and supervisors all were indicted and were functioning with a vigilance committee supervising everything that was done. Hiram Johnson came to great prominence as a prosecutor in these events. The outcome was typical. Nobody was convicted but Abe Reuf, the political boss, who went to San Quentin. Reuf and I were old friends. When I was a young reporter in San Francisco his practice was in the police courts. I was able to give him the publicity so necessary to a young attorney, and we used to take in the prize fights together.

After a couple of years Hearst called me to New York, ostensibly to do editorials for one of his campaigns. I did not know it, but while I was on my way East, my successor as managing editor was on his way to San Francisco. This was typical of my adventures in the field of journal administration. Before a great while I was ordered to Chicago and became the managing editor of the *Examiner* there. Arthur Clark, an old San Francisco colleague, was managing editor of the *American,* Hearst's evening paper. At unscheduled intervals we traded jobs. I think this happened a half a dozen times during the eight years I was associated with the papers. Every now and then my titles were taken from me and I'd be back on the editorial staff. During one of these periods of degradation there was a plague of economic experts that swept over the Hearst world, and my salary was reduced one-third.

I got a job with the Essanay moving picture producers, and for a year or two I wrote scenarios at double my previous salary, with a contingent interest in certain pictures. One of these, a disreputable production entitled "The Little Girl Next Door," netted me about twenty thousand dollars. At the time my contract with the moving picture people expired, the First World War had broken out in Europe. I encountered Mr. Hearst in the lobby of the Blackstone Hotel and suggested to him that I'd like to cover the war front. He was agreeable but asked me to go on to Washington for a few weeks until he straightened out matters of censorship with the British. So on I went, and after working in his Washington office for about a month I found myself back at my old inkstained desk in New York writing Hearst editorials. His policy was anti-war, particularly anti-Wilson, so I was glad to shift again and become the Washington correspondent of the *Chicago Herald* which Jim Keeley, ex-managing-editor of the *Chicago Tribune,* had started, with the help of some of the big advertisers, to buck the McCormick publication. A year or so later Keeley's paper crashed and was bought in by Hearst, so I was sold down the river with the rest of the outfit.

Fortunately for me, Herbert Bayard Swope had become the big chief on the New York *World* and tendered me the headship of his Washington bureau, which I gladly accepted. Then began the pleasantest decade of my whole newspaper experience.

As the *World's* Washington correspondent I naturally became their main political writer and so covered all the national conventions and accompanied presidential candidates on their various swings around the circle, from the Cox-Harding campaign down to the advent of Franklin D. Roosevelt to the White House. Some memories from those times are included in a later chapter.

With my savings from my term in moving pictures I bought a delightful old house in Georgetown, which my cynical friends, having in mind the source of the purchase money, referred to as "Whiteslave Villa."

The *World* job held me until Raskob and Shouse inaugurated their campaign for rehabilitating the Democratic party. The lure of the new job, the enticement of an opportunity to become an actor on the stage instead of a spectator, was too much for me. So over I went and remained director of publicity.

PART THREE

THE DEMOCRATIC INNINGS

8. LONDON CONFERENCE: FROM HEADACHE TO HYSTERICS

*A neat program to give Uncle Sam the short end of
a hoss trade, complicated by the Moley invasion; Hull
saved the shards.*

THE LONDON Economic Conference was a Roose-
velt headache before he ever got to the White House, though
most of the discord which came to pass there stemmed from
Roosevelt's lifting our country off the gold standard two years
after Great Britain had taken that step and while we were
wallowing in the slough of a depression that was rapidly growing worse. The English had enjoyed the advantages of the
inflationary course for this period, and Roosevelt's view was
that we should get our prices up, for industry's sake, before we
entered into any stabilization agreement. The situation was
complicated with the old war debts, which the other fellows
insisted should be part of the economic agenda and which our
incoming President was bent on keeping separate. Our position
was that these debts should be handled individually with each
debtor nation.

Great Britain had paid her current installment, but with
the proviso that that payment must be counted as part of
whatever settlement was finally arrived at. France had made
motions but had paid nothing. Ultimately the whole matter of

the debts went up in smoke, every debtor except little Finland frankly defaulting; but at the time the economic conference was broached, the debts were, theoretically, at least, still alive.

President Hoover had agreed to the conference and had sought to have his successor sit in with him and share in the preliminaries. As the President and the President-elect were wide apart in their ideas, the negotiations among Hoover, Ogden Mills, and Secretary of State Stimson, on one side, and Roosevelt and Ray Moley on the other, got nowhere. Roosevelt was adamant in refusing to accept responsibility until he had authority.

According to Moley's account, after the conferees had wrangled to a declaration of the events of their meeting, Stimson tried a hurry-me-quick trick to commit Roosevelt to the course he had refused to follow. Roosevelt was peeved, but the bull was caught in time so that the new executive was able to assume office without either embarrassing explanations or any commitment.

Because the economic conference had been agreed upon after many diplomatic conversations, congressional debates, etc., he had to go ahead with it, though he did succeed in postponing it a month or two beyond the date that President Hoover had set.

I was called to the White House and informed that I was to have charge of the publicity relations of the American commission. However, some personal matters forbade my agreeing to be absent from Washington for a period whose closing date nobody could predict. (At least, so it seemed to me. The British had explained with perfect gravity that if the conference was postponed too long, its sessions would run into the grouse season. I did not realize at that time the immutability of the social obligation of British statesmen to participate in the bird shooting, and did not know that of course no reasonable person could dream of the Prime Minister and his colleagues continuing to officiate at an international meeting when the guns and the grouse were calling.) A compromise was effected. I was to go over and get things started, from the press-agent angle, and

I was given a deputy—my former chief assistant from the New York *World* bureau, Elliott Thurston—who could take over when I had to come home. However, as things developed, Secretary Hull insisted on my remaining, and so I officiated until the final week of the conference.

It was no easy job. All of the European press was hostile to the American commission. Europe had figured that all the related matters would be acted on, stabilization, tariffs, international trade generally. Their program presupposed that the United States would yield everything: our dollar would be geared to the pound and to the franc at a figure that would make it impossible for us to profit as England had profited by departing from the gold standard. Our balking at this was ill received.

The commission had its program outlined by the President before we sailed, but in mid-ocean we received instructions modified so as to make the body little more than an exploratory organization without authority to enter into any definite commitment.

The change was due to events at home: various recovery measures were beginning to take hold, prices were timidly advancing, and the obvious fear was that international compacts would disturb this trend. That circumstance was the real reason for the halting progress of the commission. There were unnumbered international conversations with Argentine over wheat and cattle, with Australia over wool, etc. The conference was opened with all the pomp and circumstance of a world congress. King George addressed us, making half of his speech in English and half in French; but the show had hardly started before we got our first jolt.

It was clearly understood, as a result of the preliminary talks over here between the British and our State Department, that the debts were not to be mentioned. Congress had reserved to itself the handling of that question and had specifically resolved that there could be no cancellation or anything tending in that direction. Had debts been on the agenda, their forgiveness, or re-composition, would have been made the price of any concession by the debtor nations.

In almost the first speech of the session Ramsay MacDonald plumped in the debts. I looked over at Secretary of State Hull and thought he was going to have apoplexy at this breach of the agreement. However, he made no comment. At one of our executive sessions it was agreed that we should ignore the Prime Minister's statement. Thereafter the conference sessions were pretty dull. The proceedings were diversified by all manner of social observances, royal garden parties at Windsor, dinners at Cliveden, all of which were very enjoyable, for Their Majesties were particularly gracious. At the garden parties the King approached pretty much every group with the hope that we were enjoying ourselves and that we would avail ourselves of the opportunity to look over the old castle and inspect its thousands of historical relics. With the normal instinct of a newspaper reporter I circulated from one group to another and heard the same royal utterance, without the change of a word, at least six times.

We were under strict orders from the Secretary of State to reveal nothing of a consequential nature. It turned out that whenever Mr. Hull had a low-down conference with the high British officials—the purport of which he would afterward explain to the assembled commission—we found a full report of the intimate chat in the next issue of the London *Times*. Whereupon I felt that it was my job to be equally indiscreet, and the American press was given an even break on these state secrets. Mr. Hull is still wondering how the American newspapers got their information.

There was one little incident that endeared the then Prince of Wales—subsequently King Edward VIII, now Duke of Windsor—to the Americans. There was a young, charming American girl there who was looking forward to a court presentation; her costume had been revealed to the folks at home, and she had spent hours, if not days, in learning the correct procedure for making her bow to Their Majesties. It so happened that there were quite a number of American ladies, for the most part relatives of the commissioners, who had similar ambitions. To their horror the court chamberlain uttered a ukase that, on account of the number of ladies who sought presentation, it had been decided that daughters of the commissioners would not be included in the presentation ceremony. All our high officials interceded with the court authorities, pleading that it would be a tragedy if this young girl had to go home and confess to her friends, who had given her parties in celebration of her expected honor, that she had been turned down. The court chamberlain was adamant, but Bill Bullitt came to her rescue in knightly fashion. He went to the Prince of Wales and told him the situation, His Highness straightened it all out, and the young girl made her bow radiantly.

Just about this time the newspapers announced that Professor Raymond Moley was coming over to London as the President's personal representative. The British and other continental delegates promptly construed his position as superseding that of the Secretary of State.

Moley's progress across the ocean was reported daily by radio, and we even learned that a plane had been chartered to bring him from the landing port to London. The Moley party did not use the plane, and paid for its hire themselves (perhaps because of some shrill newspaper criticism). The Professor came in state all right, with a courier, secretaries, and Herbert Bayard Swope, former Executive Editor of the New York *World*. I have never been able to understand exactly why Swope was of that party. There was no mystery in Moley's desire for a companion, for, regardless of the nature of the enterprise, any principal would be fortunate to have at his elbow such a forceful, experienced second. Perhaps Swope came for no other reason than a wish to accommodate a friend, or simply because, as an eminent journalist, he wanted to be in the center of events; for despite his being a successful financier as well as a great newspaperman, I hardly think my former boss on the *World* would qualify as a monetary technician, and it was with monetary affairs that Professor Moley concerned himself. His only reward, so far as I know, was that the Professor named him as the author of Jim Farley's statement to the press after the '36 election—an attribution that did anything but please Swope, who said ruefully that he was not in the habit of accepting compliments for somebody else's work. Farley's statement was notable for its lack of any triumphal boast and its promise that there would be no reprisals on those who had so viciously assailed the President during the campaign, and was hailed by the business world as an administration declaration of peace with industry.

Well, the European press and the European statesmen were regarding Moley as the real American factotum, even though officially he was an assistant secretary of state and the actual secretary, Cordell Hull, was on the job. Moreover, Hull had advised them that currency stabilization was apart from the conference agenda; yet along came Moley, officially, and obviously intending to deal with that very question. The circumstance that the Moley party was quartered at the American embassy while the Secretary of State and the commissioners were domiciled at a hotel—Claridge's—added to the British belief that the Professor was the man to whom attention should be paid.

Moley had the President's written assignment to the London mission, but there is reason to believe that he suggested it himself and that the President, knowing full well that his administration was not going to agree to any stabilization plan that threatened to interfere with his own processes for raising prices in the interest of the restoration of American industry, acquiesced on the theory that it could do no harm. Possibly there was a deeper strategy involved, having to do with disassociating the Secretary of State from stabilization negotiations that were never intended to be consummated.

If there was any such strategy, it was without Secretary Hull's knowledge, for he started on his mission thinking the economic conference promised great accomplishments. I have no doubt his initial belief was that the outcome would be something approaching the reciprocal treaties which were a later accomplishment of the State Department. Naturally he must have realized what was going on when the functions of the delegation were cut down, and the coming of Moley confirmed his uneasiness.

Hull had troubles enough, with the increasing limitations that had been put on his mission, without the vexation of the Moley incursion. There was not even perfect harmony in the commission itself. Senator Couzens was a high tariff man. Senator Pittman was concerned more with the status and prospects of silver than with economic accord in any other area. Governor Cox was an extreme money conservative. Nearly all of the commissioners could not resist the temptation to go on the air in speeches for home consumption. There were American newspapermen representing papers in the states from which the commissioners hailed, and quite naturally these statesmen talked pretty freely to their friends of the press, much to Hull's embarrassment.

The Moley party was not particularly welcome at the embassy. Ambassador Bingham and Mrs. Bingham were rather straitlaced officials, and while their hospitality was never stinted, their routine was disturbed by the late sessions of their visitors. Moreover, Ambassador Bingham was ailing. He was, of course, quite awake to the discord between the Secretary of State and his titular assistant.

Moley's official station of assistant secretary was a bit of camouflage. He required a dignified designation to lend authority to his discharge of missions for the President; his allegiance was to the White House, not to the castellated big building across the alley. Hull was uncomfortable at the situation, but there had been no open break prior to this crossing of wires in connection with the London Conference.

Naturally Bingham was embarrassed between his allegiance to his chief—the head of the State Department, of whom he was a worshiping admirer—and his obligation to respect the agent of the President. I visited the Ambassador in his sick room, and while there was not a definite resentful word, there was an inflection when he referred to "the embassy's guests" that was the reverse of enthusiastic.

The President was at that time away on the ocean on a vacation excursion. When I think of the way the air was congested by the flood of long radiograms and how the ocean boiled with cabled messages to and from London, I wonder that he ever had time to wet a line.

The most significant communication was the long epistle from Moley in which he expressed his disesteem for the personnel of the American conferees, and which caused the big blowup. That was really the bombshell, and not Roosevelt's final veto of the "stabilization agreement," which got that title from the British but was merely a declaration of expectations by the gold bloc.

Moley had been friendly with all the conference delegates. To each of them he conveyed his appreciation of their abilities and general wisdom, and I have yet to meet a public man who did not appreciate tributes to his honesty of purpose and other excellences.

Judge of their reaction when there eventuated on Secretary Hull's desk a copy of the Moley confidential message to the President, in which appeared a paragraph to the effect that there was no member of the American delegation, except Senator Pittman, who knew what it was all about. The message was headed by the word that it was only for the President and should not be circulated in the Department of State.

Moley has explained that the paragraph was meant to refer only to their lack of technical knowledge of the money problem; but the delegates took no such view of it. Similarly, though Moley frequently disclaimed any idea or purpose of supplanting or undermining Hull, the latter never changed his opinion and today feels as bitterly toward his ex-assistant as he did in London.

Professor Moley has expressed his disappointed surprise that a message intended for the eyes of the President alone should have been seen by others. I do not know how it reached Hull's desk. However, it was sent from the American embassy in the State Department code and had to be translated by that department's code people, and it is astonishing that so astute a person as the Professor should not have divined that such a message must reach the head of the department. This is particularly true because the whole diplomatic organization was perfectly cognizant of the state of affairs between the Secretary and the Assistant Secretary.

Apart from an introduction setting forth the various topics discussed, the long message dealt mainly with the progress of the negotiations and an exposition of the virtues of stabilization. As to the merits of the negotiation themselves, I am not able to judge. My philosophy as to the money question is that of Hugh Johnson, who qualified as one of the President's economy experts in the early stages of the brain trust, and who wrote: "I have yet to meet the man (and diligently have I sought him) who really knows, with even passable certainty, anything worth while about money. It has been the principal and the hottest incentive of the human race since the beginning of history. It is the goal of the fiercest and often the most ignoble appetite of man. If there is one subject about which knowledge should have been attained in the literal thousands of years since its appearance, it is money. But it did not work that way."

Nor am I able to tell what messages the Secretary received from the home force, who always assumed that Moley was after the secretaryship for himself—a belief which the Europeans generally accepted and the newspapers frequently hinted. We got regular reports of the way the American press was handling the confused developments. The *Baltimore Sun*, for example, headed one story while Moley was en route: "British Press Pictures Hull as Moley Aide" and suggested that they were awaiting the arrival of Hull's nominal assistant to inform the American delegation what to do at this world economic conference.

The Secretary of State, like a good soldier, made no public comment on the implied sneers but undoubtedly made his protests to the President, whose replies, typically Rooseveltian, avoided any direct sympathy with either man and kept to expositions of how much (or how little) could be done, reiterating that currency stabilization must be handled apart from the the economic conference, that no agreement between two or three powers (U.S., Great Britain, and France) could be satisfactory, as many nations would have to cooperate if the desired results were to be accomplished, and so forth.

Actually the situation was that each figure in the complication wanted the other withdrawn. No other deduction is possible from Hull's messages and private comments; similarly no hypothesis apart from this is compatible with Moley's word to the President that "Pittman is the only member of the delegation intelligently and aggressively to present ideas to the conference," that "the expert group needs strengthening," and finally that a "reconstituted delegation would be helpful."

So far as known, Moley was not commissioned to ride herd on the American delegation, but evidently felt he was obliged to do so.

Hull thought that his assistant secretary not only was knocking him and the rest of the delegation to the President but actually had our outfit under surveillance. In other words, he believed that somebody was keeping the other fellow advised of the most intimate intradelegation proceedings and reflections. Perhaps he deduced this from the correspondence which had been reported to him and seemed to embrace certain details, of no vast importance, but which nobody outside might have been expected to have. The Secretary of State was not even sure that his own messages to the President were inviolate. Actually there was no hidden mystery, and so far as I can surmise there was nothing at Claridge's that could be of particular interest to Ray Moley except the talk about himself and his purposes. There was a lot of this, even before Hull had let the delegates see the Moley message conveying his disesteem for their capacity, and they were as hurt and indignant as he was.

Finally Hull thought he had discovered the source of the alleged leaks in the person of an attaché who had social relations with some of the Moley entourage, and he had about decided to send the suspected one home. Nearly all of us knew the attaché well. The individual had been associated with me in the campaign, so I was selected to intercede. I told the Secretary of my knowledge and appreciation of the ability, faithfulness, and loyalty displayed previously by this person in various posts, which to me demonstrated incapacity of such a treachery as the suspicion entailed, and I further pointed out to him that if the individual was dismissed under such charges, it meant the destruction of a promising career. I am glad to say he listened to me and finally accepted my judgment, but I am by no means certain that he totally agreed with me. His sense of justice and his kindliness outweighed his doubts.

It was not remarkable that Cordell Hull should have been distracted, uneasy, and suspicious. The economic conference filled the eyes of the world. On him fell the burden of maintaining the dignity of the enterprise, though his final instructions made it impossible that any adequate result could come of the sessions. The gathering was a disappointment to the British and French particularly, and they thinly disguised their soreness at a program that jettisoned their ideas of trading off a debt settlement for a currency stabilization and other considerations that would be to their advantage. Naturally they were considering the relative gains to their countries, just as Roosevelt at home was following a course that would not give the United States the worst of it. Then came the Moley business, which Hull felt compromised his status and hampered his efforts to get the best he could out of an unpromising situation. There was no public display of his agitation. At the sessions, and in his conferences with the prime ministers and other dignitaries, he was the same smooth, suave, gentle, low-voiced, considerate official with whom the American people are so familiar.

Meanwhile Moley was continuing his deliberations with the Bank of England people and with others concerned in the monetary project. As fast as an apparent basis was reached, the President stepped on it, though he seemed to be willing, at one time, to accept a ratio of approximately four dollars to the pound, if it had to be done. The gyrations of those two acrobats, the dollar and the pound, complicated the business.

Incidentally, the episode throws a light on the often mooted question of how gravely Roosevelt accepts the policies of those about him, whom opposition editors and orators charge with impressing their star-gazing, utopian, socialistic, communistic, dictatorial—or whatever adjective fits the hostile viewpoint—dreams upon him. I think Moley was the most influential of any of those who basked in the presidential sunlight; but when Moley wanted words of presidential sympathy to help him in his commerce with the foreign financiers, he got only provocative controversy. After some years of observation I am satisfied that Roosevelt's course with all advice follows the same pattern as his decisions on his speeches. He ponders all views—and then rolls his own.

So with the declaration by the gold bloc, which Moley and the British so strenuously urged that the President should accept. This document presented in general terms the virtues and values of the stabilization principle. The Professor assured everybody that it set forth the President's own views, and so he prepared the fiduciary statesmen for a happy response. Roosevelt, however, retorted with the explosive message that wrecked the already shaky conference.

The message signed by the French and British representatives was susceptible of different interpretations. The authors insisted that it was innocuous: that it committed no country to anything definite. President Roosevelt construed it as a threat or ultimatum.

When the declaration was sent, with a strong plea that it be ratified without delay, the President was blissfully ensconced at Campobello Island, which had not even a telephone to the mainland, so he was spared for some hours the torrent of radiograms. To make sure that he got it, word was also sent to the Treasury officials, to Bernie Baruch, and to several others.

All hands were happy at what they assumed would be a satisfaction to the worried gold-standard nations. The Professor invited Hull to be the bearer of the anticipated cheery reply. Moley's own explanation later was that "whoever announced the news would receive the accolade of Europe and the United States. I wanted Hull, who had suffered so many disappointments and reverses and who might still believe he had suffered them because of my influence, to take the bows. Hull agreed."

On the other hand, the Hull side of the story is that it was an invitation to validate the Professor's various acts that had caused the Secretary of State so much embarrassment, and that he, having no responsibilities in the stabilization field, declined to attend the session at which the foreign representatives would be given the glad news.

Nevertheless a considerable gathering assembled to hear the realization of the hopes of sixty-five nations (I think every important diplomatic cutaway and striped pants in London was there); but after quite a wait they were told that the expected message had been delayed because of the inaccessibility of the President. Again the air was full of radio; all hands tried to get the President on the transatlantic phone. It was a jittery, nervous period, though the general expectation still was that the President must come through finally with an approval of the gold bloc's declaration. The first shock was when a message was received from Assistant Secretary of State Phillips to the effect that the President would answer as soon as possible and that no public comment should be made in London. The President, of course, had noted Moley's messages both to him directly and via Baruch et al. of the worthiness of the gold countries' declaration, and so doubtless meant to head off any public comment that might be embarrassing when the negative answer came.

Moley was anxious not only over the ominous implications but because the message came through Phillips, despite Moley's having carefully labeled his cables confidential and for the President's eye alone.

Presently Moley notified Hull that the President's reply was coming through. He caught the Secretary of State on the steps of Claridge's en route to Lady Astor's garden party at Cliveden. Moley writes that Hull "received the news coldly" and told him that he could send him the message by his secretary. I was not there, but my information is that it was anything but a cold meeting; in fact, I gathered that the comments of the Secretary of State—not on the message but on the messenger—were about the hottest in our modern diplomatic history.

There is no doubt that on many occasions Moley tried to diminish Hull's resentment and to assure him that he was neither a candidate for Hull's post nor a party to anything that might tend to assail his dignity, etc. The Secretary of State, so far as I know, maintained his composure in every case—except the one on the steps of Claridge's. When he talked with the delegation about it, however, Hull made no secret of the resentment he felt. He was hurt by the European press assumption that his titular assistant had come over to run the show, an impression not lessened by Moley's frequent conferences with Prime Minister MacDonald, who was chairman of this economic conference at which, Hull, his peer officially, was the chief of the American representatives. Moley always insisted that these contacts were at the Prime Minister's behest. The English premier could not quite appreciate the flexibility of the American system and seemed to take it for granted that when a subordinate proceeded with authority, independent of his official chief, the subordinate was the number one man.

I do not think there was any great community of spirit between our secretary of state and the British premier, though most of the official amenities were preserved. Hull was to the Englishman the symbol of a conference which balked his purposes; Moley was the hope of a realization of a program which MacDonald contended was not mainly purposed for the advantage of the British Empire but was designed to reassure the distracted gold countries, who thought they were confronted by inflation perils unless currency relations were stabilized.

It was to Moley that the Prime Minister poured out his agony at the rejection of what he and Moley agreed was an innocuous paraphrase of what they thought to be Roosevelt's original ideas, but which Roosevelt thought implied his acceptance of an unpalatable program prejudicial to what he was doing toward American recovery.

Well, all Europe was infuriated by the rejection; and solemn conclaves were initiated in which Moley and Hull joined to determine what could be done. I issued the announcement for Hull that the President had rejected the declaration in its present form and that the Secretary of State would give a statement of the President's views on Monday (this was on Saturday). The aim was to head off a movement to adjourn the conference and put the blame for its failure on Roosevelt.

"Our first thought," says Moley in his book, "when we had collected ourselves, was that we must protect him at all costs."

I have often wondered what the President's reaction was to the thought that he had to be protected from the effects of his own utterance. At any rate, the verdict had been rendered; and that night Moley, Swope, and Walter Lippmann, who was commenting on the economic conference for the *New York Herald Tribune* syndicate, sat up most of the night composing the explanation, and Swope and I had a hack at it next morning.

Moley, unable to understand how the President had departed from what Moley considered his actual aims and desires, had cabled Baruch and his associates for information of the President's attitude. He got word back that they had no information, as the President was on board the cruiser *Indianapolis* with Louis Howe and Henry Morgenthau. Now a quote from Moley's book: "It was all that we needed to know. Now the picture began to make sense. Louis, who did not know beans about money questions and would naturally be concerned with the superficial public reaction to the sagging of stock and commodity prices on Friday; Morgenthau, whose rudimentary knowledge of monetary problems was largely provided by Professors George F. Warren and Frank A. Pearson (advocates of the absurd theory that changes in the price of gold would cause commodity prices to vary proportionately)." *

Far be it for me to attempt to referee a discord between Professor Moley of Columbia, A.M., Ph.B., LL.D., and Professor Warren of Cornell, B.S.A., Ph.D., B.L.C., M.S.A. In their mutual contempt for each other's theories one may be right; perhaps both are right. It is no sea on which a layman should launch his boat.

Ray and Louis had been knife-eyeing one another from the

---

* Raymond Moley, *After Seven Years* (New York and London: Harper & Brothers, 1939), p. 257.

time the two first were rivals for proximity to the Boss. It requires no stretch of imagination to conceive that Louis would be emphatically on the Warren side, particularly with Roosevelt inclined in the same direction.

Back in London the job of explaining the President to the public and to the conference was gone through with. We were all told that the text of the President's rejection was to be kept as secret as could be and shown to as few people as possible.

It has always been a mystery to me why there was so much caution about the original communication, in which every nation privy to the conference was interested, and so much publicity to the subsequent message on the same subject. Our explanatory production was a pretty good job of softening, but Hull never had a chance to utter it, for on Sunday there came out of the air the President's bombshell. Here it is, sounding not nearly so bellicose as it seemed ten years ago:

"I would regard it as a catastrophe amounting to a world tragedy if the great Conference of Nations, called to bring about a more real and permanent financial stability and a greater prosperity to the masses of all Nations, should in advance of any serious effort to consider these broader problems, allow itself to be diverted by the proposal of a purely artificial and temporary experiment affecting the monetary exchange of a few Nations only. Such action, such diversion, shows a singular lack of proportion and a failure to remember the larger purposes for which the Economic Conference originally was called together.

"I do not relish the thought that insistence on such action should be made an excuse for the continuance of the basic economic errors that underlie so much of the present worldwide depression.

"The world will not long be lulled by the specious fallacy of achieving a temporary and probably an artificial stability in foreign exchange on the part of a few large countries only.

"The sound internal economic system of a Nation is a greater factor in its well-being than the price of its currency in changing terms of the currencies of other Nations.

"Hey, Doc, I suppose you also do whitewashing?"

(Herbert Johnson in *The Saturday Evening Post*)

"It is for this reason that reduced cost of Government, adequate Government income, and ability to service Government debts are all so important to ultimate stability. So too, old fetishes of so-called international bankers are being replaced by efforts to plan national currencies with the objective of giving to those currencies a continuing purchasing power which does not greatly vary in terms of the commodities and need of modern civilization. Let me be frank in saying that the United States seeks the kind of dollar which a generation hence will have the same purchasing and debt-paying power as the dollar value we hope to attain in the near future. That objective means more to the good of other Nations than a fixed ratio for a month or two in terms of the pound or franc.

"Our broad purpose is the permanent stabilization of every Nation's currency. Gold or gold and silver can well continue to be a metallic reserve behind currencies, but this is not the time to dissipate gold reserves. When the world works out concerted policies in the majority of Nations to produce balanced budgets and living within their means, then we can properly discuss a better distribution of the world's gold and silver supply to act as a reserve base of national currencies. Restoration of world trade is an important factor, both in the means and in the result. Here also temporary exchange fixing is not the true answer. We must rather mitigate existing embargoes to make easier the exchange of products which one Nation has and the other Nation has not.

"The Conference was called to better and perhaps to cure fundamental economic ills. It must not be diverted from that effort." * After some years the President made public his own comment on the gold bloc's proposal:

"For two good reasons, the United States could not yield to this demand: first, it would have terminated our national price-level increase which at that moment was restoring our own economic activity more nearly to the pre-depression level; and second, action on reducing trade barriers and on other impor-

* *The Public Papers and Addresses of Franklin D. Roosevelt*, II (New York: Random House, 1938), p. 264.

tant matters on the agenda had to be taken up simultaneously with the question of exchange arrangements if the Conference expected to accomplish permanent results.

"It is true that my radio message to the London Conference fell upon it like a bombshell. This was because the message was realistic at a time when the gold-bloc Nations were seeking a purely limited objective, and were unwilling to go to the root of national and international problems. The immediate result was a somewhat petulant outcry that I had wrecked the Conference." †

Meanwhile London was having its lugubrious ecstasy. There was Hull fretting under the twin burdens of his assistant's supposed predominance and the wreck of the conference through changing instructions. There was Moley distraught with his mournful efforts to convince all and sundry that Hull's suspicions were unfounded, and his distraction at Roosevelt's disregard of his advice. Finally, there was MacDonald wailing that Roosevelt had destroyed the conference and ruined what he had hoped would be the crowning achievement of his life. But the gem of this diadem of mourning was supplied by His Majesty.

"Only a day or two ago," narrated MacDonald to Moley, "the King said: 'I will not have these people worrying my Prime Minister this way.'"

Once upon a time in a New York traffic jam an automobile came to anchor close to a mounted policeman. The horse tossed his head, and an infant in the machine had a screaming fit of terror. Its mother took the child in her arms and said soothingly, "There, there, precious, mother will not let the naughty gee gee bite her precious baby."

The only item in this hysterical period that equaled the Prime Minister's lament was Moley's apologetic explanation of Franklin Roosevelt's harshness—that the President was, "under certain circumstances, a man who did not do himself full justice because of his choice of language."

Again I am moved to wonder how our chief executive, who

† *Ibid.*, p. 266.

is not usually accused of lack of literary pride, welcomed the implication that he was either inarticulate or incoherent?

The death of the conference was in sight, and I did not stay for the funeral. The agitation for an adjournment, saddling Roosevelt with responsibility for its failure, was in the air. I was told later that Neville Chamberlain, chancellor of the exchequer, went to the final session with such a resolution in his pocket; then Hull made a speech in which he set forth the arguments for continuing the life of the conference and warned what repercussions its dissolution might entail; whereupon Chamberlain arose and admitted that Hull had converted him, and moved a recess. And the London Economic Conference is still in recess.

I returned to Washington and made my report to the President, telling him that in my opinion the feud was so grave that unless something drastic was done he was likely to lose not only his secretary of state but his ambassador to Great Britain. He knew I was a Hull partisan, and I gathered that he agreed with my view of Moley's ineptness. He outlined his program for keeping peace in his official family. Ray Moley was to be invited to go to Hawaii to study and make recommendations on the law conditions there. The islands were in turmoil over a ghastly case that suggested that native juries paid more attention to racial ties than to the evidence. Moley declined that assignment but worked instead with the Department of Justice on legislation which that branch of the government wanted. He believes he helped keep Edgar Hoover as head of the F.B.I. despite efforts to substitute a Democratic politician. I never had heard of anybody's scheming to make such a shift, though ordinarily the ambitions of "Democratic politicians" came to my knowledge.

Roosevelt needed these two men—Hull because of the vast respect in which he was held throughout the country and of his eminence in international affairs; Moley because of the thoroughness of his knowledge of economics, his great skill with words, and his unflagging industry. Roosevelt had no doubts of his ability to keep both in service—and, I think, cared little about their mutual antagonism.

My mind flew back half a century to the Yorke ranch in Graham County, Arizona, where one evening the bunkhouse philosopher gave me a lecture on efficiency: "You take the Molly mule," said he, "and a squaw could handle her; but you take Buck and Eph, them two ornery buckskins, and its another story. That span kicked a buckboard and a water cart to kindlings on me. They'd ought to have been shot when they were foaled, but you take Miguel here, and he drives that span in double harness without ever getting a hoof over a trace or dishing a wheel—and let me tell you, son, when you get that kind of a driver, you've got a scholar and a diplomate."

Before very long Hull ran into another and not altogether dissimilar complication. He and his undersecretary, Sumner Welles, were at loggerheads. Again the Secretary of State felt that his putative subordinate was priming himself to succeed his chief. Welles was entrusted with various missions and functions that the head of the department thought transgressed his authority and prestige, and that he contended should have been handled either by him or through him.

Moreover, Welles, like pretty much every other important person in the government, has his friends and partisans among the publicity people. Every now and then some story would leak from the State Department, and Hull would make his own deductions. Relations became so strained that the Secretary of State and his second in command were not on speaking terms. Ultimately it came to a point where one or the other had to go. The root of this far from uncommon situation in the government, of course, lies in the custom of a president's selecting the key men of the various branches of the cabinet instead of leaving it to each head to pick his own assistants. In the absence or preoccupation of a department chief the undersecretary will become acting secretary, and therefore a president wants his own man.

Probably the sore spot would not have become so inflamed in 1943 had not Welles's newspaper supporters intimated that the friction was because of differing attitudes (a difference entirely hypothetical, I believe) on the part of the two men toward Soviet Russia. At a time when all hands had to tread on eggs in relation to our war allies, with conferences impending which would embrace Stalin's representatives and ultimately the Russian leader himself, this sort of talk insured a crisis.

It was a tough spot for the President. He likes Welles and has a deep regard for his abilities; he respects and has faith in Hull. Even if it were otherwise, he could not afford a breakup of his cabinet at this time, so Welles's departure from the State Department was inevitable.

By virtue of the President's expedient Professor Moley's severance from the administration was delayed half a year. Then he formally resigned and went into the publishing business with Vincent Astor on *Today*. Ultimately they took over *News Week* and made a success of the venture. For a considerable period thereafter he continued as Roosevelt's unofficial adviser on tough questions and tough speeches, though more and more his editorials departed from the Roosevelt policies. He finally came to Washington as a witness before the Senate Judiciary Committee to administer an extra and unneeded black eye to the President's court plan.

As for me, I went back to my desk at the National Committee, only to be pulled out to go with Hugh Johnson into N.R.A.

9. WHEN THE BLUE EAGLE SOARED

The hectic days when Hugh Johnson monopolized the headlines and finally construed a vacation as a dismissal.

MY ADVENT to the N.R.A. was not auspicious.

Unfortunately I reported in the Commerce Building before Johnson had notified the people there of my designation. They had already set up a publicity organization, and my reception was, to put it mildly, chilly.

They had no office for me; some of the officials had no time to see me. Naturally I retired until the director got back to his desk.

I was waiting my turn in Johnson's anteroom, gossiping with Miss Robinson, "Robbie," the most efficient young woman I ever met. Later I found that she was immensely more than a secretary: that she was in fact one of the chief's main advisers and had no small part in the policies of the new organization. She was intensely amused at my predicament.

Suddenly out of the front office boomed a tremendous voice. "Hell's tocsin! Did you think he was a burglar?"

Figuring that my status was being clarified, I faded out without waiting to see my prospective boss. Next day I came back and the atmosphere had cleared considerably. I went in to talk with John Hancock, who, apparently, was the personnel director. He was none too cordial but resignedly asked me what salary I expected. I told him that neither I nor my secretary would take any salary from the N.R.A. but were being loaned by the National Committee to General Johnson. He thawed a trifle. They found an office for me, and we went right to work. I think the six months I spent in that service was the most interesting job I ever held. My chief assistant was Bill Janson, who had been with

me when I ran the New York *World* bureau, had trailed along
when I took the job with Raskob and Shouse, and had remained
with me until the financial difficulties of the Democratic National Committee made it embarrassing to remain on their payroll. Bill was a marvel with details. A thousand times he caught
my mistakes and corrected them, frequently without telling me
that he was doing so. What success I have had is in no small degree attributable to his care and loyalty.

Our first hurdle in the new job stemmed from the committee
of cabinet members which was supposed to exercise general su-
pervision over all of the agencies. I had been getting out some
material in regard to increased production, reopening of closed
mills, etc., marking the progress of this great effort of reconstruction. Along came a definite prohibition of our issuing any matter utilizing statistics without previously committing them to
the supervising board.

As practically all of our propaganda was directed toward
showing concretely how the country was responding to the
N.R.A., this put a terrific crimp in my work; so I made a pilgrimage to the White House. Presently the word came back that the
order was suspended. That little episode, I think, did more toward reconciling the N.R.A. hierarchy to my presence than anything else. All hands appeared to have been scared to death of
the overhanging board, and they regarded my getting a recon-
sideration as evidence of mighty influence. This was not quite
the case, but I did nothing to controvert or minimize my supposed eminence. All that happened was that I presented a
reasonable case, and nobody needed anything further to give me
the necessary privilege.

A publicity director, if he is to be of any use to an organization, must have a free hand. It must be taken for granted that
he knows his business and possesses sufficient judgment to avoid
mistakes. My main argument in getting authority to use my
own discretion about our output was that the bulletins were
nearly all of such a nature that they had to be issued forthwith
to be of any value. If every piece of literature I produced had
to go before a supervising committee for consideration, the re-

sult was bound to be infinite delay, because the general board had many more important problems than editing N.R.A. announcements. I had seen the dire effects of such a system when it was applied by a Republican National Committee during a campaign. They had bright men, thoroughly competent, in their publicity division; but everything had to go to a half a dozen higher-ups before the latter could send their stuff around, with the natural result that they frequently missed the editions of newspapers that had been carrying my Democratic matter. I so scheduled my output that by the next day they would have a new issue to meet.

Early in the business I got intimations of the rivalries and counterambitions that ultimately wrecked the N.R.A. organization and compelled the resignation of Hugh Johnson. Naturally I kept aloof, preferring a reputation for obliviousness to getting mixed up in any of the feuds.

The N.R.A. setup was the realization of a publicity man's dream. Our picturesque chief with his pungent speeches, with his talk of being the target of deadcats, etc., made headlines in the paper without any effort from me.

Naturally I wanted to start off my new job with a bang. I conceived the glowing thought that a sky display was the thing. I visioned squadrons of airplanes over each great population center flying in N.R.A. formation—ground demonstrations would, of course, be taking place at the same time: perhaps a fireside talk by F.D.R. over the radio to a multitude of meetings celebrating the theme of the new organization that was to launch the recovery of industry. So I called up the army authority, asking him if the program was feasible, and got a prompt reply that the army planes could do it and would do it if the proper orders were forthcoming.

I sketched out the program. Then the instinct of caution, which must be part of the equipment of a publicity man, intruded itself. Again I called the War Department.

"Is there any danger involved in the flight formations I am asking for?"

"Oh," was the severely professional reply, "we might lose a few planes."

"Cancel the whole business!" I yelled, as cold chills ran over my frame. "It's a good stunt, but it is not worth that kind of risk."

I was reminded of the incident later on when the army enthusiastically welcomed the job of flying the mails when the air mail arrangements were canceled because of alleged irregularity and favoritism in the letting of the contracts and a ghastly series of disasters was the consequence.

At first the N.R.A. was everybody's favorite. They were holding parades and celebrations in a hundred cities to cheer the oncoming of the processes which were to get the wheels of industry turning again. I attended all the conferences: saw the happy parade of industrial kings to Johnson's office and witnessed their enthusiastic willingness to go along. Automobile magnates, railroad chiefs, great editors, and all the rest of the clan that had been rendered desperate by the market collapse saw in Johnson's effort the only hope of salvation. Later on, during the process of formulating the codes with their restrictions and their labor provisions, much of this enthusiasm waned. The magnates were all happy at the promise of the building up of markets, etc., but their rugged individualism was shocked by the insistence on collective bargaining and its corollaries. They were delighted at the practical sanction of what normally, under antitrust laws, might have been held conspiracies in restraint of trade; but they were shocked at the inclusion of Section A, which canceled out company unions and gave a fine break to the labor organizations.

I think I was particularly useful in heading off what I felt was a mistake in policy when I vetoed something emanating from the automobile division. Henry Ford had bucked at the regulations. He saw no necessity in his outfit of the sort of labor regulations that were coming on; and of course if Ford with his huge share in that business had been permitted to defy the N.R.A. measures, all the rest of the industry would have felt equally free. So one day there came to my desk a bulletin announcing that Ford's case would be sent to a grand jury with the expectation of an indictment. I held that up and sent General Johnson a memorandum setting forth that it was bad business to announce such procedure before it was actual; that if and when Ford or any other employer was indicted, it would be ample time for publicity on that subject. The General sustained me, and I think Ford's case was never sent to a grand jury. Ford and the N.R.A. wrangled along with negotiations and conferences, and ultimately the trouble was straightened out, to a degree at least. That was one of the rare occasions when I stretched my functions into the field of policy.

When it came time for the newspaper code, I suggested that the post of administrator for that code be given to my old employer, Ralph Pulitzer. The New York *World* had folded up, and Mr. Pulitzer was suffering from all the pangs of idleness following a very active career as publisher. Giving jurisdiction over the whole newspaper field to a publisher with the prestige of the Pulitzer name, I felt, would impress on newspaper publishers generally that the effort was not wholly directed to turning them over to the tender mercies of organized labor; Ralph Pulitzer would understand and be sympathetic with the problems of getting out a great newspaper. Ralph responded enthusiastically to my telephone call and came down to familiarize himself with the big job.

Then up in wrath rose Heywood Broun, head of the Newspaper Guild. He had quarreled with Ralph because of the latter's refusal to permit him to use the columns of the New York *World* to exploit his views in the Sacco-Vanzetti case. Broun had finally resigned rather than permit the publisher to edit his copy.

Immediately there came into play the weakness in Ralph Pulitzer's character. He was a fine, sensitive, artistic soul, but he had no stomach for a fight. Indeed he and his brother co-owners of the *World* let that paper go by the board rather than dip into their private fortunes and take care of the deficits resulting from the depression, from the slump in advertising in particular. The *World* at that time had a huge circulation, perhaps the largest in New York. It was enormously popular and in the opinion of all newspapermen could have well weathered the storm as did nearly all of the big New York journals. I had quit the paper three years before to take on my political job, but maintained intimacy with the staff and my friendship with the publisher.

Broun, an extreme liberal possibly with communistic ideals, went to the White House with his protest against the selection of Ralph Pulitzer. In vain I presented to the administrator of the newspaper code that General Johnson had assured me that he would stand behind him to the limit, with the added assurance that the President would not interfere. The prospect of criticism caved Pulitzer down. His brother, Joseph Pulitzer, the publisher of the other family newspaper, the *St. Louis Post-Dispatch,* which continued to be prosperous, argued that Ralph's part ownership of the *Post-Dispatch* made it inadvisable for him to wield the authority of code administrator, and so he quit the job.

Naturally the incident enhanced the repute of the Newspaper Guild, which up to that time had only the beginnings of influence and power. It gave a great boost to Broun and his Guild which previously had labored under the disesteem of (I believe) a majority of the higher-salaried newspaper workers. Like other businessmen the newspaper publishers had not been treating the young fellow of the trade with any great consideration. Whatever may be the faults of the Guild, it did succeed in improving the salaries of this group.

The original program was that Johnson and I would both get out when the codes were completed, leaving their administration to somebody who had not encountered the inevitable enmities of those who resented the new rules and regulations. However, when that time came, President Roosevelt insisted that Johnson remain, on the theory that nobody else was as familiar with the processes as he and therefore it would be disruptive to make a change. My job, however, was done, and I went back to my political desk. That was my last definite governmental employment.

By this time the rift between Johnson and Donald Richberg was nearing the acute stage. Johnson felt that the eminent lawyer who was general counsel of the N.R.A. was aspiring to the administratorship and was fomenting trouble in the ranks. I did not know and do not know now whether the General's suspicion had a substantial basis or whether it was his dictatorial instinct to see plots and cabals against his pre-eminence.

There came a time when the General went to the Pacific Coast, on a vacation, as I recall. There was a general strike going on out there; and either of his own motion or at the solicitation of one or the other of the factions in that strike, he jumped into it, and the strike was settled. He always contended that this was the result of his interposition. Perhaps it was. Through the codes he had at least a putative interest in labor troubles, but his action brought him the disfavor of Madam Perkins, secretary of labor, for butting in on her functions. He settled another strike on his way back East. And, according to him, the Secretary of Labor and Donald Richberg joined forces against him. The row gravitated, as all big government squabbles must, to the White House. The President suggested that Hugh take a long rest, which the General construed as a decision against him. Thereupon he resigned and this time made his resignation stick.

Then he went into business as a newspaper columnist and made a success from the beginning. Before he died, I am informed, his syndicate income amounted to $75,000 a year. He dealt hard knocks all around and illustrated his matter with such verbal salt and pepper that he became enormously popular with his readers.

The gravest fault of his matter, in my opinion, was his assumption of being an authority on all subjects, military, industrial, agricultural, and governmental. His pungent criticisms of the various cabinet heads and inferentially of the President gave him high rank as an antiadministration propagandist.

This position brought me in my capacity as a Democratic propagandist to write this:

"The inference from all of the General's writings is that, had he had charge of the agriculture problem instead of Secretary Wallace, crops would never have failed and prices would never have diminished. If he, instead of Harry Hopkins, had been intrusted with relief, the unemployed would now be all economic royalists; had he, instead of Secretary Morgenthau, had direction of the fiscal affairs of the government, unbalanced budgets would by this time be only an archaic expression.

"This leads to the very natural deduction that the only way to avoid dictatorship would be to make General Hugh Johnson the dictator. Then he would have a reasonably adequate field for his varied and manifold talents."

To this Hugh made response. "They should have used one of their other literary assassins to smear somebody else. Charlie is the champion smearer of all time. But he can't smear me. He is the old maestro who taught me nearly all I know about needling a stuffed shirt . . . but Charlie couldn't smear me. My teaming with Charlie is pretty much personal. Charlie is awfully sentimental that way. While he tried feebly to drip the old poison, he balanced each kick with a lick and the net result was a great boost, for which—thanks."

In the course of this amiable controversy I wrote, "It is true that he made faces at some of these [great corporations], and when the General makes a face, mothers put bandages over their children's eyes and everybody shudders. His scowl brings back a comment of the late Arthur Brisbane in describing an executive whose frown was terrible. He said, 'I have just discovered how you came to have that kind of a face. Your ancestors in the antedeluvian period used to stick that face around the corner of the cave to scare mammoths away.' "

To this the General made response as follows: "I know my face would stop a clock, but would the faces of Henry [Wallace], Henry [Morgenthau], and Harry [Hopkins] stop a Follies girl! And that beloved old sour puss of Charlie's—he could rent it out for gargoyle over a Chinese joss house to scare the devil away."

These quotations illustrate the relations between the tough old roughneck and myself, which never changed.

The Supreme Court shot the blue eagle down, and incidentally that decision more than any other brought about the President's crusade to rejuvenate the high tribunal.

The N.R.A., though it ceased upon the capital verdict of the high justices, accomplished a whole lot. It had started the wheels of industry again; it had instilled the spirit of co-operation and enthusiasm where there had been only distrust and despair. It had put millions of men to work, and, while it was all illegal by the court's decision, the trend it had given to industry and recovery can hardly be overestimated. It was Hugh Johnson who did this. All his rough talk and spectacular antics were calculated and were just what we needed. I am still of the belief that had the administration gone to the Supreme Court when the N.R.A. was at the zenith of its popularity and with a more definite and less involved cause then the sick chicken case, it might have stood up.

Our friendship was put to a rather severe test at the time I had to bar the General from my wrestling match with Vice-President Garner over the speech Johnson had prepared for that reluctant statesman. But he realized my difficulties and appreciated what was necessary to get Cactus Jack back on the campaign trail. We joked about it during the intimacy which ceased only with the death of the most picturesque figure I had encountered during my adventures in politics.

The story of our attempt to corral Garner in the campaign has its amusing side. We were having a tough time with the vice-presidential candidate. He had refused to be enthusiastic about his advancement from the speakership of the House of Representatives to candidacy for the second place in the government. In the lower house, where everybody was his close friend, he had been happy and had reveled there in the power of his office. Nothing interfered with his usual rite of "striking a blow for liberty," which was his description of the little sessions where he and his cronies took their drinks.

His habit of disappearing into his hotel apartment at dusk and going to bed at nine o'clock, after which hour his telephone was shut off, was more precious than any political or social honor, and he really resented the change in his routine which the new responsibilities threatened. It was because of his making himself invisible and unreachable when it suited him, when he was needed in the campaign, that the Roosevelt managers dispatched Charlie Hand, one of the leading lights of New York journalism, to Uvalde to ride herd on the horn-browed Texan. Through Hand we were able to get messages to Cactus Jack. These messages mainly concerned the desirability of his taking an active part in the battle and, sad to say, provoked little more than such statements as:

"The Captain is going to be elected and doesn't need me on the stump."

Hand's life in Uvalde was hardly happy, despite the amiable kidding he got at the hands of his originally not-overly-willing host.

In the end the pressure brought the recalcitrant around. I believe it was a personal communication from Franklin Roosevelt that finally induced him to come to New York.

It was my job to get the speech we thought we required; so Mr. Garner came to my quarters in the Biltmore.

"Whose idea is it to get me here?" was his greeting.

I explained that the opposition, which was busy describing the Democratic candidate as a Communist, was filling the newspapers with a story of a rift between him and Roosevelt, and pointed out that his aloofness from the firing line gave point to these implications and that people were beginning to believe that there was a row between the candidates, which might cause some of Garner's friends, disappointed at his not getting the big nomination, to abate their efforts if, indeed, some of them might not vent their resentment in active hostility.

This was, of course, sales talk that did not impress him. "Horse feathers," he said. Well, perhaps horse feathers was not the precise word he employed, but that conveys his general meaning.

However, ultimately he asked, "What is it you want me to do?"

I told him that we were all of the opinion that a campaign speech by him was a vital necessity, to squelch the opposition propaganda about a rift in the ticket.

"Let's see what you've got for me," was his response. By this time his hackles were smoothed pretty well, and I handed him a manuscript that had been concocted by Hugh Johnson.

He began to read it, and I could see the lines of his round face hardening and his complexion, always ruddy, becoming almost purple.

Suddenly he threw the whole thing over his shoulder, scattering the pages all over the floor, and started to stalk from the room. I got in his way and told him to hold on for a moment. We had been friends for a long time, so he did not stride over me; and finally I persuaded him to go for a walk and give me a chance to make the speech acceptable. There was nothing wrong with it, though it was evident that the writer had been thinking with his own head rather than that of the man who was to deliver it.

While he was gone I gathered up the pages and got busy with them. I began with a recital of his friendship with his Republican predecessor in the speakership. There had been a genuine and deep affection between him and Nick Longworth, who died shortly before Garner became vice-president.

I followed with anecdotes illustrating this intimacy and such things; and when he returned, in vastly better humor than he had been when he left, I handed him the speech.

As he read the tribute to his old intimate and adversary, the grimness departed from his face. He nodded approval of the complimentary references to Longworth.

Let it be known that the acrid, cynical old Texan is really a sentimentalist. By the time he had finished the sugary hors d'oeuvre, he did not mind the rest of the speech. He delivered the whole thing, including much of Hugh Johnson's production, over the radio with spirit and effect.

That was all we could get him to do, however. He went back to Uvalde, to his fishing and hunting and his banks.

In vain we appealed to him to continue the good work. We

mailed him appreciative newspaper clippings on his oration, thinking perhaps that he might be cajoled from his isolation by this evidence of the interest people felt in the Vice-President and their hunger to hear more from him. He was too canny to be swayed by a plea that would have moved almost any other politician; the lure of hearing his own voice proclaiming the great truths of democracy left him cold. We got back only salty comments to the effect that in his country when you had a steer roped and branded there is no sense in lassoing it some more.

He had never resented our assigning Charlie Hand to shepherd him. On the contrary, he regarded the circumstance as a good joke on Hand. The two became great friends, and the Vice-President saw to it that the lad from the big city was not lonesome in his exile.

Garner served his terms as vice-president amiably, doing his part in carrying out the Roosevelt policies, though privately making no secret of his lack of sympathy with New Dealisms or the palace favorites. When the third term began to loom, he let his own ambitions for the big job become evident, connived at the Hatch Act, which was intended to make Roosevelt's renomination less likely, and did not frown on the organization of Garner clubs, etc. But he was realistic all the time, telling his friends that no candidacy was "of more value than a can of stale beer" without the President's endorsement. He did not join actively in the Farley stop-Roosevelt program, for with his accustomed foresight he saw that it could get nowhere. With the election of Henry Wallace to the vice-presidency he cheerfully faded from the political horizon; and if he ever feels any interest in political developments, he carefully conceals it.

Most retired politicians attain a position akin to a professor emeritus. Candidates are supposed to come to them for advice founded on their vast experience, but Garner shows no disposition to be the Sage of Uvalde; his business projects, his guns and angling rods suffice him, and, though he is cordial to visiting statesmen, he seems to regard these efforts to restore his concern with the things to which he devoted more than half a century as a boring nuisance.

10. THE MODERN BOSS

Model Tweed has been replaced by the newer stream-lined models.

I HAVE SERVED with four democratic national chairmen. I have known most of them rather intimately, as well as every important political leader of both parties back as far as the days of Woodrow Wilson, and I have watched the evolution of the tough old-time bosses into the streamlined field marshals of this era.

The American people of today, as one may gather from the partisan press of both sides, are not sensitive to that evolution, for the newspapers, and the vocal partisans of either party, never fail to describe the opposition chiefs as monsters of iniquity. The popular idea of the boss still matches Tom Nast's Tweed cartoons and Homer Davenport's dollar-checked suit on Mark Hanna by which he characterized the Republican party or the trusts, indifferently. The accepted presentation of a political boss is that of a gross, uncouth figure usually with his feet on a desk, with a cigar hanging from his drooling lips, pouches under his too-small eyes, and the marks of sin and dissipation all over him, with side implications that his hand is out for any kind of graft.

Now let us compare that monster with the real thing. At the National Committee dinner celebrating Roosevelt's first presidential election, all eyes were on Jim Farley as we rose to drink the toast to the Chief.

He raised his glass of champagne to his lips, exclaiming, "Farley is off the water wagon."

He returned the glass untouched to the table, with the words: "Farley is on the water wagon again."

Now Farley came up in politics the hard way. He managed

to be elected town clerk at Stony Point, and solidified himself with Rockland County by refusing his ten-cent fee for dog licenses and his dollar fee for marriage licenses, etc., and so got to the New York legislature, then lost out on re-election by favoring repeal of the Baby Volstead Act, in defiance of Rockland County's rock-bound allegiance to the prohibition cause. Gradually he got into the inner circle of New York state politics, always training with Alfred E. Smith, finally attaining the secretaryship of the Democratic State Committee, which brought him into contact with Franklin Roosevelt. At that time, however, Ed Flynn, leader in the Bronx, was much closer to the Man of Destiny than Farley. In fact it was Flynn rather than Roosevelt who picked the Grassy Point lad, who by then had attained the eminence of a boxing commissionership, to do the missionary job of garnering the delegates for Roosevelt in the preconvention work in '32. The reason for this choice was that Jim was a better glad-hander than Ed, who was always a behind-the-lines operator who had no affection for crowds, and who hates to make speeches. Farley had kept his nose clean during his trek along the political jungle paths, and he was a systematic worker whose chosen career was politics, whereas with Flynn politics was a side issue. The latter had inherited a moderate fortune, was established in a fine law practice, and public office had no great lure for him. Farley, on the other hand, was poor; he had to have a job in the early period of his rise, or else to quit his activities along the line of his choice.

Roosevelt, when he was first elected governor of New York, called Flynn back from a vacation trip in Europe and with considerable difficulty got him to accept the job of secretary of state, and in that place Flynn and Louie Howe drew the blueprints that finally brought the Governor to the White House. My first intimation of it came a day or so after the election of 1928. Herbert Hoover had snowed Al Smith under, even in the Happy Warrior's own state. I was on the *World* at the time and ran into Howe on Broadway. "Al Smith isn't going to like this," said Louie. "He has lost the state and Franklin has carried it, and the country is not going to forget that when 1932 comes

around and the Democrats pick a candidate for president."
That, of course, was before Chairman John Raskob undertook
to wipe out this blot on his long series of successes by rebuilding
the party and renominating Al Smith, but it was easy to fathom
what was in Howe's never-idle mind. I went back to my normal
job as chief of the *World's* Washington bureau, and New York
politics, for the time being, ceased to be of immediate interest
to me.

I knew that Farley, as secretary of the Democratic State Committee, had smoothed and modernized that rather archaic organization, which up to that time had concerned itself mainly
with the big metropolitan vote, considering upstate New York
so safely Republican that the only effective campaigning for
Democrats was to build up a New York City vote capable of
canceling it. Farley's selection as state chairman was a natural,
and he handled Roosevelt's second campaign for the governorship so expertly that he became the logical evangelist for the
Governor's never-disguised presidential ambitions.

In that second gubernatorial campaign Farley stood exactly
in the spot of the impending rift between Smith and Roosevelt.
President Hoover's popular appeal had thinned considerably.
The prosperity of the first months of his incumbency had been
succeeded by the crash that heralded the beginning of the great
depression.

The Democratic party had been so braced up that Alfred E.
Smith emerged from the political retirement he had announced
after his defeat in 1928 and voiced his willingness to try again
for the White House. Farley had been Smith's constant supporter. Roosevelt had twice made nominating speeches for his
predecessor in Albany. But the parting of the ways was imminent, and the problem was how to accomplish this parting with
a minimum of danger; for with both Smith and Roosevelt contending for the presidential nomination two years ahead of the
convention, a party split that might ruin the chance of either
was among the possibilities. The horror of the New York convention of 1924 was in everybody's mind, and unskillful ma-

neuvering might easily have precipitated another deadlock and thrown a worthless nomination to some outsider.

Roosevelt had agreed to run for the governorship when importuned by Smith. The Roosevelt crowd felt that their man had agreed to make that race because Smith thought it would help him in his presidential enterprise, and that therefore whatever obligation there was lay on the other side. And, so far as Farley was concerned, that growing political personality had taken seriously Smith's original announcement that he was through with politics and had cast his lot with the rising star.

There was no open break in 1930. Smith probably felt that, with the Democratic organization in Raskob's hands, he had little to fear from the amateur efforts at Albany. As for Farley, Al's feeling was apparently that this was just a lieutenant who had gone astray. He did not know the real Farley; none of us in the then Democratic headquarters, which were in Washington, or more directly in Raskob's fortieth-story offices in the Empire State Building in New York, did.

Even when Farley started on his historic pilgrimage, we thought that Shouse, who was making powerful speeches throughout the country, would more than match the efforts of the pleasant, persuasive, indefatigable Roosevelt emissary, whose systematic letter campaign, followed up by chummy visits with party leaders, was harvesting instructed delegations clear across the country. Big Jim was an interesting figure. The hard-boiled, Tammany-tainted politician they expected in the West and Middle West turned out to be a genial, personable fellow who neither drank nor smoked, who carried along pictures of his wife and children, who attended church with regularity, who never obtruded his abstentions on those convivially inclined, and who, despite his own teetotalitarian habits, wanted the Prohibition Amendment repealed.

Shouse was a different sort of advance agent for a political show. He was amiable, earnest, tireless, of excellent appearance, immaculate in his dress. Shouse raced running horses; Farley only bet on them. Shouse had a fund of good stories, and shone at parties. He had perhaps a wider, but not a deeper, acquaintance with the party leaders than Farley, was equally suave, and was vastly more eloquent. His role was that of a high-class Kentuckian engaged in a work of public service. Farley's was that of a simple New York politician, modest but never apologetic in his demonstration that such a person was not necessarily either wicked or graceless. It was a curious anomaly that the aristocrat should be presenting the cause of the man from the sidewalks of New York and the commoner should be promoting the candidacy of the upstate Groton and Harvard graduate with all the traditions, if none of the reactionism, supposed to be typical of wealth and old-family prestige.

In general Farley worked with (or on) small groups. Only occasionally was he tempted into regular speech making. Shouse, on the other hand, pinned his faith on mass appeal. He was at his best when he addressed large audiences, and he did a grand job with his clarion voice and his ready tongue; for though he had a trunkful of prepared speeches, not once did he read one or even refer to a manuscript.

Now, which was the better salesman is a question. Both schools of propaganda have their advocates. But whether the victory of one and the eclipse of the other was due to Farley's simplicity, or whether the customers decided for themselves that his was the best bill of goods, is of no importance now.

It may be of interest to those who believe that a political campaign consists of invective and aspersion to learn that in none of Shouse's speeches was there a direct word of derogation of Roosevelt, or in Farley's talks a syllable other than complimentary toward Smith. This is the more extraordinary as the impulse and motive of each was to kill off, politically, the other's candidate. It would, perhaps, be stretching approbation far to assume from this that the two political evangels were actuated only by the virtuous motive of keeping the contest on a high plane, or that there was any compact to that effect between them. It was merely what the strategy of the occasion called for. They were both out to make friends, not to inflame enemies. The logic of the situation, each side realized, was that whichever won must have today's opposition with him when it came to tomorrow's election, if the nomination was to prove worth having.

Nevertheless the hostility between the two factions was present even then. It smoldered along with no public disclosure, Smith being a putative consultant and adviser of the Governor of New York, and the Governor never failing to speak admiringly of his predecessor and then present rival. The peace and courtesy did not break openly until March of 1931, when Raskob called a meeting of the Democratic National Committee in Washington, having previously issued a letter forecasting that he would ask the committee to pass a resolution making repeal of the Eighteenth Amendment a plank in the next year's platform. I had been part of the Raskob-Shouse outfit for nearly two years when this letter was decided on. I have been asked if I was not the author of the disturbing epistle. I'm sure I cannot recall that particular piece of literature, though it was generally my function as publicity director to distribute the utterances of the "Executive Committee."

At our headquarters the position was that the time for pussyfooting on the prohibition question had passed. The law's unpopularity, the openness of its evasion, and the scandals of illegal liquor withdrawals had made it, in estimation, a logical and valuable campaign issue. President Hoover's "noble experiment" indicated that the Republicans would have to dodge the issue, which made it even more valuable to us.

Viewed from the Roosevelt angle, it appeared that Smith and Raskob knew that the Governor of New York was as much in favor of repealing the Prohibition Act as they were, but were throwing in the repeal resolution at that particular time just to embarrass his candidacy. The idea conveyed was that the Southern delegates to the coming convention—bound to be against Smith—would not go along with Roosevelt if Roosevelt was put forth as another antiprohibition candidate. The theory was that the Raskob crowd did not care for whom the South voted as long as it was kept out of the Roosevelt column and so diminished the majority which Farley was already claiming for his entry.

More than a year later, at the National Committee meeting, Farley had his way. Not only had he garnered delegates in his pilgrimages, but he lined up national committeemen as well; and the body, after some of the finest rough-and-tumble, no-holds-barred oratory in the history of such gatherings, solemnly declared it was no part of its function to formulate platform planks. Thus consideration of the Raskob project—or trick (according to which side of the fence the observer was on)—was sidetracked, and Dixieland was not deflected from the bandwagon.

"You cannot write on the banner of the Democratic party, however much you may desire to do so," shouted Joe Robinson, Democratic leader of the Senate, following Raskob's speech, "the skull and crossbones emblematic of an outlawed trade."

"If the Democracy of this country would unite," taunted Senator Cameron Morrison of North Carolina, "and cease this foolishness about liquor, we could go toward great triumphs."

"If there is anything that happened here today," retorted Al Smith, "that could give greater comfort to President Hoover and his cohorts than the speech of the Senator, I would like to know what it is."

We were not particularly dismayed by our failure to get the Raskob repealer adapted by the National Committee. As I recall it, the conversation at headquarters ran something like this: "Well, when we come to the convention, we'll have it in the platform and have full credit for it, while Roosevelt will have either to trail along or to side-step it, and neither course is going to help him with the Southern delegates."

When we actually got to the convention, a ringing Wet plank was adopted as part of the Roosevelt platform and nobody remembered that it was Raskob who originated the bold step.

And Roosevelt did not lose the Southern delegates either, though Mississippi's delegation was a constant source of worry to Howe and Farley, who knew it was only hanging to Roosevelt by the slender margin of half a vote.

Someday the Democrats will do away with unit-rule delega-

tion, just as they did ultimately with the two-thirds rule—
which cost them the election in 1924. Each of the rules is not
without advantages, and not infrequently, perhaps, has resulted
in the selection of a better candidate; but since majority domination is the essential principle of democratic government,
giving veto power to a one-third minority is anything but
democratic—regardless of whether that word is spelled with a
capital or a lower-case "D." The unit-rule theory is that the
delegation represents the will of a state and not the predilec-
tions of the delegates themselves. Actually the delegations so
circumscribed represent merely the strongest or the smartest
of a couple of political machines.

Possibly the ultimate result would have been the same in
the 1932 convention without the unit rule. Farley and the
Roosevelt troops thought they had the bulk of the votes in
nearly every divided delegation, which with the instructed
delegations would have given him his initial majority. That
was their thought, but they were never sure.

They had to reckon, for example, with the dark-horse contingent—the guerrilla troops—who were as much interested in
preventing an early decision as were the Smith forces. Just by
way of illustration, there was the case of Senator Harry Byrd,
who had the favorite son's position in his state, but who
was counted as part of the Roosevelt strength. When there
appeared the possibility of a deadlock, Senator Byrd would not
turn over his delegation. He may have had the idea that if the
main contestants were forced to split, he might be the fortunate legatee, though it is probable that a vice-presidential
nomination was the limit of his real ambitions. Then Newton
Baker and Owen Young were hovering in the offing, ready and
anxious to take advantage of any break.

Our crowd—I was still with the Raskob outfit—broke their
hearts trying to reach Garner, who would not answer his
phone; and when Farley got contact with him, through Sam
Rayburn and Silliman Evans, the Smith strategists were still
vainly ringing Uvalde.

I was not in on the intimate strategy of the last struggles—

purposely, for the excellent reason that I could contribute nothing, and more particularly because all my old newspaper colleagues were bombarding me for information, and in the event of a leak I did not wish to be in a position to be charged with it. Consequently I am unable to verify the rumor that went around in the predawn hours of the convention decision that Smith wanted to offer Garner what he could deliver of the New York delegation as the price of Garner's standing firm for a specified number of ballots. Smith could have had small hope of getting Garner on his side, as Texas had violated tradition and gone Republican against the New Yorker in 1928, and the Texan candidate could hardly be expected to go against his state under any circumstances. On the other hand, the canny old Speaker could not be indifferent to the value to him of Northern delegates; for while this maneuvering was going on, Garner had not yet abandoned his hope of the presidential nomination, which, perhaps, explains why Smith could not reach him. He could not go with Smith; neither could he afford, at that hour, to antagonize the second most powerful of the contestants.

Garner never was keen about the vice-presidency, having frequently announced his belief that the speakership was a bigger job.

Farley has told with intimate detail how he and Silliman Evans, Homer Cummings, and Sam Rayburn finally lassoed Cactus Jack and herded him into the Roosevelt corral.

There were some heartburnings. Senator Burt Wheeler of Montana thought he ought to have the second place on the ticket, and has been grouchy ever since. Harry Byrd was never happy as a Roosevelt supporter and finally went clear out, though neither of these statesmen would admit for a moment that his opposition in the Supreme Court fracas and subsequent Roosevelt-sponsored legislation stemmed from a 1932 disappointment.

Like Smith and Raskob, Shouse and the rest of them, these preserved their Democratic status by supporting the party candidate in the campaign, and that support was neither perfunctory nor halfhearted.

Raskob led off. I introduced him to his radio audience, when he sounded off from Democratic headquarters at the Biltmore in New York, as the man most responsible for the strength and vitality of the Democratic party, and that was not mere lip service to my former chief. If it had not been for his shouldering the burden of keeping alive the organization—he came across with about $30,000 a month even during the stock market crash when he was reputed to be losing millions a day—it is more than doubtful if 1932 would have started Democracy's long series of victories. Few of the Raskobians stayed within the fold. They were quiescent during the early stages of the new administration, when Roosevelt was straightening out the banks, inaugurating the N.R.A., and promulgating his relief and employment measures; but after these things had started the stalled wheels of industry to rolling again, and the conservatives had caught their breath after their period of bewilderment and dismay, the movement began that culminated in the Liberty League.

So again in 1936 it was Farley vs. Shouse—in the campaign after the nomination and despite Shouse's Democracy.

Shouse was kind enough to invite me to join the new cabal, and with the formidable list of multimillionaires that were financing it, I realized that it meant more money for me. Though I had described myself as a political bravo whose sword was ready for any service that would be most profitable, I found when it came to the test that that declaration had been, to again borrow from Wendell Willkie, "only a bit of campaign oratory." I was evidently no true Hessian, for the idea of campaigning against the man whose election I had worked for with all my enthusiasm, and fighting Farley and the rest of the great crew with whom I had been associated, made no appeal. One of my friends told me that the Du Pont interests had in mind a vast publicity organization and suggested that there was, in consequence, a $50,000-a-year job open. Whether he was offering me the post with any authority, I cannot tell; I merely replied that I knew nothing about commercial publicity and advised him that there were several agencies, expert in that line, available.

The objects of the Liberty League, as set forth in their pamphlets and in the speeches in behalf of the outfit, were fine examples of restraint and logic from the reactionary point of view.

"The Constitution," orated President Shouse, "is the living voice of American Liberty. It is the shield of protection of the person, the home and the rights of the citizen. But the benefits derived from it have come to us of the present generation without a struggle, and because we have not had to fight for what it confers we have at times seemed to esteem it too lightly. Consciousness of the Constitution and of what it involved needs to be reawakened in the minds and hearts of the American people," etc.

"Founded as a nonpolitical organization by leaders of both political parties, the Liberty League, more than any other organization I know, stands for sanity and cool judgment in a time of popular confusion and muddled governmental policy," said Dr. Neil Carothers, professor of economics at Lehigh University.

"If you think that the inestimable privilege of American citizenship imposes any obligations, then join, and join at once this patriotic collective effort to defend our constitutional liberty. The American people can still save their Constitution if they will only awake from their dream of fancied security and join hands in a common purpose."—James M. Beck's speech.

Later on what might be called the infantry of the Liberty League opened fire, unrestrained by the dignity of the high officials, and spattered the Democratic administration with real invective.

The formidable quality of the organization could not but cause concern at Farley's headquarters. The volume of money represented by its directorates scared us, for every important corporation cluster—Rockefellers, Morgans, Du Ponts—was represented, and figured as contributors. A compilation at the time presented that on their executive committee there were seventy presidents or directors of corporations.

They had approximately seventy eminent attorneys on their staff, headed by John W. Davis. This division was referred to in contemporary comment as "The Little Supreme Court" of the League.

Our comeback to this legal array was to review their appearances before the actual Supreme Court and recount the times they had lost before the real tribunal.

"None of this recital," I wrote in one of my "Dispelling the Fog" letters, "is meant to suggest that the distinguished attorneys in question are not good lawyers or even great lawyers. It merely seeks to point out that the ponderous assumption of infallibility in construing the Constitution of the United States may not be wholly authentic. Appeals to the Supreme Court are expensive luxuries, and it must not be supposed that these gentlemen were putting their clients to vast expense if they did not think their view of the law must be agreed to by the grave supreme justices. So, in many instances, it appears either that they were honestly wrong in their contentions, or we must take the shocking alternative of assuming that they were trying to persuade the highest court in the land to go awry.

"Their effort to get state judges to throw in with them, as typified by the approach to the Supreme Justice of the Court of New York—and that is no isolated instance—makes one wonder if they have ever thought of approaching the members of the national tribunal of last resort?" *

With two Democratic ex-presidential candidates in their organization—Al Smith ranking as secretary and John W. Davis heading their legal department, there was color to the contention that the Liberty League was a nonpartisan body; which did not interfere with their supporting Governor Landon, the Republican nominee, in 1936. The voting that year made it

---

* Justice Carew responded to their invitation to have him join the Legal Committee thus: "Sir and to your colleagues: I regard this as impudence and I do not desire to receive this or any other communication of its kind."

clear that even these two eminent Democrats could not deliver their admirers to the opposition party.

The gold-coast complexion of the organization, instead of carrying weight with the voters, was a complete handicap. In 1936 the country was in no mood to accept the mandate of big business, and we at headquarters had no hard task beyond parading their list of directors and contributors. The revolt against Franklin Roosevelt that was, according to its prospectus, to deliver the nation from thraldom to the starry-eyed theorists, who were presented as authors of the New Deal and as the President's managing board, got no further than the billion-dollar set and a few Democratic affiliates who had always trained with them. Possibly the three-family campaign fund—about $60,000—preserved Maine for the Republicans, but it is not improbable that had they saved this money Maine would have gone the same way.

The net result of the investment, amounting in all to about a million dollars, was, as was told at the time, the conversion of America's favorite family—the Du Ponts—into political enemy number one.

It was not for any incompetence on the part of those who managed the show. President Jouett Shouse earned his yearly salary—currently reported as $54,000—by an incessant course of speech-making on the peril to American democracy involved in the subserviency of Congress to the executive, the threat to unborn millions of loss of liberty and the destruction of the Constitution—always with insistence that the Liberty League was altogether nonpartisan, was seeking to steer Roosevelt on the right path, etc. The Liberty League was pursuing what we used to call its "dupontifical" propaganda, while its constituent leaders were shooting checks to the Landon campaign funds.

When the outfit went into the silences, after the 1936 election, Editor Gannett took over, with the modest proposal that five million Democrats and five million Republicans enlist in a junta to repeal that election. As preliminary he wanted the old reliable Liberty Leaguers to come across with four hundred thousand dollars and new contributors to yield three hun-

dred thousand to finance this movement to save us from dictatorship and so on. He piled out a lot of literature between the
inception of the idea and the Republican convention four
years later, at which convention, if my memory serves, the
upstate New York publisher got two votes—from upstate New
York delegates.

The campaign of 1940 was about the longest in our history,
for with the imminence and finally the advent of the war in
Europe came the question of whether Franklin Roosevelt
would break the tradition forbidding a third term.

I happen to know that nothing was further from his mind
before the European crisis threatened to engulf the United
States. I remember his musing that his sole ambition was to
turn over his desk to his successor with a country at peace,
prosperous and contented.

We at Democratic headquarters during that period were
wondering where a candidate could be found who would come
up to the specifications—vote-getting capacity, experience, liberalism, and popular appeal. We realized that following such
a colorful figure as Roosevelt it would be dangerous to give
the Democratic standard to any mediocre man. As is inevitable,
the administration of a strong president does not conduce to
the growth of other dominant political figures. The Senate
showed nobody who had caught the public's particular attention. The only governors who had been conspicuous successes
to the extent of being known to states besides their own were
Lehman in New York and Horner in Illinois, both Jews, and
the country had not advanced to where a man of that persuasion could be elected to the presidency.

That phrase calls for a parenthesis. It is not that the Democratic National Committee has either an inclination for, or
sympathy with, religious or racial intolerance. Its job is to win
elections, and in that effort it must take cognizance of popular
prejudices as well as individual qualifications. It might be an
heroic gesture to defy a vicious sentiment; but if that meant
handing over the government to the other party, the committee
doing so would default on its job.

This brings us to Farley. The paucity of Presidential timber, without Roosevelt, naturally started a movement for the nomination of the next best advertised Democratic public character. Democratic newspapers published interviews with local leaders advocating the choice of the National Chairman. Farley took the position that he would neither work for nor discourage the movement. If it came to anything, to use his own expression, "that would be fine." If it didn't, he was still grateful for the compliment. So he wrote courteous, noncommittal notes of acknowledgment, and waited like all the rest of us for a definite declaration from the White House; for he, like Garner, figured that a candidacy without the Roosevelt countenance was not worth anything.

Long before convention time Farley realized that the third-term candidacy was scheduled. A master hand at reading political riddles, with a thousand listening posts throughout the country, the National Chairman correctly interpreted the missions of Harry Hopkins, the unrecorded conferences at the White House, and the evasiveness of some of his old friends. Nevertheless he determined to go through with his program.

He was anti-third-term; he was hurt by the President's not taking him into his confidence; he was determined to give his supporters the privilege of keeping their pledges—and when that vote was recorded, he moved to make the President's nomination unanimous, and he agreed to stand by until his successor had learned the ropes of the national chairman's job. Then he declared his intention to vote the party ticket—and thenceforth he devoted himself to the coca-cola business.

He swung back to the political field when the New York gubernatorial row came on. He beat the President by nominating Bennett, and incidentally thereby turned New York state over to the Republicans. It might with equal logic be contended that President Roosevelt made Dewey governor by fighting for the nomination of Senator Mead. In other words, if either had submitted to the choice of the other, the Empire State might still be in the Democratic column.

As these pages are being written the air is full of prognosti-

cations of Farley's course at the 1944 convention. The newspaper columnists are writing about a revolt in the South and
a merger between the Southern Democratic conservatives and
the Farley supporters to stop a fourth Roosevelt candidacy,
with intimations of a third-party movement in the event of a
Roosevelt candidacy, that would do to him what Teddy Roosevelt's Bull Moose party did to Taft.

Knowing what I do about Farley's opinion of third parties,
and having in mind his worship of the party and his oft-
expressed disesteem for bolters, etc., my surmise is that in '44
he will follow the same trail he trod in 1940 if Roosevelt is a
candidate. That is, he will amass as many delegates as he can to
stop Roosevelt in the convention; and if that fails, he will again
announce that he will vote for the tickets, and then take no
further part.

As to Roosevelt's intentions, I am in the same position as I
was five years ago when I wrote:

"Of course I am entitled to a guess, and my guess is that
Franklin D. Roosevelt would take a case of the hives rather
than four years more of the headache that being President
means. It will not be so easy a choice at that. Circumstances
might arise that would make it impossible for him to lay down
the burden. The world may be at war with or without threat
of our involvement, or some other equally acute emergency
may eventuate that would forbid a change of administration;
and the man in the White House is not the kind of individual
who would let his personal desires interfere with what seems
to him his duty."

Before the 1940 convention, while I had no more definite
information, I realized that it was inevitable that the President
would run again. Jim Farley had the same conviction but
cherished the idea that the party rift consequent on the President's attitude toward the senators who would oppose him in
the court fight and on the general feeling (to which Farley
subscribed) of the danger involved in breaking the third term
precedent, made possible a defeat of his nomination.

At one time we thought we had converted the Chairman.

Frank Walker and Ed Flynn told him that they were sure of the allegiance to the President of a majority of the convention delegates and pointed out to him that his opposition would merely result in dividing the party, with unfortunate results as to Chairman Farley's own political prestige. But Vice-President Garner came at him with counter-arguments largely to the effect that the country knew Farley's distaste for a presidential third term and that his shift at that stage would undermine the national high regard and appreciation of Farley's sincerity.

So Farley decided to go through with his original program. By this time he knew that his own hopes for nomination had vanished. My impression is that he was satisfied that even if he succeeded in stopping Roosevelt, Jack Garner would not be the beneficiary. Had he succeeded in the proposed blockade of the President's candidacy, Cordell Hull would have been the Democratic nominee in 1940. That was in the cards as they were dealt when the convention assembled.

When Farley stepped out of the chairmanship and the postmaster-generalship following the 1940 convention, Ed Flynn agreed to take the first of the two jobs for the period of the campaign and declined the cabinet appointment, which was filled by Frank C. Walker, who later, with no enthusiasm, succeeded Flynn in the political post.

Walker never had been a politician, though he once served a term as assistant district attorney in Butte, Montana, thirty years ago. He is a quiet, shrewd, very successful businessman, a corporation attorney with a flock of collegiate degrees who was catapulted into the big Democratic game by his admiration for F.D.R. I believe it was his five-thousand-dollar contribution that fostered the original Roosevelt campaign fund, and its natural consequence was the National Committee chairmanship. He did not want to be postmaster-general or national chairman, but could not refuse the President's request. He brought with him to Democratic headquarters Assistant Postmaster-General Ambrose O'Connell, who knows the political highways and byways, and they enlisted George E. Allen to be secretary of the national organization.

Walker's first positive act in his then new job was to suggest to his Republican counterpart the postponement of the national conventions to autumn, with the idea of minimizing the complication of politics with the war effort, arguing that a short campaign would answer every necessity of the two parties. That invitation was declined. However, Walker pursued his own theory with the Democratic organization. His theory is that the bombs, pinwheels, and skyrockets of politics would be wasted fireworks a year before election, particularly in a nation absorbed in the graver issues of a mighty war. Hence the comparative inaction of the Democratic mill during 1943.

11. FARLEY VS. ROOSEVELT: WHICH IS THE INGRATE?

They sparred amiably through a score of conferences and never got down to the subject that engrossed each.

THE ROOSEVELT-FARLEY feud is perhaps the most puzzling phenomenon, as well as the most important intraparty development, of the present political era. It is a combat without heat, with never a published word from either of the principals in derogation of the other. There has never been a session of the two—though at various times they came together with the planned purpose of what we in Western mining days referred to as a pick-handle talk—at which they threshed out their points of discord.

Some of the numerous book writers who have attempted an analysis of this century's political developments attribute the rift's origin to primeval hostility between the stateliness of Hyde Park and the proletarianism of Grassy Point.

"It is possible, of course," wrote one commentator, "that Grassy Point and Hyde Park, although they are both on the Hudson, are more widely separated than they appear to be on the map. Hyde Park is aristocratic and ancestral, the kind of a community that would appeal to the better grade English nobility. Grassy Point is poor and middle-class; a one-street town with its home and walls built wall-to-wall with neither design nor decoration." *

The inference does not seem tenable to me. Jim Farley never had even a vestige of an inferiority complex; and Franklin Roosevelt, though anything but oblivious to the advantages of a family tree on which cluster great adventurers and eminent leaders of American industry dating back to pre-Revolutionary days, and the prestige of a patroon county seat, is too wily a man, and too experienced a politician to lord it, even by implication, over one of the lesser born.

These two men, thrown into intimate association by the vagrant winds of politics, owe each other much. It was Farley's skill and resource that was to a large degree responsible for Roosevelt's elevation to the governorship of New York, an ideal jumping-off place to a presidential nomination. To an even greater degree it was Farley's efforts which brought about that nomination and election.

On the other hand, Farley was but a lesser light in the political firmament when Roosevelt took him from the relative obscurity of the secretaryship of the New York state Democratic organization and made him, on the suggestion of Ed Flynn, the chairman of the state organization, then—when the slip-up of the Raskob program brought Roosevelt the presidential candidacy—automatically elevated Farley to the national chairmanship and the directorship of the Roosevelt destinies up to the convention of 1940.

It is easy to argue that without Farley Roosevelt might never have attained the presidency, and equally easy to demonstrate the probability that, had it not been for Roosevelt, Farley

---

* Stanley High, *Roosevelt—And Then?* (New York and London: Harper & Brothers, 1937), p. 286.

might have remained just a local boss in a New York district instead of attaining national prestige as a great political manager, postmaster-general of the United States, etc. I doubt if either of the two great figures ever struck a balance as to the relative credit for advancement of the other, though doubtless each evaluated the mutual service as mostly in his individual favor. And it is reasonable to assume that each felt that a preponderance of gratitude was due him.

In the beginning, of course, there was not an atom of discord between them. Farley was single-minded in his service as promoter-in-chief, and Roosevelt was unfailingly appreciative of those services. He consulted Farley constantly, deferred to his political judgment in all essentials, carefully avoided anything that might be construed as a hurt to Farley's pride. That was not as easy as it sounds, in view of the congenital disesteem of Farley for the brain trusters, and the brain trusters' repugnance to practical politics as practiced by the National Chairman.

Just when the break started is a moot question. At national headquarters one school of opinion was that the germ was planted when a candidate for a minor federal job in whom Farley had a personal interest was turned down and some outsider got the job. I don't know whether this was an unintentional oversight, whether Roosevelt thought the outsider was better qualified, or whether it was a case of political expediency such as is frequently a problem for the dispenser of posts. It may be that the President, secure in Farley's fealty, thought that it was more important to placate some leader in Kansas or some other state where the political situation was precarious than to oblige his friend in this particular instance, feeling (if he thought about it at all) he could make up for it in some other direction. If this episode did rankle in Farley's mind, he gave no sign of distress, disappointment, or resentment. I am quite sure he never asked the President the whys and wherefores of the matter, and am equally sure that the President never volunteered any explanation of it.

A more tenable hypothesis is that the trouble began when

the President insisted on his campaign against the senators and representatives most responsible for the defeat of his program to modernize the Supreme Court. The attempted purge with Senators George, Bennett Clark, Tydings, and the rest of them was regarded by the National Chairman as a political error. It was not that Farley was against the court plan, though I have reason to believe that Farley felt that, had the President consulted him beforehand, he might have dissuaded F.D.R. from pressing the proposal to alter the court's make-up by appointing coadjutor justices. But Farley never attempted to guide White House policies. At bottom he was no more a New Dealer than was Vice-President Garner, who, despite a fantastic attempt by the Republicans to present him as a radical in the '32 campaign, was and is a perfect symbol of conservatism whose philosophy is that of most of the Southern senators, Democrats by virtue of their environment and their sectional traditions, whose idea of progressivism is far from the present White House definition of that term.

But Garner went along with his "Captain," and Farley conformed with his "Boss," like disciplined soldiers. It was the President's responsibility to organize and carry out policies, it was their function to follow the commands of the commander in chief.

So Farley sent his headquarters staff into the fray, to fight for the passage of the Supreme Court Bill; but when that fight was lost, he showed no enthusiasm for vengeance against the national legislators who brought the defeat about. Perhaps Farley, who is as close a student of past political history as he is adept at its modern practice, had in mind Woodrow Wilson's vain attempt to supplant Jim Reed, Missouri's prize senator, with Breckenridge Long in reprisal for Reed's blasting of the League of Nations.

It was Jim Farley's job to win elections; to make friends and not enemies within the party. It did not make sense to him to fight popular officials in their own states. He did not underestimate the strength of Franklin Roosevelt's popularity and influence among the voters, but he had a shrewd appreciation of the maxim referred to elsewhere in this narrative, that while a man may be stout enough to hold citizens to his own banner, the country has never yet found an individual who could deliver the votes to somebody else.

Out of that raid the President got but a single scalp—that of John O'Connor, Congressman from the Sixteenth District of New York City. Farley's was a politician's theory: that the advantage of a crusade against a Democratic officeholder, even if successful, would not compensate for the danger, in future elections, of having stirred up a hostile faction. One of the long-distance results of the so-called purge was the denial to National Chairman Ed Flynn of the post of minister to Australia and ambassador at large to the rest of Oceania. The men the President had tried to get out of the Senate were all with the Republicans in defeating the Flynn candidacy, though most of them were Flynn's personal friends and admirers. The opportunity to get back at Roosevelt was more toothsome than the chance to favor their political associate, whose probity, intelligence, and other qualifications for the post they knew.

Even the discord of the court fight's sequel did not result in any open demonstration of a break in the Damon and Pythias situation between the two New Yorkers.

Presently, however, presidential ambitions began to stir in the breast of the Democratic national chairman. His popularity among the party leaders rivaled, if it did not exceed, the eminence of the President. Local newspapers began to mention him as a possible, if not a probable, candidate for the big nomination in 1940. At that time, of course, it was not known that Roosevelt would run again; and the party leaders, looking for a winner, were inclined to capitalize Jim's vast friendships.

Farley's own attitude, as already mentioned, was that he would neither check nor encourage the idea but would let it run its course; if it flowered into a nomination, that would be fine, and if it did not, he would not be the loser but would realize his long-time purpose of going into business and recouping his fortunes. There was nothing illogical about Farley's potential candidacy. He had the esteem and affection of nearly every subchief of the local and national organization. He had a record unspotted by scandal. He made good speeches and delivered them with sincerity and force. His capacity for making and holding friends was illimitable. His administration of the Post Office Department was better perhaps than that of any other postmaster-general. His colleagues and subordinates in politics and in office were devoted to him, and with reason, for no department chief was ever more considerate of those under him. Perhaps some of this was mere politics, but it had the appearance, at least, of spontaneity. He never came to a town in his endless pilgrimages without personally visiting the local post office and chatting intimately with the postmaster, not only on political topics but largely on the problems and mechanism of that particular postal station.

Perhaps he was unique among politicians, but Farley would not lie—even to the newspaper people from adverse journals who came to him with awkward questions.

"Just in the room" (his modification of the familiar "This is off the record") he would admit that the party outlook was unpromising in this section or that, or agree that some particular candidate had a poor chance. I do not believe that his confidence was ever betrayed deliberately, but these unrecorded comments have a way of getting into print. The person who hears them mentions them to his editor, perhaps, or repeats them in casual conversation, and finally they come to the ears of a writer unaware of or unimpressed by the understanding that the information was only "just in the room," and so it is announced to the world.

Occasionally we expostulated with him for his excessive frankness, as for example when Farley's disesteem for members of the White House court circle and his lack of enthusiasm for the purge got into the newspapers in this way; but he only answered: "What is the use of lying to a fellow who knows he is being told a lie?"

In one of our talks I broke out with:

"Jim, you are the most honest man alive! You would not steal anything—except an election."

That, I think, is a fair exposition of the code that governs most big political guns in politics today.

Farley was ambitious not only to be named for the big job but, perhaps more, to end the theory that the nomination of a Catholic to the presidency was an impossibility. He had watched Al Smith's essay in that direction and thought he had a formula for success where Smith failed. The Happy Warrior's method of meeting intolerance was to defy it. So he staged his biggest speech on the subject in Oklahoma, hotbed of Ku-Kluxism. (We had reports of stink bombs planted in the hall where he delivered his defiant address.) Prohibition was the sorest point in the South's opposition to Smith, and he drummed into his hearers his purpose of working for the repeal of the Eighteenth Amendment. The sidewalks-of-New-York personality was the base of many sneers by his enemies, so he exaggerated the East Side twang, paraded the brown derby, and interlarded his addresses with "raddio" and similar Gothamic variations. Then there was the invariable appearance at Smith's quarters of Catholic priests. There was nothing political or planned about this. The clergymen attended the meetings of their celebrated coreligionist just as thousands of other citizens did. Their dress made them conspicuous, which in a Klan-ridden community was construed as evidence of the sheet-and-pillow-case fraternity's monstrous charge of domination of the Democratic candidate by the clerics.

Farley, on the other hand, flaunted no red rags before the bulls of intolerance, prohibition, and provincialism. As devout a communicant of the church as Smith, he attended Mass on Sunday without ostentation or fanfare—and no crowds gathered to stare at him. Of course, he was not journeying as a candidate for the presidency but was merely the postmaster-general on a tour of inspection, or the chairman of the Democratic National Committee come to discuss strategies with the local leaders of his party. Prohibition was a dead issue during most of his many visits to Dixieland, and there were few if any pronounced New Yorkisms in his vocabulary. So the South knew Farley and liked him. Moreover, the political consciences of North Carolina, Florida, Louisiana, and Texas were uneasy at their 1928 apostasy from their party, and the politicians of those states are a little ashamed of the constant charge of religious prejudice and the citing of their failure to support Smith as proof of that disposition.

Leaders of those sections frequently told Farley that he would not lose a single Southern state if he ran for the presidency. This was during the period when nobody knew if Roosevelt would be a third-term candidate. They argued success in the South not only because of his individual popularity but because the South was anxious to prove that it was Smith and not the Catholic church that was their target in 1928. That was counsel easy to take by a man in whose head the presidential bee was buzzing, however vaguely, and it explains why Farley thought there was an opportunity for him. Given the solid South, with New York surely for him and Massachusetts probably as certain, election of the Democratic Chairman apparently would have been quite possible. Obviously all these things had to click to get this result, and some people doubted their validity—among them, the President of the United States.

I have reason to believe that Farley had, or thought he had, information that the President did not intend to be a candidate in 1940. Whether the assurance was definite, or was merely another example of the President's sunny disposition to make people believe that he is with them, is beyond my information. Elsewhere in this narrative I mentioned the incident of three eminent Democrats each advising me, before the voting began in the '40 convention, that he had the President's blessing in his enterprise to get the vice-presidential nomination. All of them had talked—separately, of course—to the President just before starting for Chicago.

"He gave me the green light," said Eminent Democrat No. 1.

"He wished me success," said Eminent Democrat No. 2.

"He said 'That's fine' when I told him I would try for the nomination," said Eminent Democrat No. 3.

They were all perfectly sincere in their belief that the President had indicated that the race was a free-for-all; and possibly

Farley's interpretation had nothing more definite than some such statement as that Roosevelt did not want to run again and hoped he would not have to, which I believe he told others.

In the period of uncertainty as to the President's intentions the Democratic situation in 1940 did not look bright to me. If Roosevelt finally declared himself out of it, I visualized a scramble for the nomination, with likelihood of these rivalries developing so much bitterness and division that we might have a repetition of the 1924 experience. So I decided to go to the President and suggest a possible course. I did this without consulting anybody; and I presume that when Jim Farley reads it, it will be the first time he knows that his candidacy was discussed by me at the White House.

The conversation ran thus wise:

"Mr. President, I'd like to talk some practical politics, if you don't mind."

He nodded assent, and I continued, "This has nothing to do with your plans and purposes. I want to be the last person you tell whether you will or will not run again. It is much easier for me to look a man in the eye and tell him frankly that I do not know, than it would be to dissemble or evade the inquiry that is put to me whenever a Democrat comes into my office."

He indicated his accord, and I went on:

"But I think you will agree with me that no Democrat but yourself can be elected this year. Would it not be better—in the event of your not being the candidate—to let Jim Farley have the nomination? If he ran and was defeated, that defeat would be attributed to religious prejudice. If almost any other of the aspirants was nominated and lost, that defeat would be hailed as a repudiation of your administration and the New Deal."

"No," replied the President, "that would be most unfair to Jim. He is too fine a person to be subjected to the humiliation of a bad defeat and the setback that would involve to his prospects and career. I do not agree that our party is destitute of available candidates for the presidency. There is Cordell Hull, for example. Nobody can match the universal respect of our people that is accorded him. He has their confidence, and they appreciate his ability, his patriotism, and his party loyalty."

I do not believe the President ever indicated his idea of the hopelessness of Farley's candidacy to the man most concerned —or that Farley ever consulted the President about it. In fact, it is my understanding that both regarded the question as too delicate to be brought up, so, in their not infrequent conferences on patronage, on legislation, etc., they steered wide of the topic that was engaging the thought of most of the politicians.

As the time for the 1940 convention drew near, these conferences occurred at gradually increasing intervals.

Farley, perhaps the wisest of political managers, realized ahead of anybody else that the President would be the nominee. Ordinarily the preconvention weeks would have been devoted to consultations about the strategies and tactics of the prospective gathering: estimates of the strength of rival aspirants, who should have the second place on the ticket, platform resolutions, etc. This time Roosevelt did his talking mainly to Harry Hopkins, and what that meant was fairly obvious.

My personal view is that the President fell short of his usual political acumen in his handling of that situation. If he had told Farley that he was going to run, one of two things would have happened. Either Farley would have declined a share of the convention activities on the ground that he was against a third term on principle—how much that principle was complicated by his own ambitions, I doubt if even Farley could have been positive—or else he would have played the string out. In either event the situation would have been much less awkward than it was when the President, ignoring the titular chief of the party organization, sent Hopkins to Chicago to run things. Had the President given Farley his head, the Chairman would have turned up with perhaps a hundred and twenty votes in the convention. Those votes could have gravitated to nobody but the President, so the result would have been the same, without the bitterness engendered by levying on Farley's strength in Massachusetts. Hopkins was, and is, unpopular with the politicians—perhaps for no more distinct reason than that they resent the intrusion of an outsider and an amateur in their own field.

Hopkins did nothing to ameliorate this feeling. He did not even go through the motions of a courtesy call on the Chairman of the Democratic National Committee, and during all the prevoting period he abstained from any contact with him. White House instructions and questions came by direct telephone to Hopkins and were transmitted to the delegates as if the Chairman had been nonexistent. It was a Roosevelt convention—there never was a doubt of the President's renomination, and it could have come about just as well without the pointed ignoring of Farley. Whether the rudeness of the procedure was Hopkins' own strategy, or whether he was moving under orders, only he and the President know.

Probably the explanation of that supplanting by Harry Hopkins of the titular convention manager lies in the fact that the President takes no chances in any vital situation. He knew he had the required votes in the convention. He may have had faith that Farley, even though himself a candidate, would not be guilty of any skullduggery on account of opposing a third term. But, true to his policy, he was not content with probability. He proposed to make certain; and thus eventuated the Hopkins mission, and maybe the apparent Hopkins ineptness in steering wide of the National Chairman.

The only softening element of the episode came from Mrs. Roosevelt. She consulted Farley as to the advisability of her flying to Chicago. She saw him on arrival, and in the harmony speech she made to the convention she referred to him affectionately and with many tributes to his character, ability, and service. It seemed to us on the platform with her that on that occasion, at least, she was a better politician than her husband. She may not have killed the resentment of Farley's friends, but she did mitigate it.

Farley took no part in the campaign beyond reiterating that as usual he would vote the straight Democratic ticket. He could not be induced to make any speeches, though he remained with the committee for a month to help his successor, Ed Flynn, in the organization work. That was a trying time for us at headquarters. Flynn and Farley were old and intimate friends, and each was so fearful of treading on the other's toes that nothing was done during the joint incumbency. Farley felt that the planning should be done and the decisions should be made by the new chairman; Flynn felt that he should assert no prerogatives while the old chairman was functioning. There could hardly be a meeting of the minds, for each was bound to assent to what the other suggested. So a great friendship was preserved—and a month of campaign time was wasted.

At that, Farley did more than another presidential candidate —Jack Garner—for the ex-Vice-President did not even trouble to vote in the election of 1940. Actually it is likely that Cactus Jack was not motivated in his absence from the Uvalde polling place by pique, but rather by the practical knowledge that Texas would go for Roosevelt overwhelmingly and that, therefore, one vote did not count.

After that there was small contact between the President and the ex-National Chairman—until conflicting ideas as to the New York governorship brought them together in a futile conference in which Roosevelt sought to change Farley's determination to nominate Bennett, advancing the candidacy of Senator Mead. I think the President had no particular animosity toward Bennett but merely thought he could not be elected. In that session, I am informed, the suggestion was made, or implied, that the President would support Farley himself for the governorship if Jim would take it. Later this was proposed definitely to Farley.

The governorship of New York had been the height of his ambition prior to his being mentioned for the presidency. The nomination was his for the asking at any time when Herbert Lehman cared to yield it, and Lehman was anxious to retire after his second term. Moreover, under conditions as they were up to 1940, Farley's election would have been as near a certainty as political victories ever are.

Had that conference occurred six months earlier, I have no doubt the New York fracas could have been avoided and some sort of compromise would have been made; but by the time the two came together, Farley, other things aside, was so completely pledged to Bennett that he could not run out on him, though I imagine that as recompense for a withdrawal Bennett would have been offered some big federal post.

By this time Farley's mind as to the desirability of the governorship had changed. He was in business and was getting rid of the debts with which his governmental service had saddled him. Moreover his wife, who hates the whole political setup, was firmly opposed to his reentrance into that world—a sentiment every wife will understand, whose children have reached or are approaching college age and who wants security for them. The salary of the governor of New York is large, but the social and political obligations of the office make that salary small change. Farley himself estimated that four years at Albany would increase his debts by a hundred thousand dollars.

I argued with him for an hour on one occasion urging him to take the governorship, pointing out that the most serious objection to his presidential aspirations was that he had had no experience in administrative work. I urged that the governorship would not only afford the experience but was the best possible springboard if he had any thought of making a try for the national nomination in '44.

This was long before the suggestion of his candidacy for the state office as a solution to the struggle between him and the President over the Bennett-Mead candidacies. My talk to him was not inspired from the White House, nor had it any other source than my friendship. It got nowhere with Farley, who simply said he did not want to be governor but was determined to stick to his business.

Anyhow the Roosevelt-Farley collision cost the Democrats that election and rifted the party terrifically. Roosevelt's ardent friends were indignant at Farley. Farley's supporters were equally sore at the President, for they figured that had Bennett had a united party behind him there would have been no

American Labor party candidate, and therefore the four hundred thousand votes that went to Dean Alfange would have accrued to the Democratic candidate. Moreover, the New York City Democrats had a grouch against the President for his espousal of the La Guardia candidacy, which they believe was responsible for the defeat of O'Dwyer in the mayoralty election. The bitterness of the O'Dwyer campaigners was accentuated by the advent of Adolph Berle, who crusaded in La Guardia's cause and in the course of that crusade assailed Farley and Governor Lehman, twin gods in New York City's Democratic creed. The Democrats could understand, if they could not condone, Roosevelt's countenancing the Mayor's candidacy, for they had a certain respect for the repayment of a political obligation; but when he sent one of his pet brain trusters—and they firmly believed that Berle came with White House instructions—to jump on Farley and Lehman, it was too much!

It is difficult to see how Roosevelt could have withheld his commendation of La Guardia in view of the support the Little Flower had given him. In 1936 La Guardia made innumerable speeches for the President; in 1940 he was chairman of the National Committee of Independent Voters for Roosevelt—quite a perilous venture for a fusion mayor who had to rely on Republican votes to compass his re-election.

That mayoralty election was the most peculiar episode of the sort that I remember.

The President's tacit support of La Guardia did not prevent the then national chairman, Ed Flynn, from teaming up with Jim Farley on the O'Dwyer side. Though the President is the actual head of the party in power, all the resources of the National Committee was placed at their disposal. I was detached from the national field and sent to New York to help in the O'Dwyer campaign, and did what I could in that regard, despite a long cordial acquaintance with the Mayor—which was not interrupted by the incident of my foray against him. Nor was there any rift between the President and Flynn, even though, then and at subsequent times, these two had a series of near clashes over the appointments of Republicans to war agency posts, which were causing trouble with state chairmen and national committeeman as well as with senators and representatives, who felt they were being starved in patronage.

There has been a great deal of grumbling among the Farley worshipers because the President has not tendered him a post in the war activities though Big Jim volunteered for such service. Farley's friends attribute this omission to Roosevelt's hostility to his old-time field marshal. That is not the kind of hostility that divides the pair. I have yet to hear a derogatory word about Farley in the White House. Rather recently, when the question of a successor to Chairman Ed Flynn was up, there were dozens of candidates offered; and in the course of sifting them out the President said:

"One thing we did not have to worry about while we had Farley and Flynn for chairman was that either of them might use his post to make opportunities for his personal advantage or increase his fortunes."

An easier answer to the question is that Roosevelt is anxious to preserve the nonpartisan complexion of the war production agencies. It is not hard to realize what a barrage of criticism would come from the Republicans in Congress in the event of such an obviously political appointment: the charges that whatever agency Farley presided over would be turned into a political machine, etc. with a view to next year's election.

The mere fact of such criticism might not be regarded as a grave peril, but it would cause vast embarrassment to the head of a bureau in appointing his subordinates. No politician is credited with naming men to jobs because of their superior qualifications, if the appointee is of a party opposite to that of the critic. Farley, himself, in the early stages of the Roosevelt administration was lampooned as a conscienceless, grafting spoilsman, and that was the mildest of the hostile characterizations applied to him.

And he came out of his job, after a decade in office, fifty thousand dollars worse than broke.

Now the conundrum is, where does Farley go from here? He retains his chairmanship of the New York state Democratic

Committee. We hear of him in the South and West, in huddles with local political chiefs and satraps, and we are measurably sure that he is not merely trying to sell them coca-cola. He was against the third term, so it is reasonably safe to assume that he will be at least as active against a fourth term—if that situation eventuates.

He is a great organizer, possibly the best politician of modern American history, and he has made few mistakes since "Stretch" Farley of the Stony Point baseball team stretched himself from the town clerkship of a Hudson River village, through all the grades, to the national leadership of his party. Maybe his objective is merely to secure for himself a measure of authority in the 1944 convention; but, as has been said before, once the presidential fever strikes a man, no life is long enough for recovery.

PART FOUR

POLITICS, NOW AND THEN AND ALWAYS

12. THE SUPERPOLITICIAN GUESSES WRONG

In losing a battle and winning a war, F.D.R. sows dragon seeds.

THERE ARE certain American taboos or superstitions that are usually observed by politicians. They may not all be valid. Presidents may have walked under the political ladder without disaster, lighted three election efforts with the same strategic match, or banked their fortunes on thirteen Congressmen without misfortune. But the hoodoo is there just the same.

High on the list of dangerous things to monkey with is the Supreme Court of the United States. Abstractly the American people may know that our high tribunal is not infallible. They are aware that there have been bad justices, wrong decisions, and other flaws in the court's history; but the reverence remains.

That is why, in the course of campaign activity, we at the headquarters were startled when President Roosevelt included in the list of the Republican party's possessions the supreme bench. It did not hurt him that time, though the minority party fulminated about the implied effort of the executive to trespass on a correlative branch of the government, for the country was not thinking of technicalities but of the upswing in business that might come in with a change of administration.

It was another story when he launched his measure to rejuvenate the moss-bound jurists who were knocking congressional enactments galley west and disregarding Mr. Dooley's famous aphorism relative to the Supreme Court's following the election returns.

Naturally we at Democratic headquarters had no inkling of what was coming. The President either regarded his move as being outside the doman of politics—or realized that Jim Farley would try to dissuade him from the course on which he was bent.

The first I learned of it was at the press conference when the President disclosed the message he was sending to Congress. Though I did not know just what was coming, I had what amounted to a little more than a premonition; for Joe Robinson, who sat beside me, greeted me with a mournful shake of the head. He had been advised just before. We all knew that he was slated for the next vacancy in the Supreme Court, and when the President had unfolded his project, the thought naturally obtruded itself of the Senator's dilemma—assailing the justices he expected to join, for as majority leader of the Senate he was bound to head the fighting. There never was any doubt that he would accept the responsibilities of his job, regardless of his own views. Nobody had a clearer perception of the political perils involved. Notwithstanding that the philosophy of the Arkansas statesman was pretty much that of the other Southern senators, with all their adherence to precedent and fealty to tradition, he plunged into the fray with all the vigor of his virile soul. It is not too much to say that he gave his life to the struggle, for his untimely death was practically, if not immediately, the result of the intensity of the effort he made out of loyalty to his chief.

That press conference was the detonator that set off the big blast. The President went into more detail with the newspaper men than he had with the cabinet and the congressional leaders he had summoned to hear the first announcement of the great project. He was in rare humor, for at that time he felt no doubts that Congress, which had up to that time effected pretty nearly every thing he asked for, would continue to go along with him.

With the large majorities the Democrats held in both houses, the influence of the overwhelming Roosevelt victory in 1936, and the general feeling that Roosevelt had saved the country from depression collapse, it seemed certain that the dominant party in Congress would remain what the Republicans called "rubber stamps" and the Democrats called "loyal supporters of the nation's chief in his efforts to complete the recovery of the country."

Moreover, there was general accord between the White House and the Capitol on the necessity of having some cure for the high court's fanatic reactionism. Burt Wheeler of Montana, sworn enemy of the President—the critical observer has the option of choosing whether that hostility was born of Wheeler's disappointment in not being accorded the vice-presidential nomination, or of his intense liberalism that revolted at the infraction of congressional powers by the executive, or the executive's alleged trend toward dictatorship—was as bitterly critical of the Supreme Court's economic views as mirrored by its decisions as Roosevelt himself. So there was a flock of remodeling proposals rife at the Capitol: constitutional amendments nullifying the Marshall dicta that gave the Court authority to overrule Congress, by giving Congress authority by a two-thirds vote to repass effectively legislation nullified by the Court, and other measures of like effect.

There were flaws in all of these proposals. If Congress simply enacted a law giving it a veto function over the court, that tribunal, as then constituted, would simply declare the act unconstitutional. If the amendment program was essayed, there would be a long delay before ratification could be obtained from three-fourths of the state legislatures, if indeed it could ever be accomplished in the face of the popular awe of and reverence for the Supreme Court.

Nevertheless it does not seem impossible that, had the President called in Wheeler, George of Georgia, Norris of Nebraska, and a few others from Congress and put the responsibility on them to compass the mutual purpose, he might have obtained what he was after—perhaps even something on the order of what he finally laid before them.

But to hand them a finished bill, full of subterfuges such as making age the criterion, and stressing a nondemonstrable overload of business as excuse for the naming of half a dozen coadjutor justices in the event that the old men failed to take advantage of the retirement provision, was an invitation for trouble.

Those competent historians of the episode, Joseph Alsop and Turner Catledge, wrote an elaborate circumstantial story of the genesis of the bill. The fault in their book is the fault of practically every volume by an outsider about the intimate details of governmental happenings. The writers cannot know more than they have been told. I presume that something of the same sort will be urged against the accuracy of this chronicle, for though I was officially a member of the strategy board that worked for the passage of the measure and therefore am competent, presumably, to tell what happened there, much of the story developed apart from the committee meetings, and for that part of my narrative I must rely on the information conveyed to me by the actors in the drama.

Obviously, the news source of the history to which I refer was the skillful manipulator, Thomas Corcoran. The heroizing of him alone indicates that.

Nearly every prominent figure at the Capitol has his favorite publicist, to whom he confides supposed inside information. The current medium of exchange at Washington is news and puffs. Nobody has yet attempted to stabilize this currency, which fluctuates with the waxing or waning of the prominence or influence of the news giver—and the discretion of the writer.

Undoubtedly the root of the President's court program was supplied by Attorney General Homer Cummings, who had all the Department of Justice experts working out a bill to meet the President's demand for a measure that would modernize the Supreme Court. In the records of the Justice Department lay a forgotten proposal by the attorney general of Woodrow Wilson's first administration—James C. McReynolds, most reactionary of the Supreme Court justices when the court fight came on. He offered then that the federal courts were clogged with cases and that there were many judges of extreme age; so a bill directing the very expedients embraced in Roosevelt's was produced, but it did not apply to the highest of the federal tribunals.

The authors acquit Corcoran of any part in the preparation of the court bill. His own idea, it appears, was a constitutional amendment, and they described his horror when he finally learned what was intended, while they are lyrical in their account of his strenuous efforts to get the horrific bill through. We must take their word for this, though we knew that Judge Denman, Corcoran's intimate friend, furnished a year earlier a memorandum on the "roving judges" and the Supreme Court proctor idea, which became part of the bill. Senator Wheeler, when in the throes of his bitter leadership of the fight against the President's proposal, meant Messrs. Corcoran and Cohen when he spoke of some of the administration's bright young men as authors, and sellers to the President, of the Supreme Court plan.

The famous pair and Wheeler had been close associates in putting through the death clause of the Holding Company Bill. About that time Corcoran wrote a court-packing speech for Wheeler, which the Senator would not deliver. However, according to the historians we are referring to, Corcoran changed his viewpoint, shifted to the amendment process, and advocated a constitutional change which would give Congress the authority to override a Supreme Court decision by a two-thirds majority vote if an election had intervened between the time of such decision and the opportunity of Congress to review it.

Like other good political soldiers, Corcoran worked his hardest to get over the President's plan, while Wheeler headed the opposition to it. In fact Corcoran was delegated to lobby the bill through the Senate, with Joseph Keenan of the Department of Justice as his aide. These two were members of the White House strategy board. The other members were James Roosevelt, representing his father; Assistant Attorney-General Robert

H. Jackson; Charles West, ex-Congressman and White House liaison man with the House of Representatives; my first publicity lieutenant, Edward L. Roddan; and myself.

So far as I knew then or have been able to learn since, the President never discussed the merits of the bill with the board members—jointly or severally. Either he was indifferent to their opinions or he took it for granted that they shared his own appreciation of a smart plan to liberalize the court: a scheme that made no reference to the actual purpose but sought to arrive at the desired destination with a sonorous title of governmental altruism, a recital of the overburdens of the judiciary, and a retirement provision for justices to leave the bench on full salary, but with a left-handed care for circumstances that might move them to continue by appointing, in the case of those who did not wish to retire, a sort of partner judge who could relieve them of half their tasks but who would enjoy equal authority and vote on all Supreme Court decisions. Given the power to name "not more than six" of these coadjutor justices, the President could be sure that verdicts would no longer be shaded by the reactionary tendencies of four superconservatives. Of these justices and attorney-general recited that their verdict would be adverse to any argument for social and economic progress "if the argument were made by the Angel Gabriel."

In the early stages of the court fight the President felt no doubts of success. His overwhelming victory in 1936 had brought him an enormous Democratic majority. Labor was sore at the various turndowns of measures they had urged, but that soreness was tempered by the continued life of the Wagner Bill, which had not yet reached decision. Their pain became much less when the Supreme Court sustained it—all of which accounted for the mildness of the pressure the labor lobby put on Congress in behalf of the President's venture. The farm lobby, which like its labor prototype had taken official action in favor of the act, split up, and finally some of its chief constituents reverted to their normal G.O.P. allegiance.

But before these defections every indication was rosy. The President insisted that the people were with him, and that party loyalty and the pressure of the home folks would retain a comfortable majority for the correction of the Supreme Court abuses.

There had been no serious unfavorable repercussions of his earlier declarations in regard to the reactionary functioning of the court, notably at the "Horse and Buggy Days" press conference. Those utterances were trial balloons sent up by the President, who was feeling his way toward the goal he had in mind. The Republican editors and orators had spasms at this disrespect for the high court, but there was no indication that the public generally was excited about them. So he had every reason to believe that he would put it over. Partisan clamor was expected and discounted.

Even the swift announcement of Hatton Summers, chairman of the House Judiciary Committee, that he was off the reservation did not discourage Roosevelt's confidence. He heard the story of Vice-President Garner's holding his nose and turning thumbs down when the bill came to the Senate, and merely smiled at it. Garner never was a New Dealer, but went along because it was the "Captain's" order and responsibility. For that matter the President knew that Joe Robinson, entrusted with the leadership of the Senate situation, would not abate his efforts, however doubtful he was of the virtues of the President's plan.

The episode duplicated the League of Nations fight of twenty years ago. That event, too, started auspiciously under the guidance of a popular, idealistic president, only to be jettisoned, after long maneuvering, by skillful opposition.

Perhaps the court reorganization never could have succeeded, not even if the President had carried through the idea of going to the country as Wilson went to the country in his effort to force the opposition to conform to what he thought was the popular will. Indeed, it was only the example of the failure of Woodrow Wilson's appeal that deterred Roosevelt from making a similar attempt.

Like his Democratic predecessor, Roosevelt felt at the start not only that his cause was just but that its victory was assured.

When he addressed the Democrats at their fund raising dinner
in March, the note was one of confidence as he warned his party
that if they did not find a way to get the Supreme Court out of
the way of social legislation, the people would insist on bolder
representatives. In his fireside talk a few days later he challenged
those who questioned his motives in attacking the high court by
saying that none who knew him could fear that he would toler-
ate the destruction by any branch of the government of any part
of our heritage of freedom. He declared that, in a world in
which democracy is under attack, "I seek to make democracy
work."

The responses from his own party were satisfactory; there was
no indication of alarm at his stand in regard to the high tribunal. Probably that was the particular manifestation that made
him discard the idea of a stumping tour.

Some of the strategy board wanted him to say in that speech
that he would accept an amendment to the Constitution as alternative for the bill if the opposition would agree on an effective one and guarantee its enactment and ratification. He answered that he deemed that neither wise nor necessary.

It is curious how this idea of having the opposition guarantee
something to satisfy him persisted among the amateur statesmen
who surrounded him.

I learn that among the alibis was a tendency to blame the defeat on the National Committee's passiveness. Thus: "And there
were instances of downright carelessness, as when Joe Keenan
had persuaded Senator McCarran to speak at one of the George
Berry Patriots' Day rallies and asked Michelson to make the
detailed arrangements. Had McCarran spoken, he would have
been committed to support of the bill; Michelson forgot to prepare a speech or even to get in touch with him, and in the end
McCarran left the reservation for good." The Berry program
was part of the propagandist campaign we inaugurated to emphasize the nonpartisan complexion of the movement.

I have no recollection of any such request. Had it been made,
I would have declined the assignment, as I knew the Nevada
senator had already declared his opposition to the President's

plan. My acquaintance with him was of the slightest. My surmise is that McCarran was spoofing Keenan.

Keenan was always coming to the meetings with startling reports of progress with the enemy. For example, he electrified the gathering with the tidings that he had talked with Senator Nye of North Dakota and that Nye would be all right.

Actually the day after the bill had been delivered to the Senate, Nye's radio speech excoriating the measure was in the hands of the newspapers to be published next day when he delivered it. Nye contended that a constitutional amendment was the only legal way the court could be altered.

Eddie Roddan mildly stated the facts, but Keenan insisted that Nye was ready to come into line.

Likewise I learn that the speeches we furnished were so bad that Senator Neely of West Virginia positively refused to deliver the one written for him, a reply to Senator Wheeler. The reason for that refusal, I was told at the time, was this:

Neely had fought Senator Wheeler over the Holding Company Bill, and Wheeler had made private announcement that if Neely ever posed again as a liberal he would tear him apart. So when the West Virginian saw that the speech was a reply to Wheeler, he pulled out, and another senator delivered the address over the radio at the scheduled hour.

I would not venture at this time to defend the literary pulchritude or the convincing quality of our output. We had, I believe it was generally agreed, a fairly good ghost writers' division, and no speech went out until it had been checked for accuracy and general fitness.

From these passing references it might be deduced that the strategy board was not the most harmonious of aggregations. The brain trust contingent complained bitterly of the inactivity of the National Committee. "What was Jim Farley doing?" they asked us. Chairman Farley was stumping the country making speeches in favor of the bill, with frequent descents on the Capitol to do what he could in making converts or bracing up wavering members of the administration forces. It was mildly suggested in reply that the Chairman was not required to report to the publicity division, and they had better address their question to him.

Corcoran and Keenan had an inspirational thought that if Farley got after Senator Joe O'Mahoney of Wyoming, who was one of the administration friends who early announced that he could not stand for the Supreme Court project, it might be effective. So Farley went to O'Mahoney, who made such a blistering reply that Farley suggested that he voice his objections to the Department of Justice. This O'Mahoney did, giving notice that he regarded the measure as "obnoxious, undemocratic and an insult to the Senate."

Farley in his speeches constantly reiterated that the fight was "in the bag." This was in consonance with a proverbial political strategy which holds that harm can never be done by claiming too much, while an abstinence in claiming everything possible is generally taken as an admission of weakness. Like others of the vague principles of political strategy this does not hold water all the time. Nevertheless I have yet to learn of a political leader who did not insist that his man or his cause was going to win regardless of any circumstances. An example was Senator Fess, chairman of the Republican National Committee in 1932, who promulgated Herbert Hoover's certain re-election. In 1936 Chairman John Hamilton told us on election eve that Landon would carry everything north of the Ohio River. In 1940 the Republican chairman told us that Willkie was overwhelmingly bound for victory. True, Chairman Farley in the '32 and '36 elections was equally insistent that Roosevelt's victory was "in the bag." His zenith as a prophet was, of course, in 1936, when he announced in advance without qualification that Roosevelt would carry every state except Maine and Vermont. In 1940 Democratic Chairman Ed Flynn carried on the tradition. Obviously Farley's survey of the court possibilities was only a following out of this invariable political habit.

After the event the Corcoran-Keenan combination was scandalized by Farley's "off the record" statement that "when Senator O'Mahoney comes around for help on a sugar bill, his conscience won't be bothering him then, will it? Neither will

"Now go ahead and write like Charley Michelson!"
(Edmund Duffy in the Baltimore *Sun*)

Senator McCarran's when he wants something for his state. It's all in the point of view." This statement, the anti-Farley group of the "general staff" said, "confirmed O'Mahoney's intentions and drove McCarran off the reservation." Off-the-record words are not supposed to be published, but not infrequently they get into print somehow. Possibly somebody may have thought the two senators could be scared into compliance by the implied threat.

In my opinion these two couldn't have been brought to adherence to the Roosevelt program by anything the administration could offer. O'Mahoney was under deep obligation to Farley. He had been brought into the national field as Farley's first assistant postmaster-general, which gave him a springboard from which he vaulted into the senatorship. The implied threat to bring him around was not so different from the proposals to another senator that he would be permitted to name one of the new judges if he'd vote for the bill, or from the proffer said to have been made to Wheeler that he could have two of the appointments. None of these precious proposals emanated from the National Committee.

Most of those who had supported the President but had turned away from him on the court bill suggested various compromises, knowing perfectly well that the President would listen to nothing of the sort.

While the Corcoran wing were blaming all the trouble on the National Committee folk, we were equally positive that the error lay in the inefficiency of those who had been designated as the lobbyists to push the bill through. We felt that if the engineering had been intrusted to the experienced party chairman there would have been a greater prospect of success. Big Jim Farley was a prime favorite on the Hill. He talked the senators' language. He was the fellow who tried to get for them the patronage they felt they needed for their own political welfare. When they were disappointed he sympathized with them. On the other hand, Corcoran made no secret of his contempt for Congress. Not only did the Congressmen resent Tommy's dictatorial issuing of orders, but even more bitterly were they incensed when they found the jobs they regarded as congressional perquisites being filled by Tommy's nominees. Keenan was without either close Capitol acquaintanceship or experience. It was easy for senators to turn him down or to give him equivocal answers which he sanguinely translated into near promises.

Joe Robinson was the tower of strength. He was beloved by nearly all the senators, and in a way this accounted for the long period in which he thought he had a very slender majority for the President's bill. Because of their affection for the leader many of the recalcitrant ones gave him evasive replies rather than hurt him with a flat refusal when he appealed to them to support the President.

There is no mystery or great difficulty in ascertaining how the Senate stands on any particular question, but the poll must be amassed from something besides the statements from the senators themselves. The cloakroom conversation, a senator's confidences with close friends, the influence over local bosses must all be taken into consideration. In any close Senate fight the fence-sitters take no chances of being left off the bandwagon, which accounts for identical names on pro and con lists, especially when presidential favor is involved. In other words, the underpersonnel of the Senate can arrive at a poll much nearer correctness than can be achieved by a direct method. We had such a poll. I had Eddie Roddan at the Capitol day after day, and his reports to me presaged the results of Senator Robinson's compilation many days. The strategy board refused to listen to our unpalatable figures.

Their theory was that we were secretly against the court bill and therefore not to be trusted. Just why any personal opinion I might have had could have influenced me, I have never been able to figure. I never had a part in formulating Roosevelt policies. I was merely a propagandist and therefore naturally campaigned to the best of my ability for anything the President proposed. I never expostulated except when it seemed to me that the party's prospects were being threatened. Notably this was the case when the Hatch Bill was up, but my logic in that case failed to impress the President. Consequently I was not among the members of our board who infested the presidential office with suggestions. This produced more criticism, as the historian narrates: "They played the game of palace politics . . . except Michelson, who was too world-weary to bother—they all competed for the President's ear."

It was neither ennui nor world-weariness that made me abstain from badgering the busiest man in the world. Moreover, I studiously avoided getting mixed up in the palace politics. If there was anything the President wanted to talk to me about, he knew, and I knew, that I was on call.

The strategy board wobbled around on various alternatives. The opposition had seven votes in the Judiciary Committee, not counting McCarran, O'Mahoney, and Hatch, all of whom I had listed as part of the opposition. These three all had compromise measures to suggest to the President. Hatch's thought most nearly approached the presidential idea. He suggested seventy-five as the retirement age, advocated coadjutor justices, but would have limited the President's appointment of these to one in any single year. That notion the President turned down, as he did all the others, including the suggestion that the court be increased by two members, which presumably could have given the President a better break in divided decisions.

The resignation of Justice Van Devanter made the situation still more awkward for President Roosevelt. He had promised the first vacancy to Joe Robinson. I surmise that he realized that while as majority leader in the Senate the Arkansas statesman would work his head off to accomplish the President's desires, as justice of the Supreme Court he would in all probability revert to his natural conservatism. The President, to succeed in his desire for a liberal court, required an unquestioned majority. What he would have done except for Robinson's untimely death is anybody's guess. My own opinion is that he would have kept his promise regardless of the likelihood of its shipwrecking his whole plan.

While the pot was boiling, Corcoran mentioned to me that he had persuaded Senator Wheeler to withhold an uncompromising statement in which he blasted the President's program. Wheeler and I were old friends. So on my own motion I went up to see him. I explained to him that I was acting on my own volition, that nobody had sent me, that my sole purpose was to see if there was not some way we could avert further hostilities. I told him that it was simply my desire that two of my very good friends, working in general toward the same objective, be brought to accord and asked him whether, if I could get the President to extend the invitation, he would come to the White House and thrash the matter out with him. His reply was to hand me a copy of the statement Corcoran said he had agreed to withhold, which he had already given to the press. He said that the difference between him and the President was too wide to be bridged by any such talk as I had spoken of. I reported back to the White House committee but never mentioned the matter to President Roosevelt. Later the President asked Wheeler to the White House and Wheeler came, but their conversation was barren of results.

Things finally became so balled up, and the probabilities of defeat became so manifest, that Corcoran decided the best bet would be to let the whole thing simmer for a period while the attention of Congress would be diverted to the consideration of various important measures that were before it. That was probably a good thought, but unfortunately the anti-court-bill people figured that they had us on the run and did not see any reason why they should give us a breathing spell.

A previous suggestion had been that the proceedings before the Judiciary Committee should be shortened by giving each faction another week and then closing it up. Our side had presented all of its witnesses, but the other fellows were enjoying the prospect of headlines and would make no agreement. Then Tommy conceived the brilliant thought of closing the hearings as far as our side was concerned, probably figuring, as I believe the President figured, that the other fellow would soon run out of ammunition. It did not happen that way. The opposition had infinite witnesses and speakers poised for every opportunity.

Their tactics were very much better than ours. For example,

the resourceful Wheeler in consultation with Senator Borah
reasoned that it was their best policy for the Republicans to
stay in the background, thus avoiding having the court fight
become a party matter. This policy was frowned on by many
of the Republican leaders including, I was told, ex-President
Hoover, Alf Landon, and John Hamilton, whose calculations
were that the assault on the Supreme Court would make the
finest kind of a campaign issue and therefore that the Republicans should grab and hold the ball and get full credit in the
next election. The antis refused to budge from their position.
Our side realized the advantage this stand gave the enemy, and
among the suggestions offered by the President when he did
have his conference with Wheeler was that the Democrats, even
though they differed from the administration, should put the
Republicans on the fighting line. His argument was that a party
rift should be avoided regardless of what method should be
employed to accomplish their common objective. Naturally,
the Montana senator turned that down. He was riding high, was
getting the best of the newspaper headlines, and so the squabble
wobbled on.

Our next effort was to shift the battle to the House side on
the theory that the representatives were more amenable to
administration influence than the senators—even though the
House committee dealing with the Senate Judiciary Committee was clearly against the Roosevelt proposal. Speaker Sam
Rayburn and Majority Leader Bankhead rebelled. They admitted that the House might be dragooned into accepting the
measure but insisted that it would put so many of the members
on the spot that their re-election would be jeopardized. In
addition there was the danger that when the Senate refused to
concur, it might be impossible to get the House majority to
stick. So that program fell to the ground in turn.

I think that by this time the President began to entertain
some real doubts, though he still insisted that the country was
with him. He held stoutly to that hypothesis. He, like most of
us at headquarters, expected the Supreme Court to follow con-
sistently the line of its decisions in such cases as the New York

Minimum Wage Law, the N.R.A., and the Agricultural Adjust-
ment Act—in which they had knocked down the whole structure of the government's recovery measures. He anticipated that
the court would invalidate the State of Washington's Minimum
Wage Act, which paralleled the New York bill, and would treat
in the same way the Wagner acts that provided for collective
bargaining and set up federal machinery for elections to determine the bargaining labor agency.

The President, and the rest of us, believed that when the
expected adverse decisions were rendered, the labor lobby would
crack down on the senators and representatives, instead of resting on formal declaration with such minorities as Bill Hutchinson's carpenter's union taking the other side. Hutchinson had
headed the Republican labor committee in the 1936 election.

Well, it did not happen. The Supreme Court under the
leadership of Chief Justice Hughes awoke to the necessity of
getting into step with the liberal movement and astonished the
country by a complete judicial somersault, reversing its judgment on the New York Minimum Wage Law by deciding in
favor of the similar Washington state law, and upholding the
Wagner acts, though to do so they had to go absolutely contrary
to their previous holding that labor was a state and not a national problem.

One man was not surprised. Senator Wheeler had prophesied
the verdict. He had been close to the court ever since he got
Chief Justice Hughes to write the letter that took the props
from under the ostensible purpose of the Roosevelt bill dealing
with the congestion of the tribunal, and kindred bases, and
made it certain that the Senate committee would report that
bill adversely.

All hope that the labor lobby and the farm lobby would
really get to work on the President's side vanished with the
new attitude of the justices.

That was really the end of any prospect for the success of the
President's bill, though he did not admit it, and there followed
a lot of maneuvering toward having the bill go over to the next
session: discussion of suggested compromises and other face-

saving expedients. But the opposition knew its strength too well. It was prepared to filibuster indefinitely, if that was required, to defeat any measure that would permit the President to hold that he had won anything.

Vice-President Garner, who publicly stood by the President and privately expressed disgust with the bill, decided to go home to Uvalde in the midst of it—leaving Joe Robinson, on whose health and strength his violent efforts were already telling, to fight it out practically alone. Robinson by this time was convinced that the slim majority he thought was with him had faded, and ultimately the President admitted that there was no hope for his measure and was willing to talk compromise. The earliest of the substitute measures that he considered was the Andrews amendment, a clumsy expedient that provided for a court composed of justices from ten regional divisions, associate justices, and that, moreover, would have eliminated Robinson as a member of the court, for Justice Butler was from the same district. When the Andrews bill went into the discard, they took on the measure suggested by Senator Hatch, which raised the retiring age to seventy-five and provided for coadjutor justices but limited the President's power of appointment to one a year.

There came the episode of Jimmy Roosevelt's being called to the Capitol for a session with Robinson, Barkley, and Harrison. They told the President's son that there was no chance for the original bill to be passed, and finally Robinson told Jimmy to tell "poppa" that he had better put the situation into their hands and they would get the best they could of it. Jimmy reported the conversation to the strategy board, but Robinson never did believe that he carried the unvarnished message to his father. Thereupon Old Joe became a little crusty and did not go to the White House for some time. He was miffed at the delay in appointing him to the justiceship, though he had been advised of the President's reasons for delay and Jim Farley had brought him the tidings that he need not worry, that he would be on the bench regardless of any development.

The President himself showed signs of the general peevish-

182 THE GHOST TALKS

ness when Pat Harrison and Jimmie Byrnes called on him and urged the necessity of Joe's appointment at once, pointing out that even the President's staunchest supporters were in revolt at the delay and at a rumor that Robinson might not be appointed at all. Franklin Roosevelt's dilemma was neither illogical nor unreal. He intended to carry out his promise to Joe, even though he understood that by so doing he was simply substituting one conservative for another; but, thinking apparently that Harrison and Byrnes had come at Joe's solicitation, he objected to having his hand forced. They told him—rather bluntly—that no compromise on the court bill was possible unless Joe's friends were pacified, but they got no definite pledge of swift action. Within a day or two Joe Robinson collapsed in the midst of debate and was found dead in his apartment the next morning.

A factor that added to the certainty of the bill's defeat was the election of Alben Barkley to the leadership made vacant by the passing of Senator Robinson. The Senate wanted Pat Harrison for that job. He was probably the most popular member of the body; one of the old-timers, witty and politically wise, fellow of the poker and golf-playing set; a fairly consistent supporter of the President, but a favorite of the President's opponents notwithstanding. It seemed evident that Barkley had the administration's support, and the senators, apart from any other consideration, resented the President's meddling in one of their purely domestic contests.

The President was warned that his espousal of the Kentuckian's candidacy was bad policy while the Court fight was on, for he needed Harrison influence. So he had Pat Harrison at the White House and assured him of his neutrality—but there was the episode of the "Dear Alben" letter, as well as the statements of some of the senators that administration agents had put pressure on them; so Harrison—defeated for the leadership by one vote—was rather chilly thereafter, and, though he went along, did not break his suspenders in behalf of the White House.

As our campaign's failure became manifest, tempers became

strained, misunderstandings multiplied, and the disposition of everybody to blame somebody else increased.

Joe Robinson and Joe O'Mahoney, erstwhile close friends and mutual admirers, almost came to blows in the course of the Senate leader's last-minute effort to compromise. O'Mahoney was obdurate, naturally. Robinson hazarded some remark to the effect that the Wyoming senator was trying to be a little Huey Long. The response was that if Robinson would put a cold towel on his head, he could himself be a fair replica of the abominated Huey. There followed a dressing down, not all printable, perhaps unmatched in governmental circles until Cordell Hull reverted to the Tennessee feudist line from which he sprang and told what he thought of Ray Moley.

The two senatorial Joes were flying at each other when Joe Keenan stepped between them and finally got things down to a sober basis.

Keenan, however, misplaced though he may have been as a White House ambassador at the Capitol, could never be accused of lying down on his job. He was indefatigable in striving to fulfill his mission. Part of his trouble was resentment on part of the Democratic senators, close friends and admirers of Jim Farley. They were all aware of Jim's distaste for Keenan, resulting from reports that had come back to Farley of Keenan's knocking him at the White House and elsewhere. That, I presume, was only part of Tommy Corcoran's effort to horn in on the National Committee. He was, in characteristic courtier fashion, jealous of anybody else who had access to the President, though his ostensible objection to Farley was that the latter was no true New Dealer. Sometimes—not always—the President listened to Farley when Corcoran's leftism tended to interfere with the practical politics of a situation.

The wrangling and essays at bargaining went on, but the best the President's friends could gain for him was that the resubmission of the Supreme Court Bill to the Judiciary Committee— the polite method of executing the death sentence on a Senate measure—should not mention the Supreme Court.

Even that was denied him, for Senator Hiram Johnson, ignoring the agreement of the Judiciary Committee, insisted on having it stated openly that the Supreme Court issue was totally out.

The President got back on the Senate part way by naming Senator Hugo Black for the vacancy that Robinson was to have filled. Black had infuriated the Senate conservatives by the passion and fervor of his New Dealism. They regarded him as one of the hillbilly group that had eventuated from the political revolution in the South which had eliminated such solons as Oscar Underwood.

The Senate's most sacred tradition is that of standing by its members whenever one of them becomes a candidate for advancement. They did not like Black's Ku Klux record; many of them were shocked by his conduct of investigations. Once he had summoned all the messages filed at a telegraph office to get something on the interests he was investigating.

The President put the senators on the spot, but they remained loyal to their fraternal tradition and confirmed Justice Black, not unanimously but with a comfortable majority.

And Black astonished them, and perhaps many others, by turning out to be one of the ablest lawyers and one of the most conscientious and conventional wearers of the robe. His fellow justices, who received him coldly, presently became his close friends and even admirers.

There was no question that he had joined the intolerant sheet-and-pillow-case order; he admitted it after he was named for the bench. However, he was following a well-known principle of politics—that of joining any society or group that could help him. Indeed he would not have been elected if he had not fraternized with the outfit that was then running politics in Alabama. He was not thinking of the high dignity of the Supreme Court; he was simply a politician running for office. The psychology suggests another comparison with Wendell Willkie's thoughts when he described an utterance at variance with his postelection statement as "merely campaign oratory."

I have not paid strict attention to sequence in this recital of incidents picturing the court fight, but in the retrospect it seems to me that we on the President's side were sliding downhill from the beginning.

Nor am I sure that the theory is tenable which claims there would have been a very different result had the President been willing to accept a compromise bill. In his "Dear Alben" letter he stressed that he would not insist on any specific bill as long as a substitute provided for the same objectives he had laid down, which, he averred, were those the country wished to obtain. In other words, a bill that would satisfy the opponents of the measure would have been as unacceptable to him as his bill was to them.

Time has taken care of the President's objectives in the court plan. He has now the liberal court he envisaged when he formulated the elaborate program that disrupted his party and induced him to undertake his well-nigh futile purge. Consequently he is able to say—and says it not infrequently—that he "lost the battle and won the war."

The scars of the fight will be long in healing. The senators he tried to "defeat," not because of any lack of esteem for them but as a simple matter of having senators who are in sympathy with the great cause of the "common good," have neither forgiven nor forgotten the ordeal to which he subjected them.

The result of the purge was a demonstration of the inability of men, however great their power and popularity, to transfer their strength either for or against someone else. Senator George, for example, could not, if he would, take Georgia out of the Roosevelt column, any more than Roosevelt was able to take his senatorship away from George.

One question remains unanswered. Will Roosevelt be able to realize his ideal of being on such terms with the Supreme Court that he can have consultation and co-operation with the justices about laws in advance of their enactment? He made a proposal for that sort of a coalition to Chief Justice Hughes when he first came to the White House. The idea of his talking over—even with a President—cases that might become before the court almost paralyzed the Chief Justice, so that he barely was able to tell the President that he considered it vital to the preservation of our system of government that the executive and judicial branches remain entirely separate from and independent of each other.

Had there been no Supreme Court incident, there might never have been an open break between the President and Jim Farley. The rift that ranged so many of the big men of his party outside the breastworks encouraged the Farley insurrection, but it is easy to overestimate the power of such an alliance.

If Roosevelt runs again, most of the rebels—probably all of them—may be expected to support him—not enthusiastically, perhaps, but resignedly.

13. PALACE FAVORITES

Those who dwelt in the shadow of the great, and thought they were driving the machine.

GENERAL HUGH JOHNSON has been credited as the actual author of the economic phases of the New Deal, but perhaps the roster of Franklin Roosevelt's confidential advisers ought to be prefaced by the name of Edward M. House, that shadowy satellite who appeared and reappeared and disappeared in the Woodrow Wilson orbit during the First World War and the Versailles Conference period.

House and Franklin Roosevelt were both consultants with Wilson, and their friendship did not terminate when the unofficial ambassador at large went into eclipse.

Right after his nomination in 1932 the presidential candidate visited Colonel House. Twenty years before, there appeared an unpretentious little volume of fiction, anonymous, telling the story of Philip Dru, a gentle, forward-looking dictator, who had seized the government to rid it of the blighting domination and practices of an unscrupulous plutocracy.

The method and philosophy of that starry-eyed brain truster in the exercise of his dictatorship were startlingly like the New Deal. He promulgated the doctrine that every man or woman that desires work shall have it even if the government has to give it. He arranged for the eight-hour day, collective bargaining by unions, bank security, the destruction of holding companies, the reform of the Supreme Court, with compulsory retirement at the age of seventy, and old age pensions; and Philip Dru even employed fireside talks to get his message to the people.

I don't know that Franklin Roosevelt ever read the book, but it is probable, at least, that in his many talks with Colonel House the philosophy indicated in the volume and subsequently in President Roosevelt's policies were mulled over.

The life of that book, like the career of the author, was shadowy and mysterious. I have been told that after five hundred copies had been printed, the plates were destroyed. We know who the author was because Frederick Collins, who some years ago disclosed the startling coincidence of the thesis with subsequent enactments, found, on the title page of the volume that came to his attention, a presentation paragraph to the person to whom the book was given, "who honors me with a request for this hastily and poorly expressed statement of my view in 1911 —E. M. House."

While the inspiration of many New Deal measures may have come from Colonel House's philosophy, the pattern was not followed all the way, for the fictional dictator enacted such changes as making the "executor," who was to be chosen by the House of Representatives, perform most of the offices now appertaining to the office of president. The presidency becomes, under the Philip Dru system, more like the existing vice-presidency, for the incumbent, elected for a period of ten years and ineligible for another term, has none but formal and ceremonial functions.

House members are to serve six years, subject to recall after two years by petition of one-third of the electorate.

The Senators are given life terms, one from each state, subject to recall at the end of any five-year period, and must retire at the age of seventy; but the Senate has no power to initiate legislation. If it rejects a law passed by the House, that body can dissolve and appeal to the country; and if the country sustains the measure by returning a House favoring it, then the measure becomes a law.

These examples are cited merely to indicate how far from conventional governmental thought was the man whom we regarded as the conservative balance wheel to the Wilson progressivism.

If Colonel House may have been the first of the White House courtiers, and possibly the one who most influenced the policies of Franklin Roosevelt, he must yield in point of permanency to the eminence of Harry Hopkins. That welfare worker has been on top—or near the top—ever since he came to Washington to administer the W.P.A., that organization charged with putting to work those who but for its offices would have been on direct relief. He perhaps did as good a job there as anybody could have done, notwithstanding the jibes at the leaf rakers, and the boondoggle stories, and the reiterated charges from the Republicans that he was using his huge agency to promote Democratic election success.

His first big blunder was when he announced one day when Gillette and Wearin were contesting for the Iowa senatorship that if he had a vote in Iowa he would cast it for Wearin. That gave point to the charge of partisanship, for Gillette was one of those on the purgee list by reason of his position during the Supreme Court fight, and the Republicans construed Administrator Hopkins' utterance as a warning to the reliefers that they had better vote for the administration candidate. His role, in view of his particular job, should have been to steer as wide from a political comment as he could get. Whether in his ingenuous mind he conceived the idea that flaunting his colors would help the administration candidate, or whether he failed

to realize the possible imputations of an inconsequential remark, it was stupid politically. Hopkins probably had nothing
more in mind than to illustrate his loyalty to his chief, but it
indicated his lack of political wisdom, as it compelled certain
awkward and not quite convincing explanations.

Organization Democrats were generally hostile to him anyhow, for they said he preferred Republicans to Democrats when
he was appointing his key men to the big jobs under him both
as relief administrator and as boss of W.P.A. Actually it must
be assumed that he was politically nonpartisan in these matters
and named his individual friends and associates—which may or
may not be an improvement on the more conventional spoils system. During his New York career in various relief activities he
was credited to no party. Indeed the apparent type of his mind
when he came to Washington seemed to preclude definite devotion to any set of economic principles beyond a shadowy faith
that virtue was inherent in poverty and absent from wealth. In
his later environment he seems to have drifted far from those
unstable mental moorings.

The hostility of the political regulars did not diminish during
his term as secretary of commerce but did not interfere with the
President's high regard for him and for his abilities. When the
cabinet was shuffled again, he emerged as chief of the lend-lease
activities, and finally moved into the White House as special
assistant to the President. Once there was a move to make him
the Democratic candidate for governor of New York. Farley is
credited with having spiked that.

Hopkins has done nothing to increase his popularity with
Congressmen or other Democratic officials—rather the reverse,
as they complain that he will not answer his telephone calls,
even when the caller tells his secretary that the President had
directed him to talk to Hopkins. Whether this manifestation is
due to exaggerated ego or to preoccupation with his official
duties, the effect is the same.

There is nothing new about the lack of cordiality at the Capitol for the President's contact men. Hopkins is perhaps no more
anathema up there than was Tommy Corcoran, whom, by the

way, the present special assistant is credited with eliminating from the White House circle.

The President's liking for Corcoran was quite understandable. Tommy is able, witty, companionable, entertaining, and, when he cares to be, courteous and obliging. His trouble with Congress was that he did not bother to exercise his pleasant qualities on the members thereof. They resented his phoning them orders without even sugar-coating the dose. They were irked at the idea that it would be wise to consult him about patronage. There was no question as to his influence; and whether that came to him with authority or whether he was running a tremendous—and successful—bluff, nobody was quite sure. The White House people insisted that he was merely useful to the President as confidential messenger and as an aide with a gift for speech writing, but even the underlings there were not so certain that that was the limit of his status as to cross him. He is a capable lawyer, though in the writing of laws delivered to Congress Ben Cohen did the heavy work.

Whatever is the truth—or rather whatever was the truth— about his authority, there is no question that he not only had but exercised the power. Under the guise of supplying real experts where they were needed at the beginning of the Roosevelt regime, he made Jim Farley look like a tyro in staffing the offices. In this way he had his key men in every branch of the government—a circumstance invaluable to his present sphere of activity, that of "practicing law" in the district. No man looking for a fat contract, and no one who is having difficulties with the government, could employ a more useful attorney.

Lest there be some suspicion in the lay mind that his activities while he was the star member of the White House inner circle were those of the common or garden variety of lobbyist, it is only just to say that there was no immediate money profit for himself involved. He was after power, not pecuniary gains. Whether he had in mind what would come when he departed from the palace guard, nobody knows but himself. As brilliant a mind as Corcoran's could hardly have failed to look that far ahead. He is reputed to have piled up a fortune—and not a small fortune—in fees during the year or so that he has been in private practice.

As to his qualifications it is sufficient to state that he was picked by Felix Frankfurter, and was taken into the office of Justice Holmes in conformity with that great jurist's habit of choosing as his law secretary the banner graduate of the Harvard Law School. He worked indefatigably at his strange job. He is credited with keeping the brain trust of his period harmonious but felt no call to exercise his skill in that direction on persons who could not be of use to him.

Naturally he had no affection for the party organization, and Farley was often exasperated when he got reports that Corcoran and one of his running mates, Assistant Attorney-General Keenan, were "knocking" him in the course of an effort to build up an anti-Farley organization.

Corcoran and I had a mild friendship, never an intimate one, and I quite understood the Chairman's sentiments, for upon one occasion I felt obliged to say to the young man:

"Tommy, you ought to know that the radio world is one vast whispering gallery, and that when you tell a radio magnate that I am a superannuated incompetent, he calls me within ten minutes and tells me about it."

He made no reply, and the conversation turned to pleasanter topics.

I only asked one favor from him, which he, probably quite properly, refused. This was in the matter of a lawyer who had been presented to me as a particularly bright young man with aspirations to a minor judgeship. He was the son of a Congressman who was helping me in my futile effort to prevent the passage of the Hatch Act. A Congressman was of no importance in Corcoran's scheme of things, and neither was I.

He served the President longer than anybody with a similar relationship except Harry Hopkins. Those two were supposed to have an understanding that so long as their activities did not clash there would be no hostility. I gather that this truce—for there could not be anything more than a truce, where there was rivalry for primacy in their relationships with the Big Chief—

terminated when Hopkins was entrusted with important political missions, which explains the story of Hopkins' part in the withdrawal of Corcoran, who is one of the few of his order to quit of their own accord.

The story is that "Tommy the Cork" decided that he would like to be appointed solicitor-general, and that "Harry the Hop" advised against it. It may have been that the latter had in mind the bitter feeling at the Capitol toward the other, and feared that the appointment would fail of confirmation by the Senate. It was not a question of qualifications, for worse lawyers than the versatile Corcoran have at times conducted that office, which is really the most important in the Department of Justice. The story goes on that his next ambition was to be assistant secretary of the navy, a post held by Franklin Roosevelt under the Wilson administration and by Teddy Roosevelt, the younger, under Harding. That failed by reason of a prior commitment, and an alternative assistant secretaryship in charge of naval aviation did not come to pass for lack of congressional appropriation.

Whereupon Tommy shook the dust of the White House from his feet. His enemies wonder if the divorce is permanent, and nobody would be surprised if he reappeared after he has accumulated money enough to satisfy him. He is that kind of a fellow, and, in my opinion at least, his desire to be in the thick of things, to have the glory of domination, is greater than any lust for millions. Moreover, he is really a New Dealer, perhaps even farther to the left than the average of that order.

Incidentally, another palace favorite, Stanley High, is supposed to have lost out for making public the amusing nomenclature of the inner circle—the "Tommy the Cork" stuff. (Occasionally, though I could not qualify as one of the brain trust, I have moved under the designation of "Charlie the Mike" because of my supposed affinity to the microphone over which speeches are delivered.) It was not that any particular damage could result from the disclosure of these whimsicalities, but any tendency to repeat what goes on privately at the White House is taboo.

Actually High signed his dismissal when he authored a maga-

zine story intimating a presidential desire to separate himself
from such wheel horses as Democrats Joe Robinson, Vice-President Garner, et al., carrying out the theory that what the
President would like to see is a new party alignment, with the
liberals on one side and the conservatives on the other, instead
of the present Democratic-Republican setup with a progressive
wing to the G.O.P. and standpatters among the party of Jefferson and Jackson.

Stanley High, an ex-preacher, was as able an evangelist as any
of the group. He did a journeyman job with the Good Neighbor
League in the '36 campaign, his work culminating in the great
Negro mass meeting at Madison Square Garden. He was a forceful and picturesque writer but could not keep his feet on the
ground. I still have in mind his prancing through Democratic
headquarters at the Biltmore proclaiming that he was off to
write a speech for the President—a rather shocking violation of
the rules of the game, as a ghost writer is never supposed to
admit that he is the author of a great man's utterances.

High has the distinction of being the only member of the
particular hierarchy now being discussed whose departure from
his niche was announced officially. Moley and Corcoran simply
faded out of the picture, but Secretary Steve Early handed the
White House correspondents this statement:

"The President announced the death of the 'official spokesman' in March 1933." (The White House spokesman was a
Coolidge press-conference expedient.) "He now announces the
passing of the so-called authoritative spokesmen—those who
write as 'one of the President's close advisers'!"

The *Saturday Evening Post* in blurbing the High article
used these words: "Dr. High, who here, in a manner of speaking, reads the Democrats out of the Democratic party, has the
Washington reputation of being one of the President's close
advisers."

There were repercussions at the Capitol. Vice-President
Garner joked about it, but Senator Robinson was furious.
Probably it was Robinson's indignation which caused the offi-
cial disclaimer.

The passing of Dr. High caused no mourning among his one-time confreres. Indeed it is typical of that order that each departure is a welcome relief of those who continue to bask in the President's favor.

General Hugh Johnson was a disturbing member. The old cavalryman, with his pyrotechnic expletives and his blistering comparisons, jarred the professors. His roaring voice dominated their meetings. His tone was that of a commander of troops ordering a charge. There was no disrespect involved; it was simply the emphasis of an intensely positive man, and behind the bluster was a lot of good hard common sense. The General's appointment as head of the N.R.A. was enthusiastically applauded by the remainder of the group. They always regarded him, as an economist, with much the same attitude as a regular physician regards a faith healer. I am afraid their enthusiasm for the N.R.A. was more because it took him from their midst than for its promise as a recovery measure.

Perhaps a better comparison of their estimate of the General would be the feeling at Democratic headquarters toward the professorial approach to political questions.

Contrary to the popular estimate of Hugh Johnson as merely a violent master of brimstony epigrams and pungent allegories, always in a furious temper, he was, or had been, a deep student of the abstruse problems of the day. Perhaps he overestimated the depth of his researches and covered too wide a field in his dogmatic dissertations.

Rex Tugwell and Adolph Berle, of the original brain trust, graduated into serious official posts. Berle showed a capacity to mold himself into the classical officeholder status with only a few more controversies than are normal to men so circumstanced; but poor Tugwell seems to be always in hot water. Perhaps nobody could have made Puerto Rico happy, considering that that island is still in the throes of democratic birth pains, with a heavy hangover of the old haciendero philosophy, and with an inherited Latin tendency to direct methods in politics superimposed on its economic misery. Incidentally, the situation was not helped by the mainland habit of calling every

exponent of liberalism a communist or socialist—Puerto Rico
is prone to believe that we mean our epithets and that they are
not merely campaign currency.

It appears that in appraising the qualifications of the "inte-
grated body" grouped about the President, I have been rather
fulsome as to the abilities of the individual members. There
were among them, of course, stargazers as well as stuporous
book worms, but each had the stuff the President wanted. Ray
Moley was, in my estimation, the ablest of them, even though,
when he had ceased to be the Rasputin of the administration,
he showed a startling indifference to the sacredness of confidences and backtracked from his symbolism of liberalism into
the advocacy of the causes against which Roosevelt had, with
his assistance, ranged himself. So we find him critical of Frankfurter's law, and Brandeis's assay of bigness of corporations as
a menace to the nation's welfare.

Corcoran was, in a lesser degree, perhaps, not dissimilar in
his psychology to the dean of the original brain trust, but he
was less assertive in their councils and more domineering in
his contacts outside.

I think Tommy rather enjoyed the slings and arrows the
columnists and others, including the Congressmen, flung at him
during his period of exaltation. He generally classified his
assailants as business stooges, Silurian mossbacks, and frustrates,
whose aspersions contributed to the appreciation of his eminence. The only occasion I know of where he was actually disturbed was when Evie Robert, "Chip" Robert's irrepressible
and iconoclastic wife, ribbed him on his carelessness of the
amenities. She was doing a column, and in it she said:

"I'm going to look for the most complete book on manners
I can find. This book I'm going to send to Mr. T. Corcoran. . . .
Of course, he's so busy running the country, with the assistance
of a few cabinet officers and others, that I dare say his shaggy
head is full of his own importance (for who dares say that the
the country could exist without Him). . . . If his self-admit-
tedly great and overworked brain should happen to read this,
I guess he'll remember what I'm talking about."

The occasion that provoked this was, I believe, a dinner, given by the Drew Pearsons in honor of Tommy's birthday. Corcoran and the columnist were intimately associated at that time, Drew being reputedly a star member of Tommy's propaganda staff.

The party waited a long time, and finally, assuming that some vital summons, probably from the White House, had intercepted him, proceeded to eat. The honor guest I was told arrived as they were finishing their dessert, tarried a few minutes, and departed.

There is nothing invidious in this reflection on Pearson's status. It is the business of a columnist who essays to give the low-down on administration acts, to be as close as he can be to those who are supposed to know the secrets.

Harry Hopkins is the one member of the court circle who has ridden the tumultuous seas of favoritism and remained not only afloat but at the peak. No outsider has been able to point to any single episode in which he displayed remarkable talents; but, on the other hand, he must have something, for Roosevelt has little patience with incompetents, yet has pushed the welfare worker to one important post after another. He carried him along even to Africa and Asia, where military acumen and diplomatic expertness were the demanding requirements, though Hopkins has had no soldier training, and, as indicated by his contacts with the high politicians and the members of Congress, his lack of tact, as well as his incapacity to bring harmony where there is discord, has been demonstrated.

He is the only member of the group of theorists and economists that the President has lifted to a cabinet position. Most of the others, though spurned or ignored by the practical fellows whose job it is to get out the votes, were experts in their own lines, as exemplified by their positions in the college world. I have mentioned Hopkins' ineptitude in connection with his political announcement on the Iowa primary controversy at a time when he was being accused of bending his influence or power with the relief people, and his clumsiness in handling the 1940 convention.

During the '40 campaign he came over to New York highly excited over a big batch of letters of at least doubtful authenticity, supposed to be from Henry Wallace. Their general purport was silly rather than evil. Hopkins assured us they were forgeries. Doubtless some of them, perhaps all, were fabrications. The Republicans had bought them, we were advised, but were afraid to put them out and could find no publisher daring enough to take the responsibility, though they were shoved in turn to every publisher hostile to Roosevelt. This being the situation, the obvious strategy of the enemy was to get us to take notice of the dossier, by denial or other mention, which might either provoke an unfavorable curiosity or give an excuse to force a revelation of its contents without the danger of liability. Hopkins suggested expedients that would have made admirable chapters in an Oppenheim novel (for he regarded the matter as of tragic importance) but fitted into no conception of practical politics. Ed Flynn, veteran of a hundred political battles, refused to be rattled. He felt that it was just one of the incidents of a campaign to be handled like any other foray by the foe.

The opposition could not find a publisher, the Democratic national organization gave them no opening, and so the storm passed without hysteria at headquarters and never figured in the campaign.

14. IDEALS AND UNETHICAL ETHICS

In which the reader may ponder the holiness of alliances, and learn when political sins are virtues.

WHENEVER THIS COUNTRY has become involved in war the project of a coalition government has been advanced on the perfectly tenable theory that such a national emergency requires the support and sympathy of all the people, regardless of the political complexion of the administration in power.

Roosevelt was the first modern president to accept this logic. He did so in the face of the stiff opposition of his party leaders, whose contention it was that while minority chiefs might ostensibly accept the idea of a political armistice, individuals, particularly in Congress, would take advantage of every opportunity to bomb the administration, regardless of members of their own party in that administration. That was the position taken by Jim Farley and Ed Flynn.

The coalition theory was stoutly advanced at the opening of World War I. Woodrow Wilson, although anything but a machine Democrat, rejected it. His view was that the war job was the responsibility of his administration and his party, and he had no mind to attempt to pass along any of that obligation. He retained all his Democratic cabinet, but made appointments to the headship of the various civil war agencies regardless of party: for example, Herbert Hoover as food administrator, and Julius Rosenwald as a member of the advisory committee to the council of National Defense and as chairman of the Supplies Commission. Nor was it because he was a Democrat that he made Bernard M. Baruch chairman of the War Industries Board. I don't know how often presidents have tried, unsuccessfully, to make Baruch secretary of the treasury.

There were the usual charges of dictatorship, but he got along fairly well during the war period. He tried a little purging of the "twelve willful men," with varying success, and he turned down General Leonard Wood and named General Pershing to the supreme command of the American forces. It was told at the time that Wood, when he was summoned to discuss taking the high post, said something derogatory of his old chief, Theodore Roosevelt, and Wilson thereupon rejected him on the theory that the candidate's precarious loyalties did not recommend him. Wilson was having his own troubles at the time with the ex-President, who was asking a military command for himself and the privilege of leading a force in the fray overseas.

Wilson's foes attributed his failure to grant the commission to his fear of rejuvenation of T. R.'s political plans for a comeback. My recollection is that the application was denied on the ground of physical unfitness.

Coalition government is idyllic, but it has not worked out particularly well politically. If Franklin Roosevelt thought it would soften the hostility of the minority party, he was disappointed. All it afforded was an opportunity to present his absence of partisanship in the war effort by citing that he had placed control of the War and Navy Departments in the hands of two eminent Republicans.

Instead of applauding the appointment of a Republican candidate for vice-president to the directorship of the marine branch and a Republican ex-secretary of state to head the military department, the opposition spokesmen regarded these two almost as party traitors and linked them with the confusion they were attributing to the war administration. I cannot recall a single expression of satisfaction from the G.O.P. leaders, in or out of Congress, at the inclusion of these two in the cabinet.

Roosevelt was able to fill the two posts without having to disturb his cabinet setup. The secretaryship of war was vacated as a result of a feud between Secretary Harry Woodring and Assistant Secretary of War Louis Johnson. Woodring, after serving a term as a Democratic governor of Kansas, lost out to Alfred

Landon (Republican candidate for President in 1936) in the next following election. Woodring was a quiet, unsensational war secretary. His assistant, big, energetic, full of plans and impatience, campaigned openly for the secretaryship, which was no happy condition on the verge of a great war, so both lost out and Stimson was appointed. Charles Edison resigned from the navy branch to become governor of New Jersey, which left the opening for Frank Knox.

The departure did not come unheralded, and the Democratic politicians recorded their objections. Here is an argument by one of the party chiefs which I believe was presented to the President:

"A coalition government is possible in England, where the premier has to appear before Parliament and answer for the policies of the ministry. On the parliamentary vote rests the fate of the ministry. If it sustains the premier, the ministry continues; if it votes the other way, the ministry falls. In this country, however, we work under the two-party system, which leaves no excuse for a hybrid administration. The government is unchallengeable by Congress for four years, except through impeachment proceedings. The people entrusted us with the task, knowing full well that a great war was among the imminent possibilities during the administration to which they had given authority. A coalition government will not strengthen the war effort and will weaken our party."

If that thought was planted at the White House, it was totally ineffective.

The two Republicans doubtless have rendered as good service as Democrats would have given. They have accepted their share of criticism, chiefly emanating from members of their own party —but they have remained Republicans.

Secretary Knox owns a newspaper in New Hampshire as well as one in Chicago. The *Manchester Union Leader* bitterly fought the election of the Democratic candidate for senator in the 1942 election, and New Hampshire Democrats say that the newspaper's influence was sufficient to defeat him.

During the 1940 campaign Candidate Franklin Roosevelt devoted much of his sarcasm at the hypothetical firm of Martin (Joe), Barton (Bruce), and Fish (Ham). The Navy Department had a big advertising campaign when it started recruiting. I think the estimated expenditure was something like a million dollars, and the Secretary awarded it to the Bruce Barton advertising agency. There may have been no exclusively political intent; Colonel Knox is a publisher. He had had many dealings with the Barton agency to their mutual profit, and knew that the agency was efficient. Nevertheless, Democratic agencies of equal repute felt, and still feel, that they were entitled to the advantage of such advertising by a Democratic administration.

To be realistic on this subject: I know that if I had had the placing of such a contract, it would have redounded to the benefit of the Democratic cause, and I do not mean by this that an agency controlled by the members of our party would have been any more partisan in its discharge of its function than was the Barton agency in the other direction. It would have motivated a Democratic agency to more emphatic friendliness to the administration, and such Democratic publications as got the advertising would have been encouraged in their support.

It might be urged that a coalition government is in itself a move in the strategy of partisan politics. While its first objective is to present an united front to the war foe, it implies the purpose of softening the asperity of a campaign and neutralizing, or at least minimizing, the criticisms of the minority party.

Secretary Stimson sent a heroizing letter to Henry Cabot Lodge, Republican candidate for the Massachusetts senatorship on his return to the national legislature. Presumably Senator Lodge deserved the encomium for his war service, but I do not know that other members of Congress who had continued with the fighting forces until the President directed that they return to their legislative duties, or to remain with the combat divisions for the duration of the war, were honored in the same degree. The Massachusetts senatorial contest was close, and the Bay State Democrats believe that Stimson's letter was the thing that gave victory to the Republican. Lodge used the letter extensively in the campaign, and it was not until the day before election that the Secretary of War permitted the publication of his statement deploring the use of the document for political purposes.

It is logical to assume that President Roosevelt had in mind, when he inaugurated the principle of a nonpartisan cabinet, that it would serve to promote harmony between him and the Congress in which the Republicans made many gains in the last election. There are, of course, quite a number of anti-Roosevelt Democrats in both houses, including the objects of the purge. As long as the Democrats maintained their large majority, he had little trouble in getting most of his important suggestions enacted into law. When these majorities were cut, the administration measures were at the mercy of the non-Roosevelt Democrats. The President had in mind the accord he had obtained as governor of New York with a Republican legislature. The principle did not work with Congress. The coalition cabinet did not bring him a single Republican congressional convert. In other words, he has been no more successful in effecting his legislative objectives than he would have been had he kept his cabinet wholly Democratic. There is no implication in this that the Republicans defeat every piece of war legislation he offers; but the minority determines the virtue of his offerings, and where there is a question of the necessity or validity of a given proposition, that minority is able to cast the ballot its way without violation of their patriotic consciences.

Despite constant insistence to the contrary, the mind of Congress is heavily on the election of 1944. That goes both ways, for congressional seats as well as the presidency are at stake in that election, hence the dominating influence of the farm lobby and the labor lobby as well as the long conflict over tax measures.

The platform of the minority, plus the anti-Roosevelt Democrats, might be epitomized thus:

When in doubt, hit the President; when it is politically safe, hit the President.

Let me illustrate this by an example of comparison and contrast:

An eminent and wealthy politician, Pat Hurley, was nominated for minister to New Zealand and ambassador at large. The candidate had been chairman of the Republican State Committee of Oklahoma. He contributed largely in campaign donations as well as organization and oratory to the Hoover candidacy in 1928, and was rewarded for this service by appointment first to the assistant secretaryship of war, later being promoted to the full secretaryship. His war appointment by Roosevelt was confirmed without opposition by the United States Senate, in addition to which he was commissioned a brigadier general. He did a marvelously good job, not only as a diplomat but in carrying out his unannounced mission of getting blockade runners through with ammunition and other supplies to our beleaguered forces in the Philippines.

Later on an eminent and wealthy politician, Ed Flynn, was nominated for the post of minister to Australia and ambassador at large. He had been active in Democratic politics, and as a reward for these services Franklin Roosevelt, when he became governor of New York, appointed him as secretary of state for that commonwealth. On Roosevelt's nomination to the presidency for the third time Flynn became chairman of the Democratic National Committee. He declined an appointment as postmaster-general, retired from the political chairmanship, and was named by the President, when he volunteered for war service in any capacity, for the Australian ministry, with identical responsibilities to those given General Hurley.

The Republican minority and the anti-Roosevelt Democratic senators ganged up on him so formidably that at his own request the President withdrew the appointment.

Hurley is a lawyer, graduate of Bacone College, with a lucrative law firm apart from his other large interests. Flynn is a lawyer, graduate of Fordham University, with a lucrative law firm, apart from the fortune he inherited, his cattle ranches, and other assets. Both owed their eminences to political service rendered. Each made good in every post given him. In fact it would be difficult to find two public careers so nearly alike; and yet, as candidates for almost identical governmental places, the Republican was enthusiastically indorsed while the Democrat was turned down—merely because this action afforded an opportunity to take a fall out of the President.

Of course, those who opposed Flynn did not put their opposition on such grounds. Instead they invoked an absurd scandal, which grand juries before whom his political enemies brought the charges promptly ignored.

The putative charge was that Flynn had used city-used paving blocks, handled by city employees, in the beautification of his country home. The alleged offense was committed by a minor Bronx County official, who thought he was doing the National Democratic Chairman a favor, while the Chairman was absent on the Pacific Coast. Flynn, as soon as he learned of it, sent checks to pay for the material and labor. Dignity and position aside, what likelihood is there that a man with a five-figure income—perhaps a six-figure income—would stoop to filch a few dollars' worth of junk from a city dump?

Lest this recital may be regarded as an expression of partisanship, let me confess that were the situation reversed the Democrats would probably do something along the same line. History does not recall any great consideration of President Taft by the Democratic House of Representatives that came in to plague him in 1912, though the Republicans got more than even, with Woodrow Wilson as the victim, when they won the congressional election of 1918.

Nobody has ever been able to formulate a political code of ethics. Despite the fine, altruistic language of party platforms, the habit has always been to smite the opposition, regardless of Marquis of Queensbury rules, whenever and however the opportunity offers. Had Woodrow Wilson had a working majority in the Senate when he brought home the Versailles Treaty, he might have gained the requisite two-thirds confirmation of the League of Nations. But, as Josephus Daniels phrased it: "The Republican majority is out on bail"—referring to a Senator who was charged with spending too much money to accomplish his election. Therefore the two-thirds goal was impossible of attainment. The Republicans almost without exception voted against Wilson.

They were out to get Wilson. The purely political character of that episode was revealed by Senator Jim Watson of Indiana. When Henry Cabot Lodge, one-time coworker with Theodore Roosevelt for such a League, approached Watson to handle the fight against the treaty, the cynical Indianian demurred, saying that the country was strongly in favor of the League. To this Lodge replied, "Oh, we will kill it with amendments"; and the practical politician saw how it could be done and gaily took up the task.

On the other hand I cannot recall that the Democrats, who had attained a sizable number of seats in 1930 and won the Congress two years later, did anything to ease the dying days of the Hoover administration.

I would put the genesis and results of the Hatch Act among the examples of the wide difference between ordinary and political ethics. During the period of doubt as to whether Roosevelt would or would not defy the third-term tradition, Vice-President Garner, as well as Postmaster-General Farley, had aspirations. The Vice-President, annoyed by the inability to get an answer to the nation-wide query, exclaimed, "The candidacy isn't worth a can of stale beer, unless the President indorses it!" Now, the Hatch Act was devised with the idea that, by keeping federal officeholders—postmasters, etc.—out of the 1940 convention, the business of stopping Roosevelt would be much facilitated. Let me repeat what I have previously written:

"That idea rebounded to the benefit of Vice-President John Garner, who, I believe, was never quite happy at the shift in the 1932 convention that gave us the original Roosevelt-Garner ticket. That was the development that finally lined up Speaker Sam Rayburn, of Texas, for the Hatch Act, and perhaps had a bearing on the appearance of Senator Morris Sheppard, also of Texas, as coauthor of the bill. However, when I expostulated with Senator Sheppard for his advocacy of the party-crippling measure, he assured me that he had never read the bill. His story was that Senator Hatch had come to him with the statement that he had framed a measure to take the relief people out of politics and asked permission to sign Sheppard's name to it. Everybody was in favor of eliminating the unfortunates on relief from political coercion—which sentiment was embraced in the bill's title—nothing being said then of the other provision which barred all minor executive federal employees from political activities, excepting, of course, congressional officeholders, which left every Congressman's cook, chauffeur, secretary, stenographer, and messenger free to work for his boss's election and, incidentally, the security of his own individual job.

"The young federal officials, the shock troops of every political battle, did not dare get into the campaign. They are the lads who, because of minor party service, have been rewarded with assistant district attorneyships, and man the desks in the offices of collectors of the port, revenue collectors, and the multiplicity of other posts that make up the federal establishment. Out of their ranks, as they develop, frequently come the future congressmen, senators, governors, etc. They are in the main the most competent people available, for their political careers, their speeches at small gatherings, connote with ambition, and, popular opinion to the contradiction notwithstanding, no department head would be willing to make up his staff with inferior material.

"Well, the Hatch Act puts a crimp in their activities while allowing full freedom for the people who, through a change in administration, expect to supplant the officeholders. In other words, a man may not campaign to hold his job, but there are no restrictions on the men who are striving to take that job away from him." *

The law branched out into the field of political finances. Not only does it limit the amount that can be spent by a politi-

* Charles Michelson, from an article released by North American Newspaper Alliance, Monday, December 7, 1942.

cal party, but it decrees that nobody can contribute more than five thousand dollars to the national organization. It construes loans as gifts. Where the National Committee, of which I was an employee, in the past had borrowed whatever we needed to discharge its campaign obligations, under the Hatch Act no bank could lend us what we required. During various campaigns we spent sometimes a million dollars more than we had; our radio bills alone sometimes amounted to half a million.

Our credit was established, for as contributions came in, and with what we realized by Jackson Day dinners, etc., we paid off our debts as rapidly as we could and usually within a year after election we had a clean slate.

The result of the legislation was to make constructive criminals of all the officials of the two great parties. Checks of eastern seaboard financiers for huge amounts turned up in Republican treasuries like Nebraska or the Dakotas. State organizations, to which the act does not apply, assumed national organization obligations in some form or another. So with evasions, subterfuges, and obliquities, the national organizations got along in some fashion. Not since the Volstead Act has there been so general a side-stepping of law by people who normally are classed as decent citizens. One favorite form of getting funds was to have the man who would cheerfuly contribute twenty-five thousand dollars to the cause of his party send in his legal quota and have his wife, son, daughter, brother-in-law, and secretary send in the rest. But these expedients are cumbersome and fall far short of efficiency. It is a simple thing to invite a wealthy man, interested in the success of his party, to give from his abundance; it is another thing to ask him to squirm along the troublesome path he now must take if he is to get the gift into the party treasury.

The advent of the Hatch Act involved me in my only real job of lobbying. The bill had passed the Senate, and the House subcommittee had reported it favorably before I became cognizant of what was cooking. So I went to the House and labored with the Speaker, and with the members of the full committee, with the result that the full committee presented a report that stripped the measure down to barring political influencing of voters on relief.

Then Senator Hatch moved in. The newspapers started their barrage and their threats on the Congressmen. Ninety per cent of the important journals outside of the South were and are antiadministration—Republicans either declaredly or actually, though they announce themselves as "independents." Few are the Congressmen who will not wilt before a general newspaper bombardment. So my amateur lobbying failed.

Obviously the act is hostile and dangerous to any party in power, inasmuch as it bars from party activity nearly all the government officials except, of course, congressional jobholders, while leaving free those who aspire to the jobs, whose only chance to get them is to oust the administration. I once suggested to Senator Hatch that it would even things up if his act also would make ineligible to government posts all who participated in political activities, by contributions or otherwise; but, as it was plain that he could not get his bill passed with such limitation, my suggestion fell to the ground.

To paraphrase the announcements of certain distinguished radio commentators, "my prediction is" that if and when the Republicans get in, the Hatch Act will be swiftly repealed. And, may I add, I miss my guess, if, when that time comes, the Democrats do not resist repeal as enthusiastically as they now curse the Hatch Act.

These shifts, tricks, or chicanery, as interest directs, violate the canons of true morality, perhaps, but have a near justification. What the moralists do not realize is that politics is a game for keeps, and, like other games when the stakes are high, the purpose is winning. In poker, for example, it is considered no departure from the code to deceive the opponent. So we hold a third card with three aces, to make the other fellow believe we have only two pair. We vociferously put down a big bet and stand pat on nothing, hoping the bluff will scare the man with only a minor hand. I presume, though I have not any recollection of having read it, that politics is a peaceable substitute for civil war, as its purpose is either to maintain a government or to effect a revolution. So the application of the rules of war is not incomprehensible. In war not only is every misleading or bewilderment of the enemy excusable, but combatants earn decorations and promotion for making a feint to distract attention from the actual objective, for laying a successful ambush or pretending to be an innocent merchantman in order to decoy a hostile submarine into range of camouflaged guns.

When General Eisenhower was poised for the descent on North Africa, our government permitted publication, if it did not plant the story, that the General was bound for the United States to report to the commander in chief. I am none too sure that Wendell Willkie's pilgrimage, with its resultant doleful reports of dissatisfaction in Russia and China with America's contribution of combat material, was without significance—whether, on the pilgrim's part, conscious or unconscious—in the successful effort to avert the foe's mind from the African project.

Now, I am not contending for the validity of the analogy between military and political strategy and tactics. I am merely reciting a phenomenon and suggesting an explanation of the coincidence of questionable—to put it politely—methods with nonpolitical high ideals on the part of otherwise exemplary individuals. There was more truth than humor to my comment to Messrs. Farley and Flynn about their incapability of stealing anything but an election.

The system seems to get support from the circumstance that once the fenagling is accomplished it is accepted, without more than a perfunctory expression of shock by the losers. To go back a couple of generations, the jockeying that deprived Governor Tilden of the presidency to which he had been elected and bestowed the great office on Rutherford B. Hayes produced no national convulsion. Since that time it is probable that there has been no election without a crop of ballot box stuffing or other election frauds, and yet none but underlings have gone to jail for these doings. Even the jettisoning of Woodrow Wilson's League of Nations program produced no immediate consternation. The country rocked along as usual under President Harding and his close successors, and it was only when we were precipitated into just the sort of war the league was designed to prevent that the public dismay reverted to the old disappointment.

When Wendell Willkie referred to one of his political combat declarations that went wrong as only "a bit of campaign oratory," it was a shock to the whole political world; for while the rest of the folks in the great game understand perfectly that viewpoints may change, it is flatly against the traditions of the business to admit spoofing the voting public.

The disparity between platform pledges and postelection performances illustrate the point. These give a legitimate excuse for the losers to express their horror and indignation that the promises of the convention resolutions have been defaulted, which figures in subsequent campaign oratory; but I have yet to know of a man, once he is safely in office, confessing that he was guilty of insincerity or deception when he subscribed to the platform on which he was elected. There is always the explanation that conditions have changed and that the new state of affairs made the suggested remedies for alleged ills outmoded or inadequate.

Franklin Roosevelt before the 1940 election promised that no American boy would be sent abroad to fight in a foreign war. When we began shipping our soldiers and naval folks to Iceland, Australia, and wherever else they would be useful, his opponents were vociferous in their charges of violation of his pledge. The obvious answer was that when the Japs blasted Pearl Harbor, the struggle became not a foreign but a domestic war.

When stated baldly, some of these things might suggest that there are no morals in politics. That is hardly an accurate reading, for our people have become accustomed to exaggerations in oratory and editorials. When somebody says it is "raining cats and dogs," it does not mean, and nobody takes it to mean, that there is a deluge of animal pets from the skies; just so, nobody should take unseasoned the fulminations of a political battle. I never knew an election to be won or lost by a platform; and who ever remembers one of those declarations of principles, purposes, and aspirations, except the people whose business it is to traffic in those goods?

An election campaign is a debate wherein the decision may not go according to what is said by the speakers but more likely is directed by how it is said. People vote for men rather than for principles, I think. As to the candidates themselves, it is their business to get votes, just as it is the business of political organizations to win elections. Once in high office, the chosen man does, almost invariably, what he deems is best for the country, regardless of the smoke and steam incident to the pre-election fray. True, he may be biased by the thought that his continuation in office, or at least the successorship of a man from his party, is what the country needs; but it is the country that ultimately determines that. If he has served to the nation's satisfaction, he gets his wish; if he does not, out he goes, which gives a measure—but only a measure—of validity to the cynical political maxim that people vote not for but against somebody.

15. "DISPELLING THE FOG"

Democratic barrage, and answers by the G.O.P. artillery.

DURING MY New York *World* activities I ran a column which we titled "The Political Undertow." When the newspaper commentators began their barrage on Roosevelt as preliminary to the '36 campaign, it seemed a natural thing for me to counter with a pro-Democratic column. So I got out my commentaries, under the heading of "Dispelling the Fog."

There was no subterfuge about it, no pretense of nonpartisanship: every issue proclaimed the authorship and carried the letterhead of the Democratic National Committee. Likewise I issued a clipsheet, consisting largely of short statements of business revivals under the Roosevelt régime, and there was always one article modestly headed "Editorial Suggestion," which was the best editorial I was capable of writing. It was quite a boon for harried little newspaper publications with their small and overworked staffs, and some thousands of them used the editorial without mentioning its source, to our gratification and, I hope, to the advantage of our party.

At the height of the enterprise nine or ten thousand dailies and weeklies carried much of our matter, and the publicity bureau was helped enormously by the suggestions from these journals.

My most frequent target in this barrage was the columnist crew, which, though posing as independent, were truly anti-Roosevelt. Naturally these opponents—old colleagues in the world of journalism—objected to their being classed as partisan, for they marketed their wares among newspapers of every political persuasion.

My opposition in the publicity branch of the Republican National Committee took note of "Dispelling the Fog," and one day came out with a circular announcing that they had "thought of getting out a daily or weekly political letter out of Washington and could arrange for this if there were a sufficient demand," but—there followed a list of syndicate writers, and the trio I had labeled the Three Musketeers led the list. The word was: "Most of you, however, undoubtedly would prefer to run the letters of Mark Sullivan, David Lawrence, Frank Kent, et al." The circular, addressed to all editors, recited, "Here is your chance to get exactly what you want in the way of Republican campaign material."

There was considerable commotion over my comment that "the Republican National Committee has formally taken over the Three Musketeers of antiadministration." Mr. Lawrence threatened to sue me for libel, though in my retort I wrote:

"There may be an ethical question involved, for either the Republican organization has justification for its listing these writers as elements of their publicity campaign—in which case, of course, it is hardly ingenuous for the writers to continue to pose as nonpartisan observers conveying information to the public—or it had no license to so list them and consequently did them a considerable disservice in conveying to the editors that their work was Republican propaganda."

Some of the newspapers came to the defense of their contributors and in so doing had to mention "Dispelling the Fog," which gave us much-needed advertising, and more papers asked for our service.

It frequently worked out that way. Few of the big metropolitan papers printed the Democratic output, so it was up to me to make my attacks in such form as to invoke replies and retorts, and by quoting "The Fog," however disparagingly, they gave their readers my arguments, which was my real objective.

A case in point was an article, here reproduced:

For Release Sunday, May 10, 1942. To the Editor: This letter is not copyrighted; it comes to you without restriction for use, in whole or in part, and either with or without credit.

DISPELLING THE FOG
By Charles Michelson
Director of Publicity, Democratic National Committee

You are worried about the gasoline and rubber shortages. You wonder how you are going to get Junior to school and get to your own job when your tires are worn out.

You perhaps do not trace your troubles to the circumstance that more than twenty years ago you voted for an isolationist House of Representatives. You were war-weary then, and thought possibly that it was just as well to have a Republican Congress for a change.

It is not a matter of paramount importance, with the safety of the nation at stake, that you might have to adapt yourself to a non-motor condition; that you have to register if you want a rationed pound of sugar, and that your taxes are at the peak and may go higher. There are graver elements in the picture.

Because you raised your boy in the faith that an American's first and deepest duty is to serve his country, you saw him inducted into our armed service with pride—even though your heart was wrung by the perils that beset him at an unknown destination. Did it over occur to you that you are subject to that inevitable choice because you listened to the arguments of the enemies of Woodrow Wilson that a League of Nations meant a supergovernment? That the destruction of the independence of the United States was in question, and equally wild suggestions of the import of our participating in the effort to prevent future aggressions that could menace world peace? The falsity of the theory that we could rest secure in our insular abstention from world affairs has been disastrously demonstrated by the events of the past two years. We tried to make it work with our embargo of our trade with belligerents, and by keeping our ships away from combat zones—only to find that the Nazi powers made the rules, and that to them the wide world was a combat zone. When Japan joined the Axis and assailed us from the Pacific, we were in it up to our necks.

When the Trouble Started

A Senate—two-thirds Republican—jettisoned the League of Nations, including the famous Lodge Reservations, which we had been assured protected us against the spectre of a supergovernment, and which turned out to be merely a bait to induce people who believed in the principle of world cooperation to join the wreckers.

Once in power, the isolationist principle was worked to the limit. Within a few years our country from being at the top of the world in military strength declined to fourth or fifth place. They flattened the Army and all but destroyed the Navy—first by the sinking of our ships through the disarmament conference formula and then by refusing to replace others as they became obsolete.

Of course, the American voters did not realize that when they voted in a House of Representatives hostile to the administration twenty-four years ago, they prepared the way for all this destruction and laid the foundation of the present war.

The average voter, particularly in a congressional election, is likely to look no further than the election of his local candidate.

He, perhaps, knows neither of the candidates but votes for one to oblige a friend, or a political associate, or simply to go along with his own party as a routine habit. Such procedure might not do any harm in an ordinary election, but the present is a time when the familiar social or political leaning falls short of national duty. It has been pointed out that a careless vote—or it might be an emotional one—a generation ago produced a repercussion of dire consequences in the world's history.

"Minding Our Own Business"

It destroyed the hope for an international concord that was planned to make such wars as the present one impossible; it brought us to the Harding administration and its scandals; to the amiable do-nothing policies of the Coolidge regime. We thought we were minding our own affairs, never realizing that it was leading to the great depression of President Hoover's term, and, indirectly, promoted the practicality of the rise of Hitler and Hitlerism, with the results already of the loss of millions of lives and the prostration of all that was best of civilization in central Europe.

It brought on the jingoism of Japan, for it furnished the opportunity of the yellow empire to embark on its career of conquest. That piratical foray would never have eventuated had not our country—the one agency that could have forbidden the Japonification of the Far East—been tied up in the war of the Atlantic, so that it had to divide its forces to meet the Asiatic threat.

It is to be hoped that the voters next November will keep this picture in mind when they go to the polls.

The only policy that is important now is to win the war—as soon as it can be won We have had the unfortunate experience of delayed preparation, with a minority in Congress opposed to the administration. If that minority should happen to be increased by the November elections, who can estimate the new difficulties and damage?

Our foreign enemies are eagerly assuring their people that disunity is rife in the United States, and would hail any political reversal as proof of their contention. We know that there is no basis for that particular example of Nazi propaganda. There is promising indication that the Hitler-Mussolini-Hirohito combination is already restive at the failure to realize the early triumph that was promised. That trend would be discouraged if anything eventuated that could be hailed as American disaffection.

It isn't a question of a Republican or a Democratic victory. As the President has pointed out, the issue between candidates must be the relative devotion to the Nation's cause—and in estimating this, the record of the candidates—regardless of party—must be the deciding factor.

———

Here are some excerpts showing repercussions from the foregoing article. They exemplify the process of getting attention to a propaganda argument from a huge group of newspaper readers who otherwise could not be reached.

It is of greater value to stir up doubts among those who get their political food from hostile newspapers than to present the propaganda to people who are, theoretically at least, already convinced.

That is really the basis of political philosophy from a publicity man's viewpoint. As to the epithetic missiles, the political press agent must have a hide thick enough so that they glance off. Indeed these barbs must be construed, if not as applause, as a token that the propagandist has hit his target:

Editorial from Chicago Tribune (Ital.) May 12, 1942:

CHARLIE THE SMEAR

Charlie the Smear Michelson, boss press agent for the Democratic party, has betrayed the political desperation of the Administration by the venom of his attack on the Republicans. . . . The Democratic leaders are forced to any expedient, however low, to save themselves in the November election. They are trying to use the blood and sweat of war for their personal advantage. . . . Michelson's false and ill-timed attack was a malicious contribution to disunity. The Democratic party must either disown it or accept the responsibility for this attempt to pervert the war effort to partisan ends.

"Well, gang, who's next?"
(Parrish in the *Chicago Tribune*)

Buffalo Evening News (James L. Wright) May 11, 1942:

MICHELSON FINDS THE VILLAIN IN GAS AND RUBBER SHORTAGE!

. . . After all these years Charles Michelson, director of publicity for the Democratic National Committee, the man who sits beside and counsels President Roosevelt at every one of his White House press conferences, has pulled the covers off you in his weekly publication which he calls "Dispelling the Fog." . . . After arguing that the whole course of history might have been changed if "an isolationist House of Representatives" had not been elected more than two decades ago, he says of the forthcoming elections, "It is to be hoped the voters next November will keep this picture in mind when they go to the polls."

Editorial from the New York Sun, May 14, 1942:

ELEMENTARY, MY DEAR G.O.P.

The plan attributed to Charles Michelson, master mind of Democratic propaganda, to use "Blame the Republicans for the war" as an effective 1942 campaign slogan is a house built on sand. The ingenious Mr. Michelson goes back only to 1918—when the voters of the United States refused to heed a command from the White House to elect a Democratic House of Representatives—to lay the groundwork for his indictment. . . .

Arthur Sears Henning in the Washington Times-Herald,
May 25, 1942:

"SMEAR" CHIEFS SEEK WHITE HOUSE PROTECTION

. . . President Roosevelt, through his political mouthpiece, Charles Michelson, had called for the purging of Congress of all prewar noninterventionists in the congressional elections this year. The left wing New Republic and the communistically affiliated Union for Democratic Action had named three prewar noninterventionist senators and forty-four representatives for political liquidation. . . . Michelson recently called for the defeat of all prewar noninterventionist candidates for Congress in a statement blaming the Republicans for the war, for Pearl Harbor, for the depression, and for all other misfortunes of the nation in the last quarter of a century. . . . Michelson himself was once in the boat in which Flynn finds himself, but survived by virtue of the President's favor. For several years Michelson received a $20,000 annual retainer from a radio concern which needed a friend at court in connection with delicate negotiations with the Federal Communications Commission. . . .

Editorial from the Washington Times-Herald, May 15, 1942:
MICHELSON

. . . The thing for us to do, according to Mr. Michelson, is to elect a House made up exclusively of (1) Congressmen who were interventionists and administration rubber stamps before Pearl Harbor and (2) new Congressmen whose chief campaign promise has been to yes-yes every war move the Roosevelt administration makes. . . . What Mr. Michelson is thus delicately asking for is a House of Representatives made up of men and women who have promised to object to nothing the administration may do, even when they think it is making a mistake; who have surrendered their independent judgment to the leader in the White House for the duration of the war. . . .

George Van Slyke in the New York Sun, May 13, 1942:
CHARLES MICHELSON DRAWS UP BLUEPRINT FOR COMING POLITICAL CAMPAIGNS

. . . The political strategy for the elections this year is outlined in detail in an official communication just issued by the Democratic National Committee from headquarters in Washington. The author of the document is Charles Michelson, director of publicity for the Democratic party and the White House.

It marks Mr. Michelson's entry into the congressional campaign and carries authority. The high-powered publicity man who, through nine years of the New Deal, is credited with having written more speeches for officials than anyone in that field, and to have outlined campaign policies, is on the job again, and that means the campaign is opened.

Following the old Michelson technic of claiming everything and conceding nothing to the opponents, the publicity director in effect outlines the framework for campaign oratory which Democratic candidates will be spreading throughout the land within the next few weeks. . . .

Editorial from the South Bend Tribune, May 17, 1942:

FOR THE RECORD

. . . Unless the political acumen of somebody in the White House has been greatly overestimated, the Democratic National Committee press agent will be told "let's skip that." Press Agent Charles Michelson perpetrated a major blunder when he blamed Republicans for the lack of military preparedness when the Japanese struck last December. . . . The pre-December 7, 1941, record need be cited only as conclusive proof that Chief Press Agent Michelson is trying to promote serious dissension in a narrow partisan spirit. Will he be rebuked by somebody in the White House? One guess.

Editorial from The Chicago Daily News, May 13, 1942; (Frank Knox, ex-Republican-vice-presidential candidate and now Secretary of the Navy, publisher):

ED AND CHARLIE

. . . We want to go on record to the effect that Charlie is no Machiavellian spider of politics. No, Charlie was a good reporter once, and is today a hard-working press agent trying to make good with his boss. Mr. Edward Flynn, Tammany-affiliated boss of the Bronx and chairman of the Democratic National Committee, is Charlie's boss. . . .

Some might have thought that the previous announcement by President Roosevelt, who is the head of the real Democratic party, that this is an all-out war and all-American, too, might have cramped the style of Ed and Charlie, but they don't know Charlie. What's a mere war president to Charlie? . . . As to history, Charlie's headline should read "Disseminating the Fog."

New York Herald Tribune, May 17, 1942:

MICHELSON PREDICTS DEFEAT OF ISOLATIONISTS IN BOTH PARTIES AS CHIEF CHANGE

. . . Mr. Michelson's statement was made in his weekly campaign letter, "Dispelling the Fog," in which he renewed the discussion begun last week in explanation of President Roosevelt's attitude toward the first congressional election since the United States entered the war. . . . Of the *Chicago Tribune's* charge that Woodrow Wilson's League of Nations was defeated "as much by Democratic votes as Republicans," Mr. Michelson said: "The fact is that the actual Wilson proposal was submitted for vote on December 13, 1919. In that balloting forty-five of the forty-six Republicans participating voted against ratification of the treaty. As it takes two-thirds of the Senate to ratify a treaty, it would not have made a particle of difference if every Democratic senator had voted for it. Actually thirty-seven of the forty-four Democrats present voted for the Wilson measure. . . ."

My ventures on the turbulent sea of politics brought me no serious clashes with the members of my own party. Three times I found myself at a sort of loggerhead with Senator Joe Robinson. The first discord was when I wrote a satiric story for the *American Magazine,* telling the Republican party where it fell down and what it was expedient for it to do. The Democratic Senate leader took it seriously and rebuked me severely, maintaining that I had no more right to advise the enemy than he had and that the President was very angry about it. As Roosevelt had laughed with me over the article, this did not distress me, though the Senator was very short with me for some time.

Our second run-in occurred when I went to him after the Philadelphia Convention and suggested (as I was directed to suggest) that he had made a wonderful speech, had presided over the Convention, and wouldn't he consent to grant Pat Harrison a little patch of spotlight by yielding to him the privilege of delivering the formal notice to the President of his re-

Advising the Republicans
(Talburt in *The American Magazine*)

nomination. The Senator stormed out of the room and did not talk to me for a week.

The third event of the sort was over the *Saturday Evening Post* article describing with exaggeration my feats as a ghost writer. Senator Robinson insisted that I had incited the story and that it was aimed directly at him. I was in Coventry for a full month after that. But when the Senator's attention was called to one of my syndicate letters in which I ridiculed the idea that the Senate leader, who had to be on his feet twenty times a day fighting for Democracy, needed the assistance of a ghost writer, he softened and we were as close friends as ever.

16. PRESIDENTOLOGY

The habits, customs, and instincts of the genus. Candid shots of some who were and some who aimed to be boss man of our government.

MOST OF MY professional life has been spent either in or on the fringe of politics. Naturally I have known many presidents—some fairly intimately, others as I might know an eminent actor on the stage, with the privilege of an occasional visit behind the scenes.

They do not constitute a homogeneous or consistent tribe, but one characteristic is invariable among the species. I never knew one that left the White House willingly at the expiration of one or more terms. I might go farther in this direction, having known every candidate for nearly half a century, and add that I never knew an aspirant for the high office who was ever able to abandon the ambition.

Having this abiding principle in mind, an observer may be

able to decipher some of what appear to be riddles on the political front.

The first president I ever saw was U. S. Grant. I must have been about seven years old when he came to Virginia City, Nevada, on some sort of swing around the circle. The welcoming parade was southbound up C Street. Now C Street is hardly a boulevard; so the open carriage containing the President and General Sherman had to move close to the west curb. The procession was halted, perhaps because an eight-mule ore team got in the way, and the carriage of the notables came to anchor in front of the Delta saloon. On the curb was this writer, mounted on the shoulders of his big brother, which placed me above the distinguished visitor. Honorable K. B. Brown, chief of our fire department, came to the side of the carriage to entertain the passengers. So I overheard the conversation. General Grant evidently was casting about for something complimentary to say about the ragged ramshackle town perched precariously on the slope of a sagebrush covered mountain and, looking up at the bare-legged ragamuffin who, open-mouthed, was glorying in his first contact with the great, enunciated these historic words: "Well, it seems like a fine place for children." I regarded that as a personal tribute to my small self and never forgot it. Incidentally, I was many years older before I learned that the K. B. of Chief Brown's name did not stand for Kittle Belly, by which he was always referred to, and that the U. S. in Grant's name did not stand for United States, which seemed like a fitting appelation for a president.

A little later on I was introduced to politics. We had hot elections on the Comstock Lode, and my brother used to take me to the meetings at National Guard Hall to listen to the eloquence of the leaders of the Comstock bar, who all practiced politics as a side line. I do not remember their names but was particularly impressed by one with a magnificent handlebar mustache. From that adornment I figured that he was some kin to the Delta bartender, who was decorated in the same way. The latter was a friend of mine, for he ran his fighting

game roosters in my father's chickenyard. However, all I remember about the oratory was when Counselor Handle-Bar
stormed out that "we will confront the solid South with a
solid North!" It was probably the Hayes-Tilden campaign. He
must have been a Republican, which puzzled me, because on
the sign at his law office was "Notary Public," which I assumed
to be a legal contraction of "Not a Republican." Doubtless my
presence at the speaking was due to brother's desire to help
my education beyond what was being drilled into me at the
Third Ward School.

The next president with whom I had contact was Benjamin
Harrison. By that time I was a reporter on the *San Francisco
Examiner*—matured, ripened, and cynical. I must have been at
least twenty years old. I had lost my awe at eminence. I called
the Governor by his first name, and mere senators were com-
monplaces in my professional life. President Harrison was not
an imposing figure when I was assigned to cover the big meeting at Mechanics Pavilion. I do not recall that the President's
speech excited me very much. Nevertheless I got my thrill out
of that meeting, for the newspaper put my name over my story
—the first time that name appeared in print. Nowadays that
particular glory has been dimmed, for the newspapers sign
every tale longer than your finger, but in that glamorous time
it was an accolade.

Later, in New York, whence I was transferred when Mr.
Hearst started his papers there, I had occasional chilly contacts
with ex-President Cleveland—who did not encourage newspaper intimacies and particularly not with Hearst people. I
don't know just how their quarrel started. There was a tale
current in San Francisco that it began with the refusal of the
government to permit Hearst to buy a building site on the military reservation on the north side of San Francisco Bay. It
would have been a glorious place for a castle, but whether
there was foundation for the gossip I do not know. There may
have been no definite reason for the break, for I have never
known a president, governor, or mayor—even those we helped
elect—that retained the publisher's friendship for his full term.

Naturally I participated in Mr. Hearst's various campaigns —for the presidency, governorship, and mayoralty. He always thought he had been counted out when he ran against McClellan for mayor, and perhaps he was. In those days they counted the ballots pretty much as Tammany wished. Hearst was intermittently for or against Tammany Hall. They finally gave him a seat in Congress from a Tammany district. That gave me a cross to bear. I was managing editor of the *San Francisco Examiner* at the time, and with throbbing sensations breaking all around, I had to give first-page prominence to my boss's congressional speeches. Charlie Murphy, Tammany's leader, sensible of the influence of the Hearst papers, which by that time had accumulated enormous circulations, agreed to nominate the publisher for governor or senator, leaving it to Al Smith to choose which post he wanted himself. But Smith would not forgive Hearst for the long barrage of abuse to which he had been subjected, and he threatened to take the floor of the Syracuse convention and oppose the nomination if Murphy persisted. They sought to placate the publisher by nominating and electing his friend Dr. Copeland to the senatorship.

This kept Hearst off their backs in the ensuing election, but he was sore at the Democratic party thenceforth. He organized the Independence League and had a convention at Chicago. I was editing one of his papers there at the time, and we handled the show like a real convention, with interviews, biographical articles on the candidates, a platform, committee, contested delegations, speculations on how the votes would go as between Honest Tom Hisgen and John Temple Graves, cartoons, editorials, and all the rest of the trimmings. The Hearst papers printed pages on the proceedings. I do not think any other newspaper bothered to print a line of it. I had never heard of Honest Tom before the convention and never heard of him after it, but he was duly nominated, and voted for, and so is entitled to be on this roster.

I got into the Woodrow Wilson orbit soon thereafter. Some party tycoon—it may have been Vance McCormick, Democratic

national chairman—asked me to lunch with him and Senator
Gore of Oklahoma. The purpose of the meeting was to effect
a peace between President Wilson and Mr. Hearst, and they
thought I would be a fitting emissary. I was not able to interest
my boss in the proposal, but the luncheon occasioned an interesting little adventure later on. Years had elapsed and I was
in Washington as the New York *World's* correspondent. Coming down from the Capitol in a streetcar I noticed that the blind
senator sat opposite. Never imagining that he would recall the
only time we had met, I did not greet him. Suddenly he raised
his head and exclaimed: "Isn't that the voice of Charley Michelson I hear?" I often told the story as a marvelous example of the
memory of a voice the sightless senator had only heard once,
many years before. Unfortunately I told the story once too
often, for the gentleman to whom I was narrating it gently responded: "Oh, yes, I was sitting with the Senator and told him
you were over there."

I had only a few routine professional contacts with Presidents McKinley and Theodore Roosevelt during their presidential terms, though as a New York reporter my job took me
frequently to Albany when the latter was governor. He was a
newspaperman's politician. There was the usual feud on between Mr. Hearst and Theodore Roosevelt, which never
interfered with the Governor's helping me on a story, but he
invariably indicated his disesteem for the publisher. Though
he had his tilts with individual members of my craft—never
hesitating to elect them to his Ananias Club when their product displeased him—he got on better with the press people than
any of his successors except his fifth cousin.

When he was making his tentative bid for a third nomination—not the Bull Moose episode that elected Woodrow
Wilson, but the 1920 convention nomination—he summoned
his old friends among the Washington correspondents and
talked politics. He did not need to detail his intentions but
discussed the relative strength of General Leonard Wood and
Governor Lowden, and foresaw the deadlock impending between those candidates. Had he lived, in all likelihood he

would have won his third term and the country would have escaped the unfortunate Harding administration, for T. R. was still the idol of his party, if not the idol of his party leaders.

Woodrow Wilson was a third-term candidate that year, an undeclared candidate, true, but nevertheless a receptive one. Like many of his predecessors he hoped, and probably expected, to be drafted.

On our way to San Francisco to attend the convention, Ed Hurley was among the company. He was chairman of the Shipping Board, and as nearly a close friend to Woodrow Wilson as that president's austere personality permitted. Wilson was not inclined to intimacies. Even Colonel House was more a political than a social confrere. Wilson's voluntary solitude is illustrated by his remark on one occasion that he had never had a nickname. He was not Woody Wilson, or even W. W. in print or conversation. Hurley was nearer to him than any of his cabinet, for example. Hurley had come to the train direct from the White House and mentioned that he had the platform with him. Naturally, in pursuit of news, I asked him to let me have a look at it. Just as naturally he refused, for the platform is supposed to be secret until it is reported to the convention.

"But," he said, "you may guess it is framed just to fit one man."

"Did the President type it himself?" The President's one-finger exercise on a writing machine was one of the classics of his administration.

"Never mind," he replied, sensing the obvious oblique foray by this questing reporter; "you'll have to do your own guessing when the platform committee reports."

It got into the newspapers later that the President had sent an incensed message to his son-in-law, William Gibbs McAdoo, when that statesman essayed a little nomination prospecting on his own account.

We came out of that hopeless convention with Governor Cox and Franklin D. Roosevelt as our candidates. I vibrated during the campaign between Cox's train and Harding's.

Only once, I think, did the Democratic nominee have an idea that he might win. We had come through New Jersey and into Delaware. The crowds were huge and the enthusiasm apparently intense, and, as is always the case, some of that permeated the train.

"Now," said the Governor, "it looks as though we have a possible chance."

The episode on the opposition train that stands out in my memory occurred when we were traversing Ohio. Harry Daugherty, later attorney-general, called a number of correspondents into his drawing-room to advise us of a coming story. He told us that the candidate was writing a statement on the tale that he had colored blood in his veins. We were discussing where the train should stop long enough for us to file the matter, etc., when the door was suddenly flung open and Mrs. Harding strode in. She glared at Daugherty and exclaimed:

"I'm telling all you people that Warren Harding is not going to make any statement."

Then she went out. If Pullman doors were slamable, that one would have closed with a crash. Daugherty rubbed his chin and followed her into the candidate's car. Of course no statement was forthcoming.

The negroid yarn had been rife for some days. Professor Chancellor was reported to have written a book about it that never was published. Naturally the wicked Democrats were accused of having invented it as campaign ammunition. My surmise is that the root of the gossip lay in Marion, where the father of the then prospective Mrs. Harding, the richest man in the town, was quoted as having declared that he would not permit the blood of the Kling family to be blackened by a marriage with that so-and-so. He was supposed to have had a street fight with Harding's father over it.

The nearest to an authoritative presentation of the Harding side of the story I heard came to me from James Keeley, editor of the *Chicago Tribune*, who had been charged by the Harding manager with the job of digging into the case history, probably with a view to preparing that statement which Mrs. Harding would not let her husband make.

According to Keeley the origin of the story went back eighty years. At that time there was an epidemic of a rash in the backwoods school, said rash being known to the rural community as "nigger itch," and the Harding children of that far day were accused of having brought the infection to the school. One Harding ancestor was reported to have killed an enemy who taunted him with the distorted version that had become current through the years.

In my opinion injustice has been dealt to Harding in the two pictures that have been presented to the country—the one a wily, conscienceless conniver at the nefarious doings of the Ohio gang; the other the witless dunderhead who never knew what was going on. Actually Harding was a village man about town, with the virtues and vices of his status and environment. He would have been perfectly content to remain the country editor, playing poker with the superintendent of the Marion Steam Shovel Company and the owner of the department store, figuring, perhaps with no very poignant pain, in the small scandals of the community. Instead he was catapulted to national eminence by Fate and the effort of a dominating, ambitious wife. First she took hold of his humdrum little newspaper and lifted it into an enterprise so profitable that he finally sold it for half a million dollars. Some of his enemies questioned the *bona fides* of that deal, implying that it might have been a means of conveying to him a share of the profits of the whiskey withdrawals, oil frauds, and alien property skullduggery. There would seem to be no necessity for such an explanation, for the price does not appear excessive in view of the statement to me by Harding himself that the *Marion Star* was netting more than $40,000 a year.

She goaded him into running for political offices with varying success, until a Republican sweep landed him in the United States Senate, the victor over an eminent Democrat, Atlee Pomerene, who was important enough to be mentioned as a possible presidential candidate. Then came the Wood-Lowden deadlock. Harding was geographically right; he had shown his vote-getting capacity by defeating a big Democrat. What better dark horse could be imagined?

Calvin Coolidge was chosen as Harding's running mate, not because he had settled the Boston police strike, but because Hiram Johnson had spurned the nomination; Borah would not take it, and the long sessions and the intense heat had worn out the delegates (the temperature was so fierce that the raw pine boards used for seats were sweating pitch), and Coolidge's was the first name offered.

It was not hard to believe the story circulated in Chicago that when the struggle in the convention was at its height, Harding went to the telephone to instruct Harry Daugherty to withdraw his name, and Mrs. Harding tore the telephone from his hand.

Harding received the message that he was the candidate with the exuberant comment that he had gone in on a busted flush and taken the pot.

In the Senate he was just a run-of-the-mine member. He voted with his party, took little part in the debates, and left his mark on no legislation. Being a companionable man, he was popular and was promptly adopted into the card playing, heavy dining set.

When he became president, he wobbled between glowing hilarity at the glory of the position and bewildered gloom over the responsibilities involved. Over and over he asked if a man of average intelligence and good purpose could compass the governmental task. I heard that soliloquy a dozen times as we walked the deck of the transport that took us to Alaska. Once he mused, "I cannot hope to be one of the great presidents, but perhaps I may be remembered as one of the best loved presidents."

His loyalty to his friends was probably the reason for his blindness toward the viciousness of the Ohio gang. Who was there to tell him of the iniquities of the intimates he gambled and gamboled with? Their looting was not revealed publicly until after he was in his grave, and, if he had caught rumors, presumably he had dismissed them as just part of the fog of gossip that always clutters Washington.

He was fond of the newspaper people who had campaigned with him and covered his activities during the preinauguration period. He re-established the press conferences that had been discontinued by President Wilson, and at first these gatherings were free and easy and intimate. Then came his first cropper.

The Disarmament Conference was on, and it had voted a pledge guaranteeing the security and sovereignty of the islands of the Pacific.

At the press conference somebody asked if that guarantee applied to the homeland of the Japanese.

"Certainly not," replied the President, "any more than it guarantees the sovereignty of California or any other continental territory that fronts on the Pacific."

It developed that in the subcommittee that reported the resolution to the Disarmament Conference the Japanese delegates had asked the same question and had been assured that Honshu, Hokkaido, Kyusyu, Shokoku, and Formosa were all embraced in the beneficent pact.

Perhaps purposely there was no public announcement to this effect. Secretary of State Charles Evans Hughes had to bring the conference into accord with the President's interpretation.

Thereafter there were no more informal press conferences. We had to write out our questions in advance, and the President answered or not as he saw fit.

When Calvin Coolidge took over, he improved the process. He shuffled the questions so that any inconvenient ones were at the bottom of the pile and adjourned the conference before they were reached.

When the question of whether Mr. Coolidge would be a candidate for a third term was imminent, it was reported that, as a member of the Massachusetts legislature, he had headed a round robin against Theodore Roosevelt's running again. Obviously this was a question bound to be asked at the next press conference, and just as obviously it was destined to sink to the bottom of the pack. So some missionary work was done, and every question put in bore on the third-term round robin. The President glanced at the pile, discovered what was going on, and treated us to a glowing account of the splendid job Herbert Hoover had done in rescuing and succoring the sufferers of the Mississippi flood.

It is almost a political aphorism that weak presidents have strong cabinets, and also, to a lesser degree perhaps, that the potent chief executives have about them men of minor capacity. It is a rather fortunate president who has one outstanding figure in his official family. Harding had possibly the highest-grade cabinet of modern years, for there were three figures of national renown who sat at his council table—Charles Evans Hughes, Herbert Hoover, and Andrew Mellon. They must have pulled him about quite a bit, for it seemed to an onlooker that he was rather awed by this trio. Hoover and Mellon differed about the handling of the war debts owed the United States by its allies of the First World War. The Secretary of the Treasury naturally viewed them from the bankers' standpoint. The Secretary of Commerce, successful promoter of important enterprises, seemed to have a more practical view of the effects of those troublesome assets. Generally Hoover's advice was accepted—none of which affected the final result, default by all the nations except Finland.

In the early stages President Harding and his imposing secretary of state were in anything but accord as to the League of Nations. Secretary Hughes had been a prominent signer of the proclamation in which a score of the most eminent Republicans urged the election of Warren G. Harding as the surest method of getting the United States into the league (with, of course, the amendments offered by Senator Henry Cabot Lodge). This remained the sentiment of the ex-justice, ex-candidate for president, when he became a member of Harding's cabinet. But Harding followed the ukase of his former leader in the Senate, Lodge.

Immediately after the 1920 election I heard Lodge announce the policy.

"Now," I asked the Senator, "can we assume that the amended League of Nations will be enacted?"

"Certainly not," was his answer. "Now we don't need to have anything of the sort. The whole damned thing is out of the window."

Months later, in an interview accorded me at the White House, George Harvey, returning from his embassy at London, announced the conversion of Hughes to the isolationist theory. It could hardly have been an easy apostasy, for Hughes did not take the light attitude assumed by regular politicians toward campaign pledges.

However varied were the scandals that left such a cloud over the Harding administration, they did not touch the three departments presided over by the Big Three. Perhaps they got an early whiff of the Albert Fall—Harry Daugherty doings, for looking back I find no symptoms of social relations between the aristocracy of that cabinet and the men with whom the President played around. Nor was there any intimacy between the President and the Vice-President. Mr. Coolidge stuck pretty close to the Capitol end of the town. There was something said about enhancing the distinction of the second highest office by having the Vice-President attend cabinet meetings, but Mr. Coolidge was not interested. Harding had his cronies at the White House many evenings, and on other evenings he joined them at the little Green House on K Street, but the Vice-President flew in his own narrow orbit. He was not regarded as a political asset; rather the reverse. When the talk ranged round to the next election, Daugherty, with Harding's other political generals, never thought of Coolidge as a permanent member of the administration. The idea was to send him back to Massachusetts to run against David I. Walsh for the Senate, and to have as Harding's running mate a war hero. Colonel Tom Miller, a popular, dashing veteran with a fine combat record, was frequently mentioned in the conversations for the second place on the prospective ticket. This seemed like sound politics, but in the retrospect one is led to speculate as to whether the program had not an even more sinister explanation.

Miller was the alien property custodian who went to jail after he was found in possession of a lot of Liberty bonds that had been among the assets of the American Metals Corporation, which Miller with Daugherty's connivance, indeed on Daugherty's authority, turned over to a corporation alleged to be Swiss while, in fact, direct evidence of its German ownership was in Miller's own office. Some American financiers had, during the war, dickered with the Germans for the purchase of their shares. It was requisite for these negotiations that the trading-with-the-enemy act should be waived to enable the would-be purchasers to meet the Teutonic owners in neutral territory. The deal was made but was not consummated, because A. Mitchell Palmer, predecessor of Miller as alien property custodian, and Daugherty's predecessor as attorney-general, ruled that the agreed price was inadequate. But the whole story was in the files when Miller and Daugherty put over the job that landed one in the penitentiary while the other escaped by virtue of a single juror's having refused to vote for conviction and so hung the jury.

Miller's account of how the fatal bonds came into his possession—or rather the story Miller's friends brought to me as having been told them by him—was that he was assured by Daugherty that there was no possibility for conviction of either of them and therefore it would be unnecessary for Miller to go on the witness stand. Had he testified, according to this explanation, he would have stated that he took a large part in the Governor Lowden—General Wood contest and had expended forty thousand dollars in behalf of Wood. When Daugherty was making his effort to swing the nomination to Harding, Miller refused to enter the combine unless he was recompensed. Whereupon Daugherty (so Miller told his friends) agreed to have the Republican National Committee make good this amount, failing which he, personally, would give Miller the forty thousand dollars. This came to Miller in Liberty bonds. Some cagy official had put a red marker on the serial numbers of the American Metals securities, and when the interest coupons came in from Miller's family the picture was complete.

To get back to the presidential sequence: Coolidge served out the remnant of Harding's term, without particular incident, and was nominated for the presidency in 1924. The high spot of the Cleveland convention was the total eclipse of the Old Guard. The loneliest figure was Henry Cabot Lodge, stalking gloomily through the corridors and not even being invited to the platform reserved for the high priests of the party. Coolidge had had his troubles with the group when he presided over the Senate. They did not think highly of him, and he more than reciprocated that attitude. As president, he resented the efforts of these old custodians of Republican policy to control him. His nomination was assured, and he saw no reason to let the haughty synod run the show.

It was a listless convention. The country was indignant at the Teapot Dome affair and other frauds and scandals, and the Republicans did not think they had a chance.

I returned from Cleveland with a carload of G.O.P. leaders, and the atmosphere was that of a funeral train. I sat with Senator Medill McCormick, who had lost out in the Illinois primaries. In the course of the conversation the suggestion was made that he get Coolidge to name him to one of the high diplomatic posts and thus keep in the picture. He was young, brilliant, though perhaps somewhat erratic, and it seemed a pity that his political career should be cut off.

"Not for me," was his comment. "I don't want to be a lame duck ambassador. I'll get all the fun I want sitting back and laughing at you Democrats struggling with the insoluble questions the next administration must face."

Then the Democrats went into that hideous New York convention, which instantly became murky with Ku Klux, prohibition, religious intolerance, and all the rest of it. Long before the Smith-McAdoo struggle had wound up, the Democrats realized they had tossed a certain victory into the street.

I ran into John W. Davis in the lobby just after he had been given the nomination, and extended the conventional congratulations.

It was with a wry grin that he responded: "Thanks, but you know how much it is worth."

The gloom of the Cleveland convention was an hilarious celebration compared with the Democratic adjournment. The steering committee went into session to perform the requisite routine of selecting a vice-presidential candidate. In the course of the rather long session somebody came out and asked me if I had any suggestions. My offering for the vice-presidency was Ed Hurley, who had made a fine record in his war job, who was popular and a Catholic, which latter qualification might assuage to some extent the indignation at Smith's being turned down. And I added, "He is on the ocean bound for Europe and so cannot defend himself."

I still think it was a good suggestion, but Candidate Davis ultimately picked Charlie Bryan, brother of William Jennings Bryan—who had shown symptoms of vote-getting calibre by being elected to something in his own state.

The '24 campaign was the most listless in my experience. I churned around with the candidates as usual and cannot now recall anybody who thought John W. Davis had a chance. Clem Shaver, his West Virginia neighbor whom he picked as Democratic national chairman, did the best he could, but the party remained split with the feuds of the New York convention, and the local organizations could not stir up even an approach for enthusiasm.

If there was expectation that the plethoric clients of the candidate would rally to his support, that hope was futile. Wall Street contributed little to its pet attorney, compared with what it did for Hoover, Landon, and Willkie in subsequent elections.

Coolidge got all the breaks. His acceptance speech was delivered on a perfect evening. His harsh New England accents were somehow neutralized by the radio, and the audition was perfect. Davis, on the other hand, spoke in a deluge. His fine, resonant tones were muffled by the air mechanism; static was on the job to such an extent that there were accusations that somebody had fenagled the radio so as to hamper him.

Through the campaign the Democratic candidate made fine,

eloquent, scholarly addresses. He might as well have gone into a corner and talked to himself. His special train got into difficulties, and there was one report that he was sidetracked on a switch while an audience in Chicago, I think, waited for him. He took his dose like a good soldier, going through all the motions of a real political battle, and he accepted defeat with becoming philosophy.

To Coolidge the campaign and election was merely an episode of administration. He guyed me a little after his first press conference on his second term, telling me to keep on and sometime I might land on the winning side. The Democratic New York *World* had, of course, opposed him.

Through his administration we were on excellent terms. I think I plagued him a little with my jeers at "the White House spokesman"—Coolidge's expedient to avoid direct quotation but to clothe such news as he wished the reporters to publish with some authority. I tried to get this ghostly creation across to *World* readers as the White House *spook*sman but was never able to get that feeble jape through a vigilant copy desk which persistently corrected what it took to be a typographical error.

If there was any effect on him, beyond the twinkle in his eye as he greeted me, I never saw it. In fact, during all my contacts with government and politicians I cannot recall ever having campaign asperities result in hostility until the advent of Herbert Hoover to the White House.

Senator Bennett Clark, for example, never rises to discuss me in milder terms than as a nefarious radio lobbyist. Senator Clark was once told that I had sought to find a Missouri candidate for his seat, though picking candidates is foreign to any job I ever held. But we have been friends since his boyhood. Senator Burt Wheeler and I remain intimates despite whatever barbs I have launched at Roosevelt's enemies, in which category, particularly during the Supreme Court row, he was pre-eminent. In fact, all the Republican leaders call me by my first name, regardless of what they have been saying on the Senate or House floors as to my wickedness. We are all like actors who, having wiped off their make-up, forget the villain-and-hero struggles on the stage.

I had known Mr. Hoover since the First World War. My paper, the *World,* had announced itself in favor of him for president on any ticket in 1920. We all regarded him as being the best qualified possibility that had approached the presidency in modern times. He had done a wonderful job in Belgian relief; he had enhanced his reputation by his service as food commissioner. Eight years later the *World* went all out for Al Smith, and I naturally plugged for the Democratic candidate to the best of my ability. I never thought of personifying that situation, and when Mr. Hoover came to the White House, I tarried after the first press conference to bow my head and extend my congratulations. He did not ask me to sit down; he did not extend his hand. He answered my greeting with monosyllables and, in short, chilled me to the bone.

When, shortly thereafter, I took the job of Democratic publicity director, he attributed my work, so I was told, to individual antagonism. I have in recent years not infrequently encountered the ex-President, at the Bohemian Club in San Francisco and elsewhere, and never has he even recognized my presence.

I only mention it as a unique example of political partisanship translated into the personal field.

It is interesting to compare the reactions of various presidents to their great office. Woodrow Wilson, a natural crusader with no doubts as to his mission, accepted the duties of president as part of his manifest destiny. Warren G. Harding was alternately elated at the glory and depressed by the responsibilities of his eminence. Calvin Coolidge took it all as part of the day's work, with no great emotion. Herbert Hoover fretted at the vexation of opposition, and was moody rather than happy in the job. Then came Roosevelt, debonair and positive, with complete faith in his capacity as statesman and politician—the first president of a long series who actually enjoyed the White House. His was a long honeymoon, that only terminated when excessive belief in the impregnability of his popularity led him to challenge the Supreme Court. That struggle was his initial serious setback, though he gaily proclaimed his satisfaction that he had "lost the battle but won the war." From that episode stemmed most of his troubles. The defeat of his measure, and the nearly total unsuccess of his purge, taught those of his party who were prone to rebellion that they might oppose the President without the certainty that they would be blasted into political oblivion.

EPILOGUE

THIS BOOK was purposed to be a recital of the panorama of events. It has ineluctably become something of a commentary as well. Obviously some of the stories I have told convey evidence of flaws in our scheme and system of administration. The first conclusion must be that the chief source of our errors and faults is the circumstance that we take our Government less seriously than we do our politics. The next conclusion appears to be that nothing can be done to change this situation.

Utopian impulses will tempt the conscientiously inclined. Could we not, for instance, establish a superpolitical power, some entirely antiseptic body that would act as a jury or perhaps as a vigilance committee to keep the two great parties to the task of maintaining and improving the government? Because we are a community of human beings, virtuous in the abstract but sublimely committed to our individual political faiths, such an organization belongs in the realm of dreams. Inevitably it would be swayed into the orbit of the Republican or the Democratic outfit, or would develop ambitions of its own to run things, which would involve alliances and deals, so that all it could accomplish would be to make the quadrennial fandango a threesome instead of a twosome. The result would be minority government.

So until the misty future may develop a beatific merger of politics and patriotism, we will have to be content to balance the incidental vices of the two-party system against its tangible virtues. We must accept the circumstance that a party in power will be most concerned with remaining in power, and that a party out of power will continue for its objective the ousting of an administration. That may not be as vicious as it sounds, for those in authority know—or should know—that permanence in office, while never totally insured thereby, has its best claim in good government. And as for the Outs, though they may trespass on morality in their assaults, their job of policing the acts of those on top outweighs their departure from the straight and narrow path.

As this is written the proceedings of the executive session of the United States Senate—which means a session supposedly dealing with matters too delicate to be made public in wartime —are being spread on every newspaper page, with the serio-comic assertion that the information came from no senator —though none but senators could be present in an executive session; which suggests that it is not only the unofficial public that takes its government with less seriousness than its politics.

Nevertheless, ours is the government that suits us; with some patching, here and there, through a century and a half, it has met our needs. We have survived geniuses and stuffed shirts in our succession of presidents and have averaged up pretty well under the job our politicians have done for us. Among the politicians there have been rogues and racketeers, perhaps in the same proportion as among businessmen, labor leaders, law-yers, and almost any other group in our citizenry.

INDEX

A

Akerson, George, 18
Alfange, Dean, 162
Allen, George E., 148
Alsop, Joseph, 168
Apache Kid, 72
Astor, Lady, 111
———, Vincent, 47, 119

B

Bailey, Joseph, 94
Baker, H. F., 75-6
———, Newton, 4, 139
Bakersfield, Calif., 82
Ballantine, Arthur, 55, 56
Bankhead, Senator, 179
Barkley, Alben W., 6, 7, 181, 182
Barnes, Lieutenant, 85
Bart, Black, 83
Barton, Bruce, 201
Baruch, Bernard M., 110, 111, 113, 198
Baxter, Norman, 42-3
Beck, James M., 142
Bellmer, Mme., 69
Bennett, ———, 160-2
Berle, Adolph, 162, 194
Biddle, Tony, 63
Bierce, Ambrose, 80-1, 91
Bigelow, "Petey," 83
Bingham, Ambassador, 105
———, Mrs., 105
———, Senator, 22-3
Black, Hugo, 184
Blythe, ———, 80
Bolton, Charles J., 83
Borah, Senator, 179
Brisbane, 127
Broun, Heywood, 124-5
Brown, Edward, 43
———, Hon. K. B., 222
Broderick, Senator, 78
Bryan, Charles, 235
———, William Jennings, 92-4
Buller, Justice, 181

Bullitt, William, 103
Bull Moose party, 147
Byrd, Harry, 5, 6, 139
Byrnes, James, 182

C

Carothers, Dr. Neil, 142
Catledge, Turner, 168
Cermak, Mayor, 9, 37
Chamberlain, Neville, 117
Child, Richard Washburn, 44
Churchill, Winston, 85
Cisneros, Evangelina, 88-9
Clark, Arthur, 96
———, Bennett, 152, 236
Cleveland, Grover, 223
Clifton, Ariz., 72
Coffin, George, 89
Cohen, Benjamin, 169, 190
Coleman, Harry, 96
Collins, Frederick, 187
Conboy, Martin, 13-4
Coolidge, Calvin, 17, 31, 32, 215, 229-32, 234, 235, 236, 237
Cooper, ex-Governor, 42
Copeland, Dr., 224
Corcoran, Thomas, 13, 168-9, 174-8, 183, 189-93, 195-6
Couzens, Senator, 105
Cox, James, 93, 105, 226
Craig, General, 65
Crane, Stephen, 89
Crosby, ———, 68
Crowley, Leo, 62
Cuba, 85-9
Cummings, Homer, 140, 168
———, Walter, 36
Curtis, Vice-President, 30
Czolgosz, 91-2

D

Daniels, Josephus, 204
Dargie, William, 95
Darrow, Clarence, 93-4

0290
uf